Karen De Clercq
The Morphosyntax of Negative Markers

Studies in Generative Grammar

Editors
Norbert Corver
Harry van der Hulst

Founding editors
Jan Koster
Henk van Riemsdijk

Volume 144

Karen De Clercq

The Morphosyntax of Negative Markers

A Nanosyntactic Account

ISBN 978-1-5015-2732-6
e-ISBN (PDF) 978-1-5015-1375-6
e-ISBN (EPUB) 978-1-5015-1377-0
ISSN 0167-4331

Library of Congress Control Number: 2020934831

Bibliographic information published by the Deutsche Nationalbibliothek
The Deutsche Nationalbibliothek lists this publication in the Deutsche Nationalbibliografie;
detailed bibliographic data are available on the Internet at http://dnb.dnb.de.

© 2022 Walter de Gruyter GmbH, Berlin/Boston
This volume is text- and page-identical with the hardback published in 2020.
Typesetting: VTeX UAB, Lithuania
Printing and binding: CPI books GmbH, Leck

www.degruyter.com

Contents

Acknowledgment —— IX

Part I: Aims and background

1 Introduction —— 3

2 Theoretical background: Nanosyntax —— 9
2.1 Introduction —— 9
2.2 Syncretisms —— 10
2.3 Lexicalisation or spellout —— 15
2.4 Deriving *ABA —— 26
2.5 Conclusion —— 27

Part II: The internal structure of negative markers

3 Classification of negative markers —— 31
 Introduction —— 31
3.1 Preparing the classification —— 32
3.2 Property 1: Stacking —— 33
3.3 Property 2: Scope position —— 35
3.3.1 T^{NEG}-markers —— 39
3.3.2 Foc^{NEG}-marker —— 43
3.3.3 $Class^{NEG}$-markers —— 48
3.3.4 Q^{NEG}-markers —— 50
3.4 Property 3: Contradiction and contrariety —— 54
3.5 Property 4: Function —— 57
3.6 Conclusion —— 59

4 The crosslinguistic morphosyntax of negative markers —— 61
4.1 Some notes on the methodology —— 61
4.2 Crosslinguistic sample —— 65
4.2.1 Pattern 1 —— 65
4.2.1.1 Greek —— 65
4.2.1.2 Le bon usage French —— 70
4.2.1.3 Korean —— 77
4.2.1.4 Other language —— 86

4.2.2	Pattern 2 —— 86	
4.2.2.1	Japanese —— 86	
4.2.2.2	Colloquial French —— 90	
4.2.2.3	Turkish —— 91	
4.2.2.4	Other languages —— 95	
4.2.3	Pattern 3 —— 98	
4.2.3.1	Mandarin Chinese —— 98	
4.2.3.2	Modern Standard Arabic —— 102	
4.2.3.3	Persian —— 105	
4.2.3.4	Malayalam —— 108	
4.2.4	Pattern 4 —— 113	
4.2.4.1	Khwe —— 113	
4.2.5	Pattern 5 —— 116	
4.2.5.1	Moroccan Arabic —— 116	
4.2.6	Pattern 6 —— 118	
4.2.6.1	Hungarian —— 118	
4.2.6.2	Hebrew —— 123	
4.2.6.3	Dutch —— 127	
4.2.7	Pattern 7 —— 129	
4.2.7.1	Czech —— 129	
4.2.7.2	Hixkaryana —— 132	
4.2.7.3	Other languages —— 135	
4.3	Summary and discussion —— 136	
5	**The internal syntax of a negative marker —— 143**	
5.1	The negation sequence —— 143	
5.2	Decomposition —— 145	
5.3	Containment —— 150	
5.4	Spellout —— 152	
5.5	Conclusion —— 155	

Part III: Negative markers and their clausal syntax in English and French

6	**The external syntax of negative markers in English —— 159**	
6.1	Introduction —— 159	
6.2	Insertion of negative PRE-markers —— 164	
6.3	Unproductive affixal negation —— 173	
6.3.1	Pointers —— 173	

6.3.2	Spellout of unproductive Q^{NEG}-markers —— 174	
6.4	Insertion of negative suffixal markers —— 178	
6.4.1	*-less* —— 178	
6.4.2	*n't* —— 181	
6.5	Conclusion —— 191	

7 Diachronic change in French —— 192
7.1 Introduction —— 192
7.2 Bipartite negation —— 192
7.2.1 Asymmetry and formal analyses —— 192
7.2.2 BUF analysis —— 195
7.3 Colloquial French —— 199
7.4 Two additional notes —— 200
7.4.1 A note on grammaticalisation and negative arguments —— 200
7.4.2 A note on Afrikaans —— 200
7.5 Conclusion —— 202

Part IV: Remaining issues

8 Other syntactic perspectives on negation —— 205
8.1 Introduction —— 205
8.2 Multiple NegPs —— 205
8.3 Conclusion —— 215

9 Semantics —— 216
9.1 Introduction —— 216
9.2 Setting the scene —— 217
9.3 Extents —— 219
9.4 Context-dependence —— 221
9.5 Deriving contrariety from extent inclusion —— 222
9.6 Syntax —— 224
9.7 *Un*-marked antonyms —— 227
9.8 Conclusion —— 229

10 Conclusion —— 230

Bibliography —— 233

Index —— 249

Acknowledgment

This book is based on my PhD, but goes beyond it and was altered in many ways, adding a substantial set of languages to the typological sample and modifying the analysis so that it is a nanosyntactic analysis throughout. I owe a great debt of gratitude to my informants without whom this book could not haven been written. I owe a lot to Rachel Nye for thorough and endless discussion on the nature of question tags in English. She has been a tremendous help throughout the years, and especially during the time of my PhD. Thanks also to William Harwood, Eric Lander and Reiko Vermeulen for help with my data on English. Furthermore I want to thank Amélie Rocquet for careful discussion of the French data. Many thanks to Mansour Shabani and to Karimouy Mitra Heravi for their help with the Persian data, to Jakub Dotlačil, Radek Šimík and Pavel Caha for their help with Czech, to Adrienn Jánosi for many patient exchanges on Hungarian, to Marika Lekakou and Metin Bagriacik for help with Greek, to Hicham El Sghiar for his judgments on Moroccan Arabic, to Vadim Kimmelman for help with Russian, to Li Man for help with the Chinese data, to Fatih Önder, Metin Bagriacik, Karsan Seyhun and Jorge Hankamer for useful discussion of Turkish, to Minjeong Son and Jaehoon Choi for help with Korean, to Reiko Vermeulen, Yasuhiro Iida and Makoto Ishii for discussion of the Japanese data, to Johan Brandtler for help with Swedish, Sevda Selayva for help with Azerbajani, to Yael Gaulan for help with Hebrew, to Aleksandar Aleksovski for help with Macedonian, to Maryann Madhavathu for help with Malayalam, Hilde Gunnik for help with Khwe, Lydia Ruguru Gilbert for help with Kimeru, Anselm Theodos Ngetwa for help with Swahili and Anthony Chukwuemeka Atansi for help with Igbo. I also want to thank an anonymous reviewer for very useful comments, and the Mouton editors for their work on the manuscript that led to this book.

    A special word of thanks goes to Guido Vanden Wyngaerd, who as a close friend, colleague and co-author has influenced the content of this work in many ways. Other colleagues whose support and feedback was at different stages of the writing and thought process invaluable are Elitzur Bar-Asher Siegal, Anne Breitbarth, Pavel Caha, Jeroen van Craenenbroeck, Liliane Haegeman, Martin Haspelmath, Dany Jaspers, James McCloskey and Michal Starke.

    Finally, I want to thank my friends and family, my mother and father in particular, for their never-lasting support and help in many ways.

    I dedicate this book to my daughters, Sien and Noor, and my wonderful husband, Joris, whose daily warmth and love nourishes all parts of life, not in the least the research I do.

Part I: **Aims and background**

1 Introduction

This book explores a hitherto undiscussed link between sentence negation (henceforth SN) (1a) and constituent negation (henceforth CN) (2): the existence of syncretisms between negative markers expressing CN and those expressing SN.[1]

(1) a. She isn't happy.
    b. She is not happy.

(2) a. She is unhappy.
    b. She is dishonest.
    c. She is non-Christian.

Before we can tackle the syncretisms between CN and SN, we need to clarify what is meant with CN and SN. Klima (1964:261–270) discussed some diagnostics to test the scope of negation, i. e. whether negation takes the entire clause in its scope or whether it takes only 'a constituent' in its scope. The main diagnostics for the scope of negation are the question tag-test,[2] (3), the *either/ too*-test, (4), and the *neither/so*-test, (5).[3]

---

[1] Jespersen (1917) refers to the distinction SN/CN as 'nexal negation' versus 'special negation' and Horn (2001b), following the tradition by Aristotle, refers to the distinction as 'predicate denial' versus 'predicate (term)' negation. I come back to these distinctions in chapter 3.

[2] Question tags or reversal tags (Quirk et al. 1985:810–813) are not the only possible tags a clause can be appended with. There are also reduplicative tags or same way tags (Swan 2005). Whilst question tags reverse the polarity of the matrix clause and ask "confirmation from the Addressee for a proposition that the Speaker commits herself to, albeit somewhat tentatively (Cattell 1973, McCawley 1998, Malamud & Stephenson 2011, Farkas & Roelofsen 2012)" (Brasoveanu et al. 2014:175), reduplicative tags copy the polarity of the matrix clause and signal the speaker's conclusion by inference or the speaker's sarcastic suspicion (Quirk et al. 1985:812). Typical of a reduplicative tag is that the Speaker challenges or questions "a proposition that she feels the interlocutor committed herself to (Cattell 1973, McCawley 1998)" (Brasoveanu et al. 2014:175). A sentence with a reduplicative tag can be preceded by 'Oh so'. Since negative sentences can never take reduplicative tags, the question tag test is usually used to test the scope of negation. If applied correctly the reduplicative tags could also lead to interesting insights by making use of the 'oh so' test. However, Brasoveanu et al.'s (2014) experiment on the two types of tags showed that the results with reduplicative tags are harder to interpret and hence probably not as reliable. It is therefore important to keep the two tags apart (De Clercq 2011). The data below and in the remainder of this book always present judgments for question tags, not for reduplicative tags. So if I star a positive clause with a question tag, that does not exclude that it is most probably acceptable under a reduplicative tag-reading.

[3] McCawley (1998:604–612) provides an interesting overview of some of the tests that were first introduced by Klima (1964). He provides a discussion of the differences between them and the

The tests, illustrated in (3)–(5) below, show that constituent negation in (3c)–(4c)–(5c) patterns for all three tests with the affirmative sentences that are illustrated in (3a)–(4a)–(5a) and not with negative sentences in (3b)–(4b)–(5b).

(3) a. Hoboken is in New Jersey, *is it/ isn't it?
 b. Hoboken isn't in Pennsylvania, is it/ *isn't it?   (McCawley 1998:611)
 c. John is unhappy, *is he/ isn't he?

(4) a. John voted for Bergland, and Mary voted for him too/*either.
 b. John didn't vote for Reagan, and Mary didn't vote for him *too/either. (McCawley 1998:604)
 c. John's spouse is non-Christian, and Jim's spouse is non-Christian too/*either.

(5) a. John voted for Stassen, and so/*neither did Mary.
 b. John didn't vote for Stassen, and *so/ neither did Mary. (McCawley 1998:609)
 c. John is dishonest, and so/*neither is Mary.

These tests make a distinction between negative markers that give rise to SN and those which give rise to CN.[4] However, there is also evidence suggesting that the seemingly fundamental distinction between SN and CN signalled out by the tests in (3)–(5) may not be so fundamental at all. This seems to be the case when we look at the licensing of negative polarity items (NPIs): both SN and CN markers are able to license NPIs in certain syntactic contexts.[5] Both the sentential negative marker *n't*, (6a), and the negative affix *un-*, (6b), are able to license the weak NPI *any* in certain syntactic configurations.

(6) a. He won't be able to find any time for that.
 b. He is unable to find any time for that.   (Klima 1964:291)
 c. Unaware of any dangers he went on vacation.   (Zeijlstra 2004a:46)

---

problems related to the tests. Also Jackendoff (1972), De Haan (1997), Penka (2011), De Clercq (2020) discuss the Klima-tests from various angles.

4 I use the word 'negative marker' throughout this book to refer to markers which negate predicates, irrespective of whether 1) they are morphologically simplex or complex, 2) morphologically free or bound, 3) affixal, infixal or circumfixal and 4) whether they give rise to sentence negation or constituent negation. However, 'negative marker' does not refer to negative polarity items, negative quantifiers, negative indefinites or negative expletives in this book, unless referred to explicitly.

5 It is beyond the scope of this book to go deeper into the nature of NPIs and NPI-licensing contexts. For an overview see Ladusaw (1979), Horn (2001b), Zwarts (1992, 1995, 1998), Giannakidou (1997, 1998), Gajewski (2011), Brandtler (2012).

I take these facts to show that negative markers that give rise to SN and CN are somehow different from each other (cf. the Klima-diagnostics) and somehow very similar (cf. NPI-licensing), i. e. negative markers across the sentential-constituent divide share minimally a negative feature, but differ in the presence or absence of other features.

This brings us back to the syncretisms we started out with. Whereas CN in English can be expressed by affixal negative markers like *un-*, *iN-*, *dis-* and *non-*, (2) and SN is expressed by *not* or the clitic *n't*, (2), in Czech CN and SN are all expressed by means of the same negative marker *ne-*, (7).

(7) a. Ja ne- jsem šťastný.
       I NEG- am happy.
       'I am not happy.'
    b. Ja jsem ne- šťastný.
       I am NEG- happy.
       'I am unhappy.'

Within the group of English affixal negative markers (*un-*, *iN-*, *dis-* and *non-*) it has long been observed that *non-* does not give rise to the same type of negation as *un-* (Zimmer 1964, Horn 2001b, Kjellmer 2005). Whereas *non-*, in (8a) indicates that someone is simply not an American, *un-* in (8b) expresses that her behavior is unworthy of an American. I discuss this contrast in detail in chapter 3.

(8) a. She is non-American.
    b. Her behavior is un-American.

However, in Czech this contrast is not morphologically marked, as illustrated in (9).

(9) Je ne- americký.
    is NEG American
    'He is un-American.'
    'He is non-American.'

It thus seems that there are different types of negative markers and that the division between these types is morphologically blurred in some languages (like Czech), but visible in others (like English). What it looks like is that the dichotomy between SN and CN is too simple. On the one hand the English data suggest that there is more variety than the dichotomy suggests, whilst Czech suggests more uniformity between CN and SN than the dichotomy suggests. In spite of these observations, most formal literature on negation deals with sentence negation, pushing constituent negation to the margins of the system. In particular, within

Fregean logic all negative markers are treated similarly, as propositional negators. What the new syncretism data show is that there is a need for a rehabilitation of constituent negation and more in particular, that there is a dire need for a more fine-grained classification of negative markers. Providing this classification and looking at syncretism patterns across a sample of languages is what this book sets out to do.

The book consists of four parts. The first part provides the theoretical background and this introduction. In chapter 2 the theoretical framework *nanosyntax* is introduced and the basic tools are provided to enable a reader who is unfamiliar with the framework to follow the discussion in the subsequent chapters.

The second part consists of three chapters all centred around the typology of negative markers in copular clauses with adjectival predicates. The following research questions steer the discussion in chapters 3–4:

(10) a. What types of negative markers are there?
 b. What criteria lie at the basis of the classification?
 c. What syncretism patterns can be detected between these types of negative markers across languages?

Chapter 3 provides an answer to (10a) and (10b). In this chapter it is discussed how negative markers can be classified in four different groups: T^{NEG}-markers, Foc^{NEG}-markers, $Class^{NEG}$-markers and Q^{NEG}-markers. The classification is based on four properties of negative markers: their scope – and related to that – their ability to stack or co-occur with other negative markers, their semantic properties (contradiction vs. contrariety) and their function. Once the classification is established, copular clauses with adjectival predicates in 23 languages are carefully scrutinized in pursuit of an answer to (10c). Chapter 4 thus discusses the syncretism patterns that can be found amongst the four groups of negative markers across a varied sample of languages. It turns out that no *ABA patterns are detected in the domain of negation, i. e. within a paradigm of negative markers based on the natural scope of negation there are no negative markers syncretic with negative markers in non-contiguous cells (cf. section 4.3 for discussion and explanation). Moreover, all logically possible patterns are attested in the sample under discussion. This is an intriguing result because it shows that morphology is not arbitrary and follows the natural semantic scope of negation. Moreover, the syncretism patterns also provide insight in the functional sequence of the predicates it combines with.

Within nanosyntax (Caha 2009, Starke 2009, Baunaz et al. 2018) and other approaches to syncretisms (Haspelmath 1997, Baerman et al. 2005), syncretisms are considered meaningful. They are considered surface conflations of hidden layers of syntactic structure within what is normally considered an indivisible unit, the morpheme. A morpheme can thus be decomposed into its subatomic features on the basis of syncretism patterns. Such a decomposition has been applied to case (Caha 2009, Starke 2017), to Path expressions (Pantcheva 2011), to demonstratives (Lander 2016), to complementizers (Baunaz & Lander 2018a) etc. Following the nanosyntactic tenet that syncretisms point to hidden layers of structure, the research question in (11) is addressed in chapter 5.

(11)   What hidden structure do these syncretisms between negative markers point to?

I propose in chapter 5 that a negative marker can be decomposed into five subatomic features: negation, tense, focus, classifier and scalar quantity. These features are heads and are hierarchically organized. Depending on the scope of the negative marker, more or less features are present, but negation is always present. I discuss how these negative markers are spelled out.

Building on the syncretism patterns and the related proposal for a decomposition of negative markers, the other part of the book aims at establishing the link between the internal syntax of negative markers and clausal syntax in English and French. Much of this work is unexplored territory in nanosyntax and this is also how it should be read and treated: as an open project that should be built upon and that hopefully sparks off discussion. In chapter 6 I go beyond the nano-world and show what happens at the level of the clause in English. Crucially, this chapter shows that negative markers of different scopal types can be treated in one module of the grammar, i.e. syntax, and it provides an answer to the research question in (12):

(12)   How do the negative markers with their complex internal structure end up in different positions in the clause?

I propose that there are at least four dedicated scope projections for negative markers in the clausal spine, i.e. four NegPs. These NegPs project optionally above a QP, ClassP, FocP and TP in the main clausal spine. The negative markers of English are discussed in chapter 6, with special attention for the spellout of unproductive negative markers like *iN-* and *dis-* and the seemingly suffixal sentential marker *n't*. I argue that *n't* is lexically stored together with the auxiliaries and modals to which it attaches.

In chapter 7 I continue the explorations at the clausal level, while also illustrating how the core principle underlying the nanosyntactic tenet, i.e. that language variation boils down to different sizes of lexical trees, is perfect to capture diachronic change. I apply this to the domain of French negation and more in particular to the evolution from *ne ... pas* in le bon usage French to the use of *pas* in Colloquial French. The research question this chapter sets out to answer is in (13):

(13) How well can nanosyntax capture diachronic change?

In the final part I provide an answer to the research questions in (14).

(14) a. How does the present proposal relate to other syntactic accounts for negation?
b. How would the semantics for these negative markers work?
c. Do we need a syntactic account?

In chapter 8 I discuss three syntactic approaches to negation in more detail, i. e. Zanuttini (1997), Poletto (2008, 2017) and Cormack & Smith (2002), and I explain how these proposals relate to the current programme. Finally, in chapter 9 I discuss the semantics of one of the four different negative markers in more detail, i. e. the Q^{NEG}-marker. Moreover, I discuss why a semantic account would not suffice to capture one of the core results of the present enterprise, i. e. the fact that scopally identical negative markers cannot be stacked. Negative markers can only be stacked if functional structure intervenes between two markers, an idea also worked out in De Clercq & Vanden Wyngaerd (2019a). In the final chapter I summarize the results and I point to avenues for further research.

As a final note in this introduction, it is important to point out that—even though the scope of this book seems wide in that many different types of negative markers are looked at—this book is not concerned with all possible problems that negative markers and negation in general give rise to. This book does not study negative concord, nor does it study NEG-raising or the interaction of negation and other types of quantification. This book is concerned with something that has hitherto not been studied, i. e. the study of syncretism patterns between different types of negative markers and what these patterns mean for the internal structure of negation on the one hand and for the traditional syntax-morphology divide on the other hand. The possible implications for other domains in the study of negation remain an issue to be investigated in future work.

2 Theoretical background: Nanosyntax

2.1 Introduction

Nanosyntax (henceforth NS; Starke 2009, 2011a, 2014b, Caha 2009) is a Late Insertion theory that finds its origins in the cartographic tradition (Cinque 1999, Rizzi 1997, Kayne 2005, Cinque 2010, Shlonsky 2010).[6] The cartographic research aim is to provide a detailed structural map of natural language syntax (Cinque & Rizzi 2008:42). Nanosyntax pushes this idea further and does not stop at the level of the word or morpheme, but goes beyond it and hence inside the structure of a morpheme.

The main idea underlying Late Insertion theories is that lexical items are inserted post-syntactically, after Merge (Chomsky 1995) has created syntactic structure with bundles of morphosyntactic features. Within nanosyntax these syntactic terminals that Merge operates on are very small: they can even be submorphemic. As a consequence of Late Insertion the functions or features that were traditionally attributed to the lexicon are now distributed amongst other components of the grammar: most importantly to the syntactic component in nanosyntax.[7]

As a of consequence of the submorphemic nature of the building blocks of syntax, spellout is phrasal.[8] It is 'only after some steps of derivation that a constituent large enough to correspond to a morpheme is created' (Starke 2014b:4): this morpheme is thus a phrasal constituent.

Spellout is also rigidly cyclic within NS: at every node, after every application of Merge, spellout is mandatory. The spellout domain is thus very small, even smaller than in approaches which are considered to take a rigidly cyclic approach

---

6 NS was proposed in lectures by Michal Starke and was further developed by students and senior researchers at Tromsø University. Most of the ideas in this chapter are based on a lecture series by Michal Starke at Ghent University in November 2011, Starke (2009, 2014b), on Caha (2009), Fabregas (2009) and also on Caha et al. (2019). A more lengthy introduction to the framework is Baunaz & Lander (2018b) and Baunaz et al. (2018) in general. For more work in NS I refer the reader to: Pantcheva (2009, 2011), Taraldsen (2012), Rocquet (2013), De Clercq (2013), Caha (2013), Lander (2015), De Clercq & Vanden Wyngaerd (2019a), Taraldsen Medová & Wiland (2019), Wiland (2019).
7 In this respect NS is like Distributed Morphology (henceforth DM) (Halle & Marantz 1993, Harley & Noyer 1999, Bobaljik 2012 and many others). I refer the reader to the aforementioned references for an introduction to DM, and to Caha (2018) for a comparison of DM and NS. I will only focus on NS in this book in general.
8 Cf. McCawley (1968), Weerman & Evers-Vermeul (2002), Neeleman & Szendrői (2007) for nonnanosyntactic implementations of phrasal spellout.

to spellout, like Epstein & Seely (2002), Bošković (2002, 2005), Müller (2004), who argue that spellout domains or phases are not bigger than a phrase.[9]

An ideal domain to study submorphemic features and the relevance of phrasal spellout is a domain in which syncretisms can be observed. Syncretisms can be looked at as a mismatch between syntactic structure and the lexicon (Fabregas 2009): there is only one lexical item but it corresponds to more than one syntactic representation and therefore consists of more than one feature. Caha (2009:6) calls them a 'surface conflation of two different underlying morphosyntactic structures'. In line with Jakobson (1962), Caha (2009:17) argues that 'syncretism points to the existence of a hidden level of linguistic organisation inside an apparently indivisible unit: the morpheme'. Put differently, whenever a morpheme has multiple readings, the claim will be that those readings are structurally different and by virtue of the fact that they are realised in the same morpheme, that they are structurally related.[10]

In order to understand the internal linguistic organization of syncretic morphemes, it is crucial to understand the restrictions on syncretisms. One domain in which syncretisms are prevalent and in which the restrictions on syncretisms have been studied is the domain of case (Baerman et al. 2005, Caha 2009, Baerman & Brown 2011). In the following section I explain what the restrictions on syncretisms are and how these restrictions play a role in the organisation of the internal structure of a morpheme. In section 2.3 I explain the core principles of nanosyntax by applying them to case morphemes (Caha 2009). This all will serve as a preparation for chapter 4 and 5, where I apply the nanosyntactic approach to negative markers.

2.2 Syncretisms

In order to illustrate how the restrictions on syncretisms determine the structural internal organisation of a morpheme I look at an example from Modern Greek, discussed in Caha (2009:6–7).

(15) a. o anthrop-os
the.NOM human-NOM
'the man'

---

[9] These approaches differ from approaches which take vP and CP as spellout domains or phases, cf. Chomsky (1995, 2001).
[10] Of course, lexically homophonous words, like Dutch *bank* which can both mean 'bench' and 'bank', are not considered here.

b. t-on anthrop-o
the-ACC human-ACC
'the man'

c. t-u anthrop-u
the-GEN human-GEN
'the man'

The paradigm in 2.1 (adapted after Caha (2009)) shows three Greek declension classes in the singular and one in the plural. The table shows that syncretisms are possible between NOM and ACC in the plural of *maxit* 'figher', i. e. *maxites*, and between ACC and GEN in the singular, i. e. *maxiti*. With respect to *álpha*, there is only one form for NOM, ACC and GEN singular. The word class of *anthropos* 'human' is completely non-syncretic for NOM, ACC and GEN singular. Crucially, there is no word class which shows a syncretism between NOM and GEN that does not also include ACC. We will refer from now on to the absence of this type of syncretism as *ABA.

Table 2.1: Case syncretisms in Modern Greek.

	maxit fighter PL	maxit fighter SG	anthrop-os human	álpha álpha sg
NOM	maxit-es	maxit-i-s	anthropos	álpha
ACC	maxit-es	maxit-i-Ø	anthrop-o	álpha
GEN	maxit-on	maxit-i-Ø	anthrop-u	álpha

Cross-linguistic research on syncretisms in the domain of case morphemes (Blake 1994, Baerman et al. 2005, Caha 2009, Baerman & Brown 2011) has led to the case sequence in (16).[11] The sequence shows how case can be ordered on the basis of the available syncretisms: a language will not be syncretic for nominative and comitative without also being syncretic for all intermediate case-layers.

(16) The Case sequence (Caha 2009:10):
nominative – accusative – genitive – dative – instrumental – comitative

Caha (2009) argues that the sequence based on the existing syncretisms points to structural contiguity: NOM is structurally closer to ACC than to GEN and so

---

[11] But see Starke (2017) for an updated case sequence capturing problematic case facts in Icelandic.

forth. Structural contiguity and thus the syncretisms between cases can be captured if we decompose case in its syntactic primitives. This decomposition can be achieved by 'sub-classification' (Caha 2009:20–21). This means that all cases in the sequence are considered part of one set of cases. We call this set *W* (Caha 2009:20). When the first case of the sequence is branched off from the set *W*, a new set *X* arises, and so on. Two sub-classifications can be made, depending on whether we start splitting off NOM from the set of all cases, as in (17), or COMIT, (18).

(17)   {NOM, ACC, GEN, DAT, INSTR, COMIT}

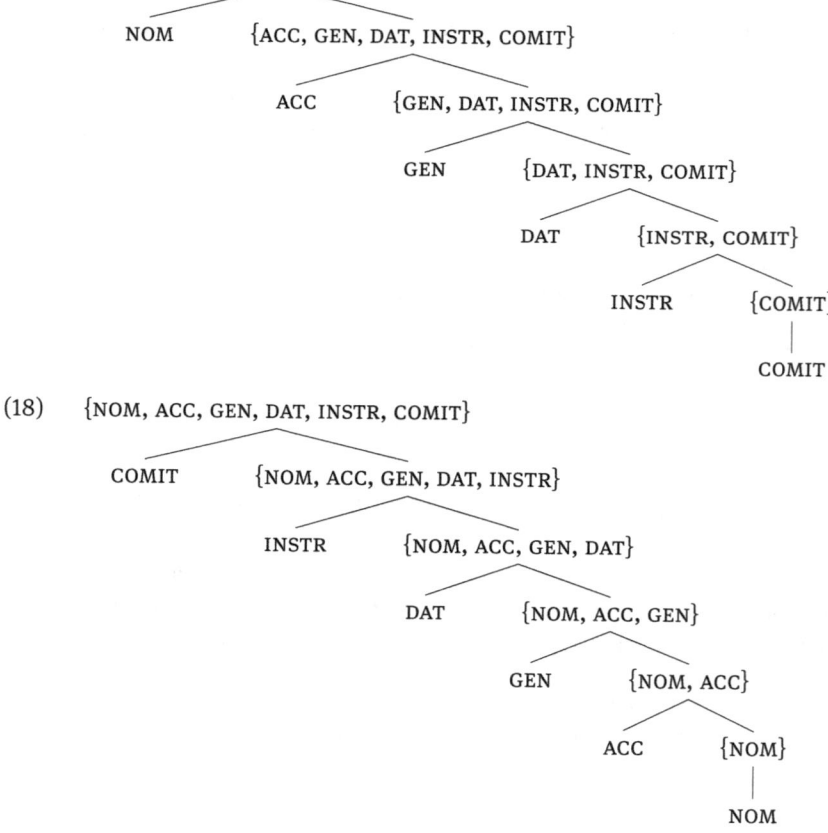

(18)   {NOM, ACC, GEN, DAT, INSTR, COMIT}

The next step is a 'cumulative classification' (Caha 2009:21). Each case is classified in terms of the number of sets it belongs to. For the decomposition in (17) the cumulative classification is in (19). For (18) it is in (20).

(19) a. W = NOM
    b. W, X = ACC
    c. W, X, Y = GEN
    d. W, X, Y, S = DAT
    e. W, X, Y, S, Z = INSTR
    f. W, X, Y, S, Z, P = COMIT

(20) a. W = COMIT
    b. W, X = INSTR
    c. W, X, Y = DAT
    d. W, X, Y, S = GEN
    e. W, X, Y, S, Z = ACC
    f. W, X, Y, S, Z, P = NOM

If a case belongs to different sets, it could be said to consist of different distinctive features. A case that does not belong to certain sets, lacks these distinctive features. In (21) and (22) the letters representing the sets have been replaced by case features: K1, K2, K3, …. Again I present the decomposition for both possible directions of the case sequence.

(21) a. K1 = NOM
    b. K1 + K2 = ACC
    c. K1 + K2 + K3 = GEN
    d. K1 + K2 + K3 + K4 = DAT
    e. K1 + K2 + K3 + K4 + K5 = INSTR
    f. K1 + K2 + K3 + K4 + K5 + K6 = COMIT

(22) a. K1 = COMIT
    b. K1 + K2 = INSTR
    c. K1 + K2 + K3 = DAT
    d. K1 + K2 + K3 + K4 = GEN
    e. K1 + K2 + K3 + K4 + K5 = ACC
    f. K1 + K2 + K3 + K4 + K5 + K6 = NOM

In line with nanosyntactic assumptions, each of these Kx features is a syntactic head. The features are organised in terms of binary branching trees. Caha proposes what he calls the Split K, a hierarchically organized 'case tree' in which case is split up in different case layers, each instantiating a syntactic feature (K1, K2, K3, …) as in (23). Even though decomposition and sub-classification are theoretically possible in both directions, Caha (2009) gives ample cross-linguistic evidence that NOM is the smallest case in the case tree and consequently also the lowest. So the decomposition in (17) and the cumulative classification in (19) are confirmed to be correct by cross-linguistic data.

(23)

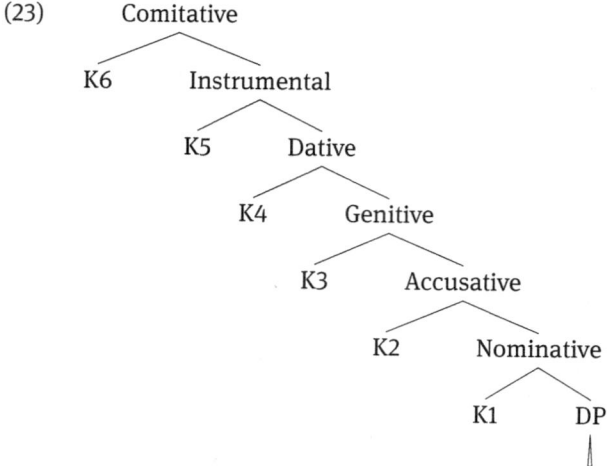

An interesting consequence of the decomposition of case and the structure in (23) is that it implies that there are structural containment relations between the different cases: nominative case is contained within accusative case, nominative and accusative within genitive case etc. Caha (2009:37) proposes the Universal Case Containment Hypothesis which also includes the Universal Case Contiguity Hypothesis:

(24)   Universal Case Containment:
    a. In the case sequence, the marking of cases on the right can morphologically contain cases on the left, but not the other way round.
    b. The case sequence: NOM–ACC–GEN–DAT–INS–COM

Morphological evidence for these hypotheses comes – amongst others – from case compounding,[12] a pattern in which one case is associated with what seem to be two case morphemes, as illustrated in table 2.2. In West-Tocharian the GEN case form comprises two morphemes: -ts and -em(-), with -ts following -em. The latter morpheme is the morpheme for ACC, suggesting that ACC morpheme is actually

---

12 Caha (2009:69) distinguishes between case stacking (cf. also Richards (2007)) and case compounding. In case stacking a noun bears multiple case markers expressing multiple case dependencies, whereas in compounding there is only one dependency relation expressed. This difference is also relevant for negation: there is negation compounding (also called negative doubling, a subtype of negative concord), and negation stacking (also called double negation).

Table 2.2: West-Tocharian case compounding (Caha 2009:69).

	horse-pl	man-pl
NOM	yakw-i	enkw-i
ACC	yakw-em	enkw-em
GEN	yakw-em-ts	enkw-em-ts

contained within GEN, or, put differently, that the genitive is an augmented accusative.

Summarizing, when one wants to account for the syncretism patterns in the case domain, then case needs to be decomposed in submorphemic features. Consequently, NOM, ACC or GEN are no longer labels for one morpheme, but they are labels or umbrella terms for a phrasal constituent which consists of several submorphemic hierarchically structured features. Phrasal spellout necessarily follows from this perspective on language: if one morpheme consists of several submorphemic features then only lexical insertion at the level of the phrase – and not at the level of terminals – can eventually lead to the output of a featurally complex morpheme. I discuss phrasal spellout and other core principles of nanosyntax in the next section.

2.3 Lexicalisation or spellout

In this section I illustrate by means of a concrete example how phrasal spellout and Lexical Insertion work within nanosyntax. I introduce the core nanosyntactic principles and the spellout algorithm whilst discussing an example.

The data I use to explain nanosyntactic lexicalisation are in table 2.3. The table presents four case forms of the N *jabolk* 'apple' in Slovene (Caha 2009, Starke 2011a). NOM and ACC are syncretic.

The way these case endings and root are stored in the lexicon is shown in (25). All lexical items (henceforth LIs) contain a lexical tree. This is an immediate consequence of the fact that nanosyntax is a Late Insertion model and that the lexicon

Table 2.3: Slovene *jabolk*, 'apple' (Caha 2009:240, Starke 2011a).

nom	jabolk-o
acc	jabolk-o
gen	jabolk-a
dat	jabolk-u

is post-syntactic, i. e. the lexicon contains stored syntactic trees. All LIs also contain phonological information, in between slant brackets in (25).[13] Only the lexical items of roots also consist of conceptual information, shown in small caps in (25a).

(25)   Lexical items
   a.   </jabolk/, [N*], APPLE>
   b.   </o/, [$_{K2P}$ K2 [$_{K1P}$ K1]] >
   c.   </a/, [$_{K3P}$ K3 [$_{K2P}$ K2 [$_{K1P}$ K1]]] >
   d.   </u/, [$_{K4P}$ K4 [$_{K3P}$ K3 [$_{K2P}$ K2 [$_{K1P}$ K1]]]] >

The lexicon of Slovene thus contains an entry for the 'root' N*, *jabolk*, (25a), with a lexical tree, phonological information and conceptual information (in small caps).[14] It also contains an entry for the case suffix *-o*. Due to the fact that NOM and ACC are syncretic, there is only one LI for both NOM and ACC. The LI for GEN is (25c) and the LI for DAT is (25d).

Observe that the lexical trees in (25b)–(25d) differ from (25a) in that they do not contain N*. Put differently, there is no lexical tree corresponding to *jabolko* or *jabolka*, but there is a tree for *jabolk* and there is a tree for *o* and for *a*.

When syntax merges N*, then—due to rigid cyclicity—the syntactic structure is checked at the level of the phrase NP* against the lexicon. The lexicon contains a LI with a matching Lexical Tree, (25a), thus N* can be spelled out as *jabolk*.

(26)   NP* ⇒ *jabolk*

When the first feature of the case spine, K1, is merged, generating the syntactic tree, cf. (26), then again the syntactic tree is checked against the lexicon, (25). However, the syntactic structure cannot be spelled out, since there is no LI matching the structure in (27).

(27)   K1P ⇒ ?
       /   \
      K1   NP*

Therefore, spellout-driven movement applies. spellout-driven movement only kicks in if Merge fails to lead to spellout. Stay thus takes precedence over Move.

---
13 For the phonological information I use regular spelling and not IPA.
14 * stands for all necessary functional material in between the root and the case layers. I assume for now that the root is spelled out without recourse to movement, simply by matching with the relevant LI.

NP* moves to the specifier position of the newly merged head without leaving a trace, (28). The reason why spellout driven movement does not leave traces is because this type of movement never leads to reconstruction.

(28)

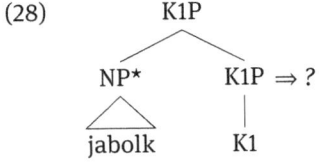

After movement has applied, the new structure is again checked against the lexicon. At first sight, there is again no LI which is a perfect match for the syntactic structure. However, there is a lexical item, (25b) that consists of a lexical tree that is the superset of the syntactic tree. By the theorem in (29), which is informally called the *Superset Principle*, the syntactic structure can be spelled out. The lexical tree in (25b) is bigger than the syntactic tree in (28) and thus contains the syntactic tree.

(29)   A lexically stored tree matches a syntactic node iff the lexically stored tree contains the syntactic node. (Starke 2009:3)

The Superset Principle naturally accounts for syncretisms. It is due to the observed syncretism between NOM and ACC in Slovene that the LI for NOM in Slovene is bigger in size than its syntactic structure: the lexical tree namely also consists of K2 (ACC).

However, the Superset Principle alone is not restrictive enough. If this were the only relevant principle for matching, then the LIs in (25c) and (25d) are also good candidates for insertion in K1P, because the lexically stored tree of these items also contain the syntactic node K1 (for this specific example). A principle is needed to restrict the matching principle. This is achieved by the Elsewhere Condition (Kiparsky 1973), as in (30). The Elsewhere condition ensures that at each cyclic node 'the most specific [LI, kdc] wins' (Starke 2009:4). This principle has been informally referred to as *Minimize Junk* (Starke 2009).

(30)   *Elsewhere Condition* or *Minimize Junk*
       In case two rules, R1 and R2, can apply in an environment E, R1 takes precedence over R2 if it applies in a proper subset of environments compared to R2 (Caha 2009:18).

Having the Superset Principle and the Elsewhere condition in place, LI (25b) is the winning competitor. Consequently, the case ending /o/ is inserted in the lower K1P, yielding the nominative *jabolko*, as in (31).

(31)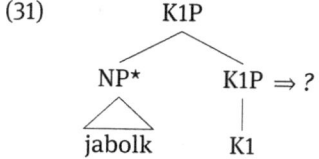

When K2 is merged, the resulting syntactic tree cannot be spelled out: there is no LI which matches the syntactic structure, (32).

(32)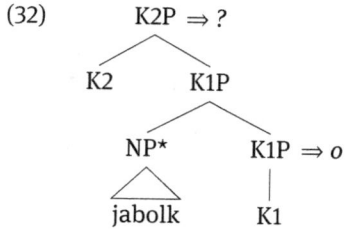

In order to spell out, NP* is cyclically moved to the specifier of the newly merged head. The lexicon is again consulted. The lexical tree in (25b) now matches the syntactic tree in (33). The accusative suffix /o/ can be inserted.[15]

(33)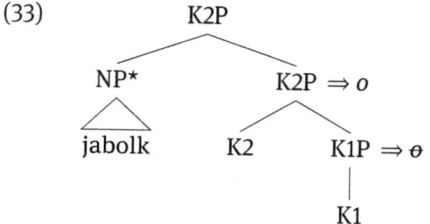

However, we need a principle here which prevents the spellout of NOM from also being preserved, since there is no form *jabolk-o-o* in Slovene. This theorem is called *Cyclic Override*. Cyclic Override follows from the theory itself. Starke (2009:4) puts it like this:

> Spellout is taken to be cyclic, with a spellout attempt after each merger operation. Each successful spellout overrides previous successful spellouts. Since merger is bottom-up, the biggest match will always override the smaller matches.

Consequently, when /o/ is inserted at the phrasal node K2P, the previous spellout is overridden. This yields the accusative form *jabolk-o*.

---

15 In the tree in (33) and the following trees, we assume that cyclic phrasal movement does not leave traces (since it does not allow for reconstruction) and therefore leads to the reduction of the previously created the spec position from which movement takes place, i.e. K1P in this case, to a single node.

When K3 is merged, (34), the structure is again checked against the lexicon. However, phrasal spellout is not possible due to the presence of N*. Therefore, N* again undergoes cyclic phrasal movement to the specifier of the newly merged head resulting in (35). The lexicon is consulted and there is a matching lexical item for K3P. The new spellout /a/ overrides the previous spellout, resulting in the GEN form *jabolk-a*.

(34)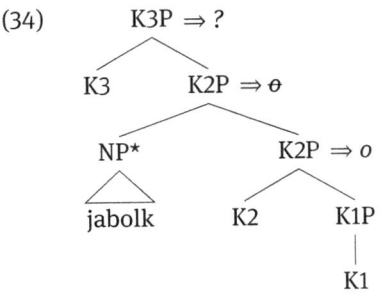

(35)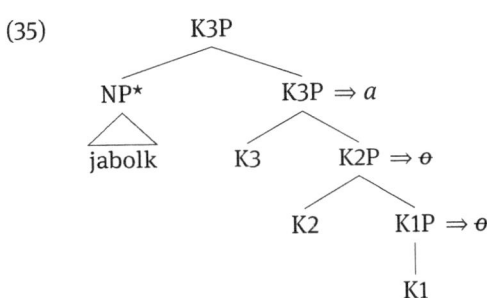

Finally, when K4 is merged, (36), the syntactic tree is checked against the lexicon. No LI is found that matches the structure. N* would intervene in the spellout of the case layer K4P. N* moves to the specifier of the newly merged head, (37), upon which the lexicon is checked again. Now K4 can be spelled out and /u/ can be inserted. The previous spellout is overridden, yielding the dative form *jabolk-u*.

(36)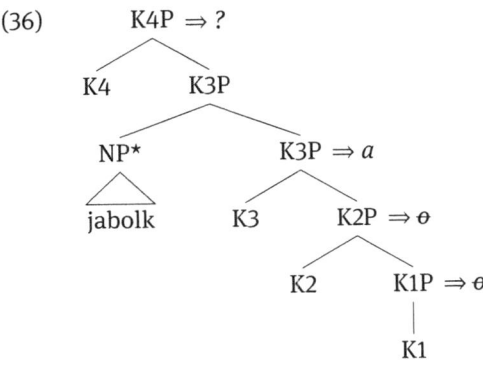

(37)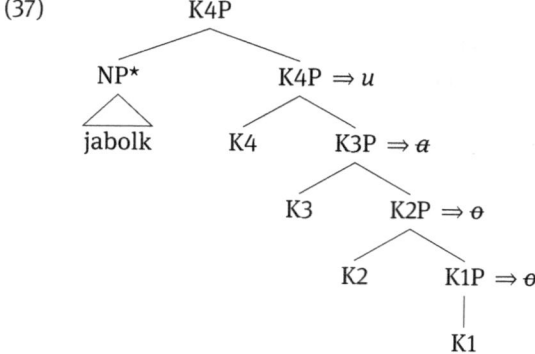

In all the trees above, when movement applied in order to be able to spell out, it was cyclic phrasal movement: NP* moves cyclically up the tree. However, another kind of phrasal movement, namely snowball movement or roll-up movement (Collins 2002, Aboh 2004), is possible if Stay or cyclic phrasal movement does not lead to spellout. Snowball movement is the kind of movement in which a phrase moves cyclically up the tree and pied pipes the projection containing its previous landing site, as in (38).

(38)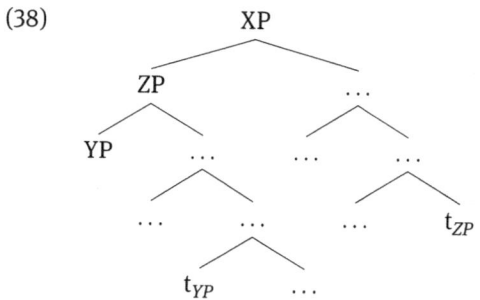

A typical situation in which snowball or roll-up movement would be necessary to be able to spell out is when there is case compounding, i.e. when two case-endings co-occur on one NP*, spelling out only one case dependency. I illustrate this for the West-Tocharian GEN. The West-Tocharian case paradigm, from (Caha 2009:69), in table 2.2 is repeated here as 2.4.

I assume the lexicon of West-Tocharian contains at least the LIs in (39).

(39) a. </-em/, [$_{K2P}$ K2 [$_{K1P}$ K1]] >
 b. </-ts/, [$_{K3P}$ K3] >

Table 2.4: West-Tocharian case compounding.

	horse.pl	man.pl
NOM	yakw-i	enkw-i
ACC	yakw-em	enkw-em
GEN	yakw-em-ts	enkw-em-ts

In order to spell out the West-Tocharian genitive of *horse*, K1 and K2 are first merged and spelled out according to the rules of phrasal spellout discussed above, as shown in (40). There is an LI (39a) in the lexicon of West-Tocharian which allows for insertion of the case-ending *em* in K2P.

(40)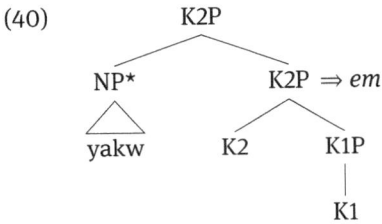

Once ACC is created as in (40), K3 is merged. The lexicon will be checked, but there is no LI to spell out this syntactic structure. Consequently, cyclic phrasal movement applies and the derived structure is as in (41). However, upon checking the lexicon, this structure cannot be spelled out either, since there is no lexical tree which contains this syntactic tree.

(41)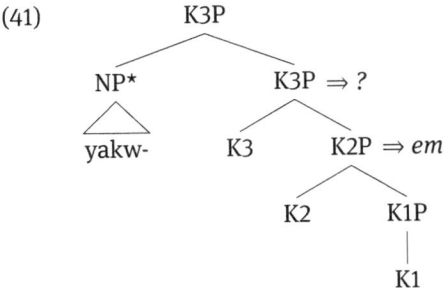

If there were no other options, this would lead to a crash. But as we saw, there is one more type of movement, viz. snowball movement. Starke (2011a) proposes that the previous step can be undone and that a new attempt at spellout can be made. NP* moves again to K3P but this time it pied-pipes along its complement, as in (42). Now there is a lexical item in the lexicon corresponding to the lower K3P in (42), namely (39b). This LI can be inserted. As a result of the snowball movement the previous spellout cannot be overridden and hence there is case compounding.[16]

(42)
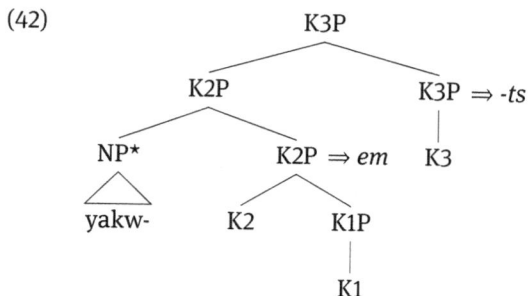

What this discussion shows is that there are different movement types allowed to get the correct spellout. Starke (2018:245) explicates the hierarchy of steps in what he refers to as *the spellout algorithm*. The order of the steps in the algorithm is based on the idea that moving less material is more economical than more material. The basic steps are as in (43):

(43) a. Insert feature and spell out (= Stay/Do not move)
      b. If fail, try a cyclic (spec-to-spec) movement of the node inserted at the previous cycle.
      c. If fail, try a snowball movement of the complement of the newly inserted feature and spell out.

If one of the movements fail, the movement needs to be undone and a new option needs to be tried, this is called backtracking.

The type of movements discussed in (43) lead to the spellout of suffixes and hence constitutes an ideal means to capture case suffixes. However, as pointed out in Caha (2009) the case hierarchy does not only spell out case suffixes but is also considered to play a role in the spell out of prepositions. Starke (2018) argues that the distinction between prefixes and suffixes is structurally anchored and parametrised. PRE-elements or prefixes, like for instance prepositions, are proposed to consist of a binary bottom, (44), whilst POST-elements or suffixes al-

---

[16] These type of movements do not cause antilocality violations (Klaus 2003, Grohmann 2011) because these movements are purely spellout driven and hence not for feature checking purposes. Antilocality is only an issue when feature checking is involved.

ways have a unary bottom, as a consequence of spellout-driven movement not leaving traces, (45).

(44)

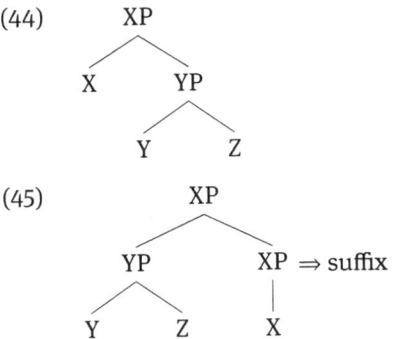

(45)

Due to this structural difference between PRE- and POST-elements, a phrase like *of* in *of sugar* for instance would never get spelled out. The reason is that the lexical tree of *of* has a binary bottom, (46) (Starke 2018:247), and whatever type of movement that would be tried, the resulting structure would be unary and it would not be possible to spell out *of*.

(46) < /of/,

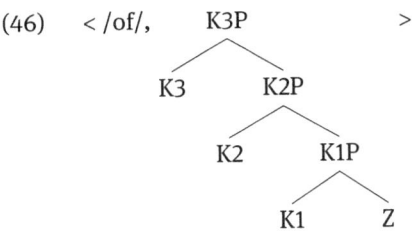

>

As such it seems that the spellout algorithm needs to be updated with another operation to be able to spell out PRE-elements as well. We again draw on operations that are familiar from regular syntax, i. e. the way subjects are merged in a derivation as complex specifiers. Starke (2018) proposes that PRE-elements are assembled and merged in the same way, i. e. elements with a binary bottom are merged as complex specifiers. Since complex specifiers are XPs and merge-XP requires a new derivation to be spawned, merge-XP is a heavy operation, as opposed to merge-f, which is light and atomic. Starke (2018:246) therefore proposes that a new derivation can be spawned in a complex specifier as a last resort option, after all options from the spellout algorithm have been tried. The feature required to be spelled out will be provided by the new derivation, which will grow with the functional sequence (henceforth FSEQ) and will grow as long as possible (given its costly nature). The updated spellout algorithm is thus as in (47):

(47) a. Insert feature and spell out (= Stay/ Do not move)
b. If fail, try a cyclic (spec-to-spec) movement of the node inserted at the previous cycle
c. If fail, try a snowball movement of the complement of the newly inserted feature and spell out.
d. If merge-f has failed to spell out (even after backtracking), try to spawn a new derivation providing feature X and merge that with the current derivation, projecting feature X to the top node.

In what follows I illustrate in detail how merge of such a complex specifier works. In addition to the lexical item in (46), there is also the lexical item for *sugar* in the lexicon with its phonological and conceptual information, (48). Moreover there is also a phonologically null accusative/nominative form of the preposition *of*, illustrated in (49).

(48) </sugar/, ZP , SUGAR >

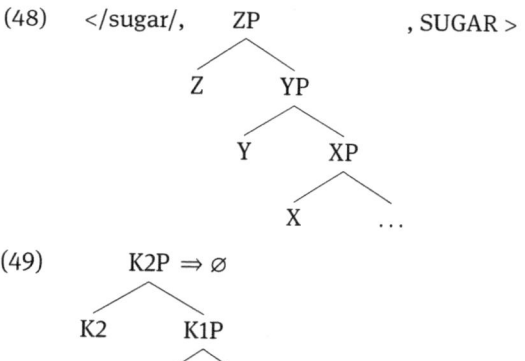

(49)

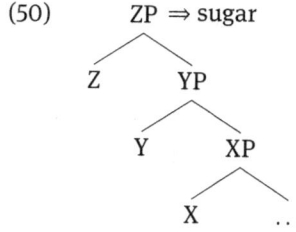

First the root *sugar* will be merged, eventually yielding the structure in (50) and spelled out at every node by the lexical item in (48) (by cyclic override).

(50) ZP ⇒ sugar

At ZP K1 will be merged, but this will not lead to any spellout, because the lexicon of English does not contain suffixes for nominative marking, (51).

(51)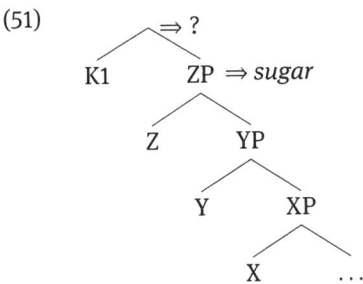

So after having tried the different steps in the spellout algorithm, i. e. successive cyclic movement (which is not available in this case since there is no spec) and snowball movement, a new derivation will be spawned in order to spell out the feature required by the FSEQ. The last feature provided in the main spine and the newly required feature will be merged in the newly spawned derivation, yielding the structure in (52), which will be spelled out by the lexical item in (49), which is phonologically null.

(52)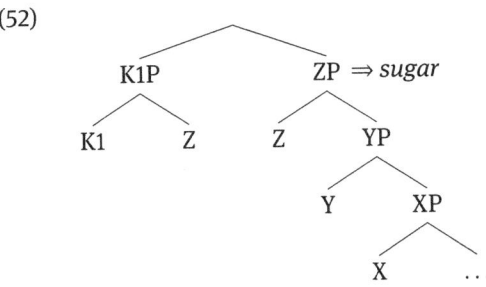

Due to the fact that spawning a new derivation is so costly, the newly spawned structure grows in tandem with the main spine for as long as possible. So K2 will also be merged in the new subderivation and spelled out by the phonologically null (49). Eventually, K3 will be merged and spelled out by (46), providing the spellout of the preposition *of*.

(53)

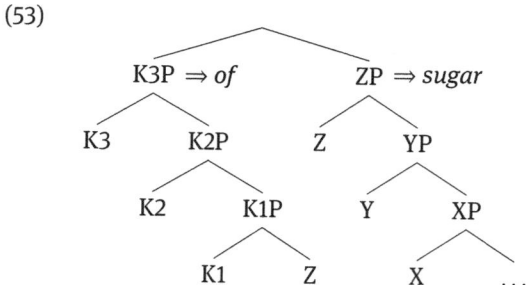

After this, the subderivation will no longer be able to provide whatever other feature may be required by the FSEQ and will be closed. The derivation continues in the main spine.

2.4 Deriving *ABA

Finally, the system of phrasal spellout complemented with the Superset Principle, the Elsewhere Condition and Cyclic Override is well-equipped to capture the absence of ABA-patterns in the domain of s, i. e. the *ABA patterns which we exemplified by means of the case paradigm in 2.1. Let me briefly explicate why. Imagine a lexicon with the following lexical items, (54).

(54) a. </A/, [$_{XP}$ X [$_{YP}$ Y [$_{ZP}$ Z]]]$_>$
      b. </B/, [$_{YP}$ Y [$_{ZP}$ Z]]

If syntax merges Z, then at the level of ZP, both (54a) and (54b) are candidates for insertion due to the Superset Principle. However, due to the Elsewhere Condition, (54b) will be inserted. Spelling out B, instead of A.

(55)   ZP ⇒ B
        |
        Z

However, if we defined the lexical item for A as in (56), then A would be inserted at the level of ZP, (57), but would not be a candidate at the level of YP, as in (58), nor at XP. Only B would be a candidate at YP in that case.

(56)   </A/, [$_{ZP}$]$_>$
(57)   ZP ⇒ A
       |
       Z

(58)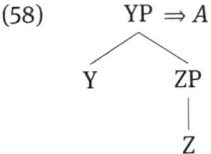

There is one way to derive an ABA-pattern in this system and that is by postulating two lexical items with a different lexical tree and the same phonology, i. e. one with the structure in (54) and one with the structure in (56). Whilst this can be useful for certain cases of accidental homonymy, it is not the type of approach one wants to promote, because if this were the right way to deal with syncretisms the lexicon would consist of numerous lexical items consisting of the same phonology and different lexical trees.

2.5 Conclusion

In this chapter I explained how the core principles of nanosyntax, namely phrasal spellout, the Superset Principle, the Elsewhere Principle and Cyclic Override together provide a theory which can capture attested syncretism patterns and excludes unattested ABA-patterns. The approach allows one to look inside a morpheme to lay bare the distinctive features a morpheme consists of.

I will discuss and highlight more aspects of nanosyntax as we go along. The basics laid out here should, however, be sufficient to follow the ideas and analyses presented in this book.

In order to detect the submorphemic features inside a negative morpheme I investigate in the next part of this book syncretism patterns within the domain of negative markers across a varied sample of languages. This leads to the postulation of a negative spine, a complex NegP.

Part II: **The internal structure of negative markers**

3 Classification of negative markers

Introduction

In the introductory chapter on nanosyntax we discussed how syncretisms between different case markers can be used to diagnose underlying and hidden structure. More concretely, it was proposed, on the basis of the detected syncretisms, that one case morpheme consists of submorphemic features with cases being contained within each other.

In this part I argue that a similar approach can be taken to negative markers, i. e. meaningful syncretism patterns between different types of negative markers exist and are a reason to decompose negative markers. As far as I know, negative markers have never been looked at from this point of view and hence this observation and its implications are the main empirical contribution of this book. What looks like one negative morpheme – English *not* – can – on the basis of the empirical work done in this study – actually be subdivided into submorphemic units. In addition, the decomposition of the negative morpheme explains why there are morphologically different negative markers with different scopal properties.

The aim of this part of the book is to develop a nanosyntactic approach to negative markers or to put it differently to look at the internal syntax of negative markers. In this chapter I propose a classification of negative markers into four types based on four different properties. In chapter 4 I examine how these four types of negative markers are encoded cross-linguistically and I discuss the absence of ABA-patterns across these four different types. Finally, in chapter 5 syncretisms will be accounted for as a consequence of the internal structure of the negative morpheme/marker itself, i. e. the negative morpheme is decomposed by means of nanosyntactic tools.

For expository purposes, I limit my discussion to negative markers that combine with adjectival predicates in predicate position and with the copular verbs these adjectives can combine with. As already mentioned in footnote 4 in chapter 1 'negative marker' refers to markers that negate predicates, irrespective of whether 1) these markers are morphologically simplex or complex, 2) morphologically free or bound, 3) affixal, infixal or circumfixal and 4) whether they give rise to sentence negation or constituent negation. However, 'negative marker' does not refer to negative polarity items, negative quantifiers, negative indefinites or negative expletives in this book, unless referred to explicitly. Some languages, like Khwe, Hixkaryana and Chinese in the present sample, lack -or are said to lack- real adjectives. In that case copular constructions with nominals, adverbs or deverbal adjectives were considered, because I assume that in these languages adverbs or verbs are syncretic with adjectives and express properties that are typically associated with adjectives (p. c. Starke 2016). I will not consider negative markers on verbal predicates, as in *disagree*, or on nouns, as in *non-event*. I am at this point not taking other negative strategies into account than pure negation. As mentioned before, I do not consider negative indefinites like *no, nothing, nobody* in argument position nor do I consider negative adverbs like *nowhere* or *never* or correlatives like *neither*. In all of these cases negation combines with an argument, adverb or coordinator, which does not allow us to study negation proper in its purest form. Moreover, I have not run into a language where any of these other negation strategies were the sole strategy for negation a language had at its disposal. It seems that if a language has any of these negation strategies it also has the 'pure negation' strategy, which is why I believe it is warranted to try to understand the latter first before extending the account to other, more complex, negation strategies. However, it is clear that the system developed in this book can be extended to these strategies, as I show for negative indefinites in De Clercq (2019a), but I do not elaborate on them in this book. More details on the methodology and the sample are in chapter 4.

3.1 Preparing the classification

Before a decomposition of negative markers on the basis of syncretisms is possible, it is necessary to know what type of negative markers there are. The mere word 'syncretisms' presupposes namely that there are different groups of negative markers amongst which syncretism patterns can arise. This is indeed the case, as we will see, and before we discuss the different existing syncretism patterns across languages, I first need to introduce the different groups of negative markers.

With respect to the classification of case-features the literature, both traditionally descriptive and formal, provides us with a reasonably good insight into what the different classes or kinds of case markers are. For negation the different kinds or classes of negation are not so clearly delineated, though distinctions have been made and actually date back to Aristotle. A common classification is one based on the scopal properties of negative markers. Predicate denial (Aristotle's term) or propositional negation (Frege's term) are two different labels used to refer to wide scope or sentential negation, i. e. negation that scopes over the tensed predicate. Horn (2001b:21) argued that the label predicate denial is more appropriate than the label from formal logic, because propositional or external negation is not morphologically realized in the languages of the world. I come back to this discussion in section 3.3.1. Predicate negation is Aristotle's label to refer to the scope negation can have over an untensed predicate and predicate term negation is the label referring to the scope of negation over a term. All these labels refer to well-known distinctions from traditional logic (Horn 2001b:140–141).[17] The classification proposed in this part of the book is in many ways reminiscent of the old Aristotelian classification. As in the traditional subdivision, the subdivision I propose also takes into account the distinction between negative markers that take scope over the tensed predicate, the untensed predicate or the predicate term. However, unlike in the traditional division, I subdivide the group of negative markers that scope over the predicate term into two groups because of how they can be stacked (cf. section 3.2) and because of the meanings they can give rise to. In addition, the labels that I use in my classification are based on the syntactic position in which the negative marker takes scope. As such I arrive at 1) negative tense markers (T^{NEG}-markers), 2) negative focus markers (Foc^{NEG}-marker), 3) negative classifier markers ($Class^{NEG}$-markers) and 4) negative (scalar) quantity markers (Q^{NEG}-markers).[18] The classification presented in this book is based on four different properties of negative markers: 1) the scopal properties, 2) stacking properties, 3) semantic properties (contradictory or contrary negation) and 4) functional properties. In what follows I discuss the four properties which lie at the origin of the present classification. In chapter 4 I discuss the classification with respect to a cross-linguistic sample.

3.2 Property 1: Stacking

The most crucial property for the classification of negative markers, which ties in closely with the property described in the next section, is stacking. The stack-

---

17 Horn's (2001b) entire book is dedicated to a careful discussion of these concepts within the history of logic. I refer the reader to his book for a thorough discussion. Horn (2001b:140–141) provides a neat summary of the different concepts used by some of the key philosophers and logicians in the history of negation.

18 As pointed out by an anonymous reviewer, there is evidence from indigenous languages of the Americas that the morphological expression of tense can be optional or absent. On the basis of these languages (in particular Blackfoot and Halkomelem) Ritter & Wiltschko (2014) argue that INFL is a universal head in the syntactic spine and TENSE is not. Under their approach, T is argued to be one of INFL's possible instantiations. Two other instantiations are location or participants. In the languages scrutinized in this book this issue did not arise and tense is marked on the predicate. If Ritter & Wiltschko (2014)'s proposal is on the right track, then it could be that the label I use, i. e. T^{NEG}, should be replaced by $INFL^{NEG}$. However, more research on Blackfoot and Halkomelem, from a nanosyntactic perspective, i. e. paying attention to syncretisms in the INFL domain and domain of negation, would be necessary to see whether this adaptation is indeed required. I leave this to future research.

ing properties of the different types of negative markers give insight into the scopal properties of these negative markers and are immediate support for the fact that there are different positions for negation in the clause. A negative marker like sentential *not* or *n't*, let us call it N4 for now, can in principle co-occur with the constituent negative marker *not*, N3 for now, (59a). N4 can also co-occur with *non* (N2), (59b) or a marker like *un-* (N1 for now), (59c). Moreover, also several negative markers can be stacked within the same sentence, (60), combining N4, N3 with N2 or N1.

(59) a. He is not not happy, is/*isn't he?
 b. This sentence is not non-ambiguous, is/*isn't it?
 c. He is not unhappy, is/*isn't he?

(60) a. She isn't NOT unhappy.
 b. She isn't NOT nonprofessional.

Consequently, due to the fact that *n't* can stack on *not* and *not* on *un-*, but not the other way around, stacking can be used as a test to see what the scopal properties of a negative marker are and thus provides insight into where negation can appear in the clausal spine. The rule is that the negative marker which can stack on most items takes widest scope. For instance, it is clear that English *non-* belongs to a different group than *un-*, because *non-* can stack on *iN-*, *dis-* or *un-*, as in (61), but not the other way around.

(61) a. nondisenfranchized, noninfinite
 b. Nonunhappy people are the best. (Jim McCloskey, p. c.)

However, as we will see, also for other languages, it is rare that markers belonging to group N1 and N2 stack. I assume that the rarity (but grammaticality) of this type of stacking must be related to the fact that the scope of both negative markers is the same predicate term without any other substantial addition – apart from the N1 marker – to the adjectival root. We will return to this issue in sections 3.3.3 and 3.3.4.

Negative markers of the same type never stack. This constraint seems part of a more general restriction on permissible functional sequences, discussed by De Clercq & Vanden Wyngaerd (2017b, 2019a) and elaborated on in section 3.3.4. The English negative markers *un-*, *iN-* and *dis-* for instance cannot be stacked on each other nor on any other negative marker, (62), which I interpret as a consequence of the fact that these negative markers take scope in the same position and hence belong to the same group.[19]

(62) a. *indishonest, *inunhuman, *disunhappy, *disinhuman, *unnothappy, *unnonprofessional, ...
b. *undiscourteous, *undishonest, *undisagreeable (Lehrer 2002:504)

Due to the synchronic unproductivity of *iN-* and *dis-* (Zimmer 1964), I consider *un-* the productive marker of this group and *dis-* and *iN-* unproductive markers.

Summarising, the more negative markers a certain marker can stack on, the wider its scope. When a negative marker cannot stack on any other negative marker, it is necessarily a marker belonging to the group that I dubbed N1 in this section. Since the stacking properties of negative markers are a probe into their scopal properties, I will discuss the scopal properties of these negative markers in the next section and label the groups according to their scope position, i. e. the temporary labels N1, N2, N3 and N4 will be replaced. For now we can say that the classification for English is roughly as in (63):

(63)   N4   N3   N2   N1
        n't/not   not   non   un-/dis-/iN-

3.3 Property 2: Scope position

I mentioned earlier in the introduction that Aristotelian predicate denial is negation that scopes over the tensed predicate, predicate negation is negation scoping over the untensed predicate and predicate term negation is negation scoping over a predicate term. This traditional distinction is maintained in the different groups of negative markers that we distinguished in the previous section, i. e. N4-markers like *n't/not* scope over the tensed predicate, *N3*-markers like *not* over the untensed predicate and *N2*- and *N1*-markers like *non* and *un-* over a predicate term.

Keeping in mind the stacking properties of negative markers and the traditional Aristotelian descriptive labels, we now link the different types of markers, abbreviated earlier in this chapter as N1, N2, N3 and N4, each to a position in

---

[19] I consider it possible that this group, which I will label Q^{NEG}-markers in the next section 3.3, can be further subdivided. The privative prefix *a-* for instance is in complementary distribution with *un-* or *in-* and hence cannot be stacked, but it always gives rise to privation, unlike *un-* or *in-*, which tend to give rise to contrariety (see section 3.4 for an explanation of these terms). Due to their stacking properties I treat these markers as belonging to the same group, but one could argue that they should be distinguished on semantic grounds.

clausal syntax. Important to mention here is that we are not yet looking at the internal structure for these four different markers at this point nor to how this internal structure captures the syncretisms. This will be discussed in chapters 4 and 5. We are now only laying the foundations for a classification of different negative markers that will serve our crosslinguistic investigation.

The raw structure in (64) illustrates the skeleton of a (copular) clause (the structure of the clause will be refined in chapter 6.2), with four positions for negation, each position for negation will be argued to be associated with another position below it, i. e. there are positions for negation above TP, FocP, ClassP and QP. I will label the different groups of negative markers in accordance with these associated positions, i. e. N1 becomes a Q^{NEG}-marker, N2 becomes a $Class^{NEG}$-marker, N3 a Foc^{NEG}-marker and N4 a T^{NEG}-marker. It must be emphasized here that not all copular clauses contain all these projections. Apart from TP (or INFL, see footnote 18) all other projections are optional in the FSEQ. However, if they co-occur, they occur according to the hierarchy in (64). For instance, the presence or absence of Q and Class depends on the internal structure of the adjectival predicate. Non-scalar adjectival predicates for instance will be argued to lack a Q-layer.

(64)

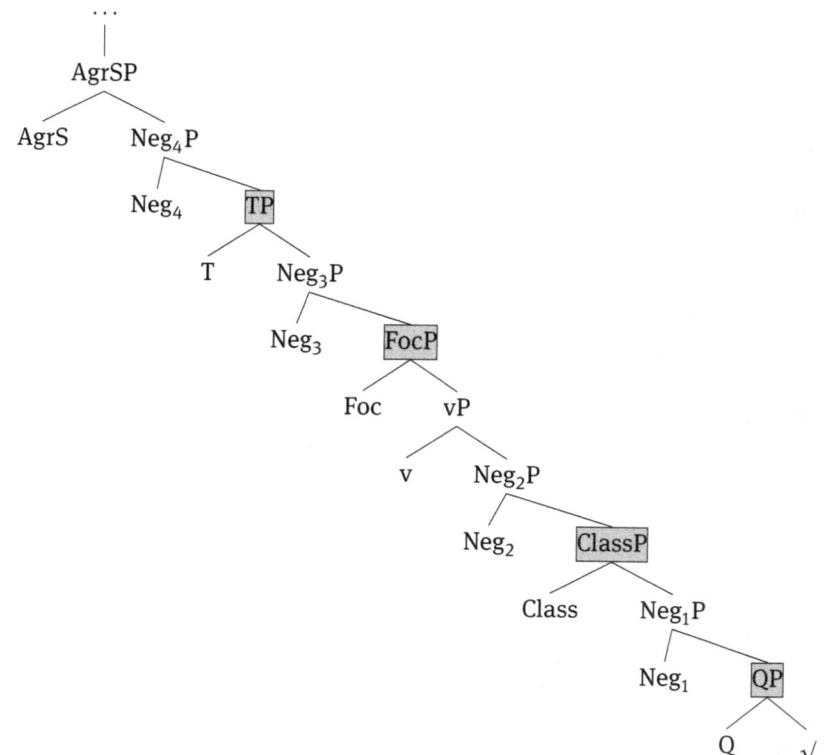

The table for English in (63) can now be updated to (65):

(65)

N4	N3	N2	N1
T^{NEG}	Foc^{NEG}	Class^{NEG}	Q^{NEG}
n't/not	not	non	un-/dis-/iN-

Before we continue our discussion of these different types of negative markers and their associated scope positions in syntax, it is important to say something more about the functional projection NegP on the one hand and about the fact that the C-domain is absent from the raw structure in (64) on the other hand.

First, before Kayne (1989) and Pollock (1989) introduced NegP as a designated position for negation in the FSEQ, negation was considered an adverbial modifier without any dedicated functional projection, much like Ernst's (1992) way of treating sentential negation in English (cf. Haegeman & Lohndal 2013). Even though some linguists only adopt NegP for languages that have negative concord and hence a negative head (Zeijlstra 2004b) or do not adopt it at all (Ernst 1992), NegP is no longer a controversial projection for most syntacticians, be it that it is mostly exclusively used as a position for the marker expressing sentence negation. NegP is sometimes referred to as PolP (Ouhalla 1990, Belletti 1990, Culicover 1992 or ΣP (Laka 1991, 1994) in accounts that want to focus on the fact that certain affirmative elements also trigger polarity effects. Pollock's main reason to argue for the existence of a NegP was motivated by a wish to account for bipartite negation in French. Under his proposal *ne* and *pas* originate within the same projection, with *ne* the head of NegP and *pas* its specifier, thus setting the first steps on the road to consider negation as intrinsically complex. Actually, the proposal for French negation that will be discussed in chapter 7 just pushes Pollock's idea a bit further. The relation between specifier and head of NegP in Pollocks's work will be translated in the current framework as a relation between two parts of a negative nanospine, together constituting full negation.

In line with Pollock's proposal and building on Rizzi's work on the wh-criterion (Rizzi 1990), Haegeman (1995) proposes that a negative operator needs to be in a Spec-Head configuration with a negative head, i. e. satisfying the Neg-criterion, to give rise to sentential negation. This means that any negative phrase (marker or argument alike) needs to move overtly or covertly to the specifier of a NegP above TP to give rise to sentential negation. This idea has been very influential and remains relevant for the present proposal, be it that under the present proposal this idea is extended to other types of negation. The idea of multiple NegPs as such is not new either and is present in the work of many scholars working on negation. However, the implementation in this book is different. Usually multiple positions are discerned for sentential negation, as in the work by

Zanuttini (1997), Poletto (2008, 2017) or for sentential negation and regular constituent negation, as in Cormack & Smith (2002), leaving undiscussed what is traditionally labelled as lexical negation (Dahl 2010), morphological negation (Horn 2001a:187, Hamawand 2009) or affixal negation (Horn 2001a:273–308). In this book NegPs are not only proposed for what is traditionally considered part of syntax, but also for negative markers that are usually considered part of morphology. In chapter 8 we will discuss Zanuttini (1997), Poletto (2008, 2017) and Cormack & Smith (2002)'s work and compare it – as far as this is possible – to the proposal developed in this book.

The second issue I need to address is why the C-domain is not considered in the structure in (64), since it is well-know that there is a polarity related functional head in the CP-domain that can host a constituent or particle that expresses external negation/propositional negation (see section 3.3.1) or polarity emphasis with respect to the polarity expressed in the TP (Breitbarth et al. 2013b). The reason why this position is not addressed is because 1) the nature of this position is not quite clear nor 2) is it clear what type of polarity-related constituents/negative markers it can host. The position has received many various labels in the literature: FocP (Rizzi 1997, Haegeman 2000, Butler 2003, Poletto & Zanuttini 2013, Bar-Asher Siegal & De Clercq 2019), ForceP or FinP (Authier 2013), or a left peripheral Verum-Focus position (VFoc) (Van Craenenbroeck 2010) or CP (Moscati 2006, 2010, McCloskey 2011). With respect to the negative constituent/marker in the C-domain it needs to be said that for the sample of languages that I studied there was no CP-related negative marker that is dedicated to C-negation only and/or that is not somehow fused with another functional category (like a complementizer or coordinator, as is the case with correlatives). This observation is in line with earlier typological observations that the morphological realisation of an external negator or real propositional negator is typologically rare (Dahl 1979, Horn 2001b). In addition, polarity markers like 'no', which have propositional scope and which have been argued to be generated in CP (Holmberg 2013, 2015), share properties with negation, but are in many languages rather agreement markers than real negation markers. Finally, negation that takes widest scope is often expressed by different constructions, either negative clefts or preposed negative DPs/PPs with negative indefinites or negative constituent markers (Haegeman 2000), all of which have been argued to be associated to a left peripheral Focus Position (Rizzi 1997), i.e. to a position taking external scope. For none of these constructions it can be argued that they are uniquely dedicated to the C-domain and/or independent negative markers that have not been fused with other clausal constituents. For all these reasons I focus on pure negative markers in copular clauses within TP and PredP/vP and I keep other CP-related negative constructions and the study of negative complementizers or correlatives for future work.[20]

In the following subsections I discuss the scope position for each of the different types of negative markers that can be discerned on the basis of the stacking test discussed in section 3.2.

3.3.1 T^{NEG}-markers

The group of negative markers that I label T^{NEG}-markers in this book has variously been referred to as the group of negators expressing sentence negation (Klima 1964), nexal negation (Jespersen 1917) or in Aristotle's terms predicate denial.

The label T^{NEG}-marker will be used throughout this book and I will comment on it below, but it is useful to reflect for a moment on the Aristotelean notion of predicate denial that is most closely related to what I refer to with the label T^{NEG}-marker. Within Aristotelian term logic (Horn 2001b:chapter 1) negative markers taking wide scope over the predicate are said to give rise to *predicate denial*, i.e. S is not P. In the case of predicate denial the predicate (positive or negative) is denied of the subject (Horn 2001b:31). For a sentence like (66) this is indeed the case: the predicate *happy* is denied of the subject *John* by the affixal negative marker *n't*, yielding the reading of predicate denial in (67).

(66)   John isn't happy.

(67)   For John, it is the case that he is not happy.

However, this is not usually the type of reading that is associated with sentence negation in formal linguistics. Very often it is argued that this type of negation gives rise to *propositional negation* or external negation, the type of negation argued for in the propositional logic of the Stoics and Frege (Horn 2001b:138). From

---

[20] Recently, Bar-Asher Siegal (2015), Bar-Asher Siegal (2015) and Bar-Asher Siegal & De Clercq (2019) argue that Jewish Babylonian Aramaic (JBA) developed a negator for which it can be argued that it is a morphological instantiation of an external negator. These new data suggest that there may after all be an extra type of negative marker that takes widest scope and that – in accordance with the type of analyses proposed in this book – would have to be argued to be syncretic in most languages with the T^{NEG}-marker. Closer investigation of how wide-spread this type of negative marker is remains subject to further investigation. Within the current sample studied in this book there is no language that makes use of a unique negative marker for the expression of external negation.

a Fregean point of view, a T^{NEG}-marker in a sentence like (66) takes scope over the entire proposition. The reading is illustrated in (68).

(68) It is not the case that John is happy.

In (68) the subject is also under the scope of the negative marker. Often this reading does not differ much from the reading in (67), but in certain cases the T^{NEG}-marker cannot get a propositional reading, as in (69). Neither in (69a) nor in (69b) can the negation scope over the subject. The sentence in (69a) doesn't mean that 'nobody came', cf.(70a), nor does the sentence in (69b) means what the sentence in (70b) means. It seems that for these examples only the low scope reading, as in (67), is appropriate.

(69) a. Somebody didn't come.
     b. Many arrows didn't hit the target.
(70) a. Nobody came
     b. Not many arrows hit the target.

I therefore want to argue that regular sentence negation expresses predicate denial, exemplified in (67), and is associated with a NegP above TP.

The label T^{NEG}-marker indicates where this negative marker surfaces or is assumed to take scope, i. e. in a projection above Tense Phrase, i. e. NegP (Pollock 1989, Haegeman 1995). Even in languages where the sentential negator linearly follows the tensed predicate, as in English, I want to argue that the negative marker still structurally occurs in a position that is hierarchically higher than TP when it gives rise to sentence negation (cf. also Haegeman (1995)). This position for NegP can be compared with what Laka (1990, 1994) refers to as ΣP and Cormack & Smith (2002), Poletto & Zanuttini (2013) as PolP. The idea of a high position for sentential negation, on the edge between TP and CP, is present in work by Moscati (2006, 2010, 2012) and McCloskey (2011). The sentential NegP for which I propose that it hosts T^{NEG}-markers is located in a position high up in the T-domain, below AgrSP and below FinP.[21]

The position that I take in this book with respect to negative markers expressing sentence negation deviates from the idea that the position for sentence negation is parametrized (Ouhalla 1991) and varies crosslinguistically in either select-

---

21 The idea of a very high NegP in English dates back to the very early days of transformational grammar. Klima (1964) suggested that English *not* is generated sentence initially at deep structure, dominated by a node labelled Pre-S. However, Klima's type of position is probably more compatible with a position that captures external negation/propositional negation and that we argued is located in the left periphery and is outside the scope of the present book.

ing a TP or a VP. For English it has often been proposed – in line with Ouhalla (1991) – that the sentential negator sits in a position that is dominated by TP (Cormack & Smith 2002, Wilder 2013). However, I adopt the proposal that negative markers with sentential scope universally scope over the tensed predicate and hence over T. As such, my proposal is in line with Belletti (1990), Haegeman (1995), Zanuttini (1997) and Holmberg (2003) who argue that the position preceding tense is the position in which negation needs to take scope to give rise to sentence negation. Zanuttini (1997) calls this position NegP1. For English (Klima 1964) the question tag-test can be used to test whether a negative marker outscopes the tensed predicate or not (see chapter 1).[22] In formal English T-negation is expressed by *not*, a marker that can give rise to positive and negative question tags, suggesting that this marker is ambiguous in terms of its scopal properties. The ambiguity is illustrated in (71). Whereas *not* in (71a) takes sentential scope, this is not the case in (71b).

(71) a. All the cookies [were not] eaten, were they?
     b. All the cookies were [not eaten], weren't they?   (Horn 2001b:490)

Now if we have a closer look at the question tags in combination with *n't*, the T-negation in informal English, then we see quite a different picture. The question tags for *n't* are namely always positive and there is no ambiguity possible, as illustrated by (72).

(72) All the cookies weren't eaten, {were they/*weren't they}?
(Horn 2001b:490)

It is therefore fair to say that in spite of the fact that *n't* follows the tensed predicate, the scope of this negative marker must be higher than the tensed predicate, i.e. the interaction of English *n't* with question tags and other Klima-tests pro-

---

[22] Jackendoff (1969:218) criticizes Klima's notion of sentence negation and the tests he uses to get to what sentence negation is. Under Jackendoff's definition of sentence negation, given in (i), only propositional or external negation could be considered sentence negation.

(i)   A sentence [$_S$ X-neg-Y] is an instance of sentence negation if there exists a paraphrase 'It is not so that [$_S$ X-Y]'.

Instances like (69a) would not be considered instances of sentence negation under Jackendoff's definition. Jackendoff's notion of sentence negation thus coincides with what is here referred to as external negation, a type of negation that is out of the scope of this book. I refer the reader to De Clercq (2020) for a discussion of various terms related to sentence negation.

vides support for a NegP above TP. Also the tags for *not* suggest that this marker can function as a marker taking scope above TP, i. e. it can be a T^{NEG}-marker, whilst it can also take scope lower, in a position for which we will argue it is associated to FocP and can therefore also be treated as a Foc^{NEG}-marker (cf. section 3.3.2). In other words, the idea defended in this book is that what has been regarded as a parametric difference for the base position of sentence negation is actually a parametric difference between whether a negative marker is syncretic for the expression of T-negation and Foc-negation or not. This parametric difference follows from the internal structure of the negative markers a language has at its disposal. This idea will be further worked out in chapter 5.

A well-known and often-discussed fact from the literature is negative doubling or bipartite negation, here illustrated with examples from French, (73), and Afrikaans, (74). Typical of bipartite negation is the use of two particles to express sentence negation, i. e. without one of the two particles sentence negation cannot be expressed.

(73) Il n'est pas fatigué.
 he NE is NEG tired
 'He isn't tired.'

(74) Hy is nie moeg nie
 he is NEG tired NEG
 'He is not tired' (Biberauer & Zeijlstra 2012)

Actually, for French the claim that both particles need to be present is too strong. Either one says that *ne* is optional in nowadays French or one argues that there are two different varieties of French, a written formal variety of French, that we will refer to as *le bon usage French* and that requires the presence of *ne* for the expression of sentence negation (Grevisse & Goosse [1936] 1993, Rooryck 2017) and a colloquial variety of French that does not require the presence of *ne*. Bipartite negation is not the same as negative concord. Whilst negative concord always involves an argumental indefinite like *no one, nothing* or an adverbial quantifier like *never*, bipartite negation is a label that applies solely to particle negation and more in particular to the fact that some languages need two particles to give rise to sentence negation. Under the present proposal the concomitant claim for bipartite negation languages is that only one of the two particles will scope over TP, the other particle will have lower scope. We will discuss the case of French in detail in chapter 7 and speculate there on how to analyze languages like Afrikaans.

Summarising, T^{NEG}-markers, the markers which give rise to sentence negation, take scope over tensed predicates and hence over TP, regardless of whether they precede or follow tense morphology.[23]

3.3.2 Foc^{NEG}-marker

The group of negative markers that are usually considered low scope negators or constituent negators I label Foc^{NEG}-markers, because these negative markers are hosted by a NegP that is associated with focus.

Foc^{NEG}-markers do not (usually) take scope over the tensed predicate, i. e. their scope is restricted to the untensed predicate. Support for this comes from the interaction with question tags in English as discussed above. For a sentence like (75) (or (71) in section 3.3.1) *not* can either take wide scope and hence give rise to positive question tags, but it can also scope only over the untensed predicate and hence give rise to negative question tags.

(75)   Kim is not happy, is she/isn't she?   (Horn 2001b:517)

Therefore, it could be argued that the negative marker *not* is a T^{NEG}-marker when it scopes above tense and a Foc^{NEG}-marker when it scopes below tense.

Moreover, when negation scopes only over the predicate the negative predicate is affirmed of the subject, resulting in an emphatic construction with emphasis on *not*, (76a), and/or on any intervening modifier between the negative marker and the adjectival predicate, as in (76b):

(76)   a.   Kim is NOT happy, isn't she?
        b.   Kim is NOT VERY happy(, isn't she?)

---

23 I focus on T^{NEG}-markers that combine with the present indicative tense. However, there are languages that develop different negative markers depending on Tense, Mood or Aspect (Haspelmath 2011, Dryer 2011). For instance Greek has a special negative marker for the subjunctive, namely *min* (Willmott 2008). If a language has different negative markers within the finite domain, then these markers are in complementary distribution with the present tense, indicative marker. This is an observation I base on my own experience with typological research. More research is required to investigate whether this hypothesis holds. I nevertheless assume that tense or mood-related negative allomorphs, and some aspect-related allomorphs, belong to the same group, i. e. the T^{NEG}-marker group and I leave them for future research. I focus on the present tense indicative markers, which I consider the default markers of this group.

Foc^{NEG}-markers are those negative markers that express *predicate negation*, rather than *predicate term negation*, due to the fact that they can scope over the entire untensed predicate and not only over a predicate term.

Since they are low scope negators, Foc^{NEG}-markers are often used as adverbial modifiers, as in (77), and as contrastive negative markers, as in (78).

(77)   Not long ago, he bought the house.
(78)   a.   John drank not coffee, but tea.
       b.   John drank tea, not coffee.   (McCawley 1998:613)

Moreover, if a language has small clause constructions, this negator is the negator used in small clause constructions, as illustrated in (79), and confirmed by the negative question tag.[24]

(79)   They consider it not likely, don't they?

In some languages, like Greek for instance—the same morpheme as the Foc^{NEG}-marker is also used to say *No!*, again referring to the emphatic and focal character of these negative markers. However, the study of *yes/no* from a nanosyntactic perspective will remain outside of the scope of the present study, as also explained in the intro to this section 3.3.

The label Foc^{NEG}-marker is related to what this type of negation gives rise to, i. e. focus, and to the functional projection associated with this type of negator in clausal syntax. I will first say something more about why negation is associated with focus and then I will elaborate on the functional projection the label refers to.

It is generally acknowledged that there is a relation between focus and negation (Jackendoff 1972, Kratzer 1989, Horn 2001b, Herburger 2000, Haegeman 2000, Han & Romero 2001, Butler 2003, Neeleman & Vermeulen 2012 and many others), but it is far from obvious what the nature of that relation exactly is. Whereas it is beyond the scope of this book to discuss the relationship between negation and focus in any detail and to do justice to it, I will try to sketch the interaction briefly as I see and understand it.

The focus of a proposition P is that part which would correspond to the wh-word in a wh-question (Neeleman & Vermeulen 2012:232). Pia is the focus in (80b) and John in (81b). Both attract the main stress in English (Selkirk 1984).[25]

---

[24] Thanks to Michal Starke for pointing this out to me.
[25] The entire discussion of focus in this section is based on De Clercq (2018).

(80) a. Who did John invite?
      b. He invited PIA.
(81) a. Who invited Pia?
      b. JOHN invited Pia.   (Neeleman & Vermeulen 2012:232)

Focus also triggers a set of alternative propositions, which is called the focus value of a sentence. The ordinary value of a sentences like (80b) is in (82a), whereas the focus value is in (82b) (Neeleman & Vermeulen 2012:233).

(82) a. Ordinary value: [John invited Pia]
      b. Focus value: [[John invited Pia], [John invited Bill], [John invited Sarah], [John invited Tom], ...]

Neeleman & Vermeulen (2012) argue that in case of a contrastive focus as in (83b) the alternative component always consists of negation. In what follows I explain how this works.

The meaning of a contrastive focus, (83b), can be made explicit by the construction in (83c). The semantics of (83b) is in (84a): it provides a function consisting of the background, the focus, which is *Pia*, and the set of alternatives to the focus, which is in this case the singleton *Bill*. Negation turns out to be an inherent part of the set of alternatives, because it "contributes a component of meaning that expresses that there is at least one alternative for which the proposition expressed by the sentence does not hold." (Neeleman & Vermeulen 2012:235). The alternatives component with negation is in (84b).

(83) a. John invited Bill.
      b. (No, you're wrong.) He invited PIA.
      c. John invited not Bill, but Pia.
(84) a. λx[John invited x], Pia, {Bill}>
      b. $\exists$ y, y $\in$ {Bill}, $\neg$[John invited y]
         (Neeleman and Vermeulen 2012, 236)

What I want to argue is that a negated (untensed) predicate can be compared to the alternatives component. Consider the negated sentence in (85).

(85) I am not angry with you for writing such innocent letters as these.

If we assume that this negated sentence is the alternative for which 'the proposition expressed by a sentence [in the discourse] does not hold' (Neeleman & Vermeulen 2012:235), then this sentence must be informative as to what could be the focus of this sentence, i.e. the bit that corresponds to *Pia* in our example in (83b). Typical of negative sentences is that the focus remains unclear and only the negated alternative is explicated. A potential focus to (85) could be (86a), explicated with the specialized construction in (86b)

(86) a. I am angry with you for ignoring me all the time.
      b. I am not angry with you for writing such innocent letters as these, but FOR IGNORING ME ALL THE TIME.

As such, we could say that negation turns a predicate into an alternative, which is therefore necessarily associated to an overt or covert focus. It is this reasoning that partly fed into adopting the label Foc^{NEG} for the low scope constituent negators. However, it cannot be the only reason, since also wide scope negative markers could be argued to turn a predicate into an alternative. Another reason is the fact that in languages that use bipartite negation to express sentential negation, as French, one of the two parts of the negation was in the development of the bipartite negation introduced to emphasize the original single negation. In the history of French for instance *pas* was introduced to emphasize *ne*. Apart from the fact that this emphatic focal element has turned into the main negator in colloquial French nowadays it was and still is also an independent low scope negator, i.e. a Foc^{NEG}-marker. In chapter 7 we will discuss bipartite negation and the diachronic development in French in more detail.

As shown in (64) I want to argue that the negative markers illustrated in (75)–(78) can take scope in a position for negation above a Focus Phrase (FocP). The Focus position that this book will be most concerned with is low FocP, a projection dominating vP (Belletti 2004, Jayaseelan 2001, Butler 2003, Jayaseelan 2008, Kandybowicz 2013). Naturally, this is not the only Focus Phrase negation can be associated with, but it is the one we will focus on most in this book. I want to follow Simpson & Wu (2002) in arguing that a variety of functional heads can select a Focus phrase. One of the functional heads that they argue that can take a FocP as complement is NegP. Moreover, they propose that these Focus phrases can become agreement phrases at a later stage, a phenomenon which they argue is relevant for bipartite negation. I want to modify their proposal slightly and argue that a NegP can appear on every FocP, for which they argue it can be merged as the complement of a variety of different functional projections (D, Aux, Neg). As such, this proposal is in line with the observation from Cinque (1999:109) that negation can be associated with different AdvPs across the clausal spine (see also chapter 8 for more discussion). However, the implication here is that the negative marker that is so free to occur in many different positions is the Foc^{NEG}-marker, the constituent negator and negator that can be used as an adverbial modifier, even though this negator is – as we will see – in many languages a syncretic marker, both for sentence negation and constituent negation. Simpson & Wu (2002) argue that in spite of the fact that their account predicts that FocPs can occur in many different positions, there are nevertheless positions that are more frequently associated with Focus than others, making their proposal compatible with cartographic approaches to focus. One such position they mention is the left peripheral position for Focus (Rizzi 1997), which we discussed in section 3.3.1 and for which we argued it will remain out of the scope of this book. Another position, the one I want to focus on in this book, is the FocP above vP (cf. also Breitbarth et al. 2013a for discussion of this position as a position for polarity emphasis).

The position above vP is a position for which Belletti (2001, 2004) argues it hosts postverbal subjects in Italian. Belleti's low FocP is argued for on the basis of contrasts as in (87). As a reply to a question which requires identification of the subject, only the reply with the post-verbal subject in (87b) is appropriate. The reply with the subject in preverbal position is not appropriate in the given context, (87c).

(87) a. Chi ha parlato?
      b. Ha parlato Gianni.
      c. #Gianni ha parlato.   (Belletti 2004:21)

On the basis of this contrast Belletti (2004:22) concludes that the subjects in these different positions contribute different information structural content. The postverbal subject carries new information focus, whilst the preverbal subject is a topic. She proposes that the post-verbal subject moves to the specifier of a low FocP, a position that has often been considered a position for new information focus (Belletti 2004, Jayaseelan 2001, Butler 2003, Jayaseelan 2008, Kandybowicz 2013). However, I want to abstract away from whether Belletti's low FocP or any FocP is associated with new information focus or contrastive focus and remain agnostic with respect to the precise type of focus involved. Simpson & Wu (2002) for instance treat the FocP above VP as a position hosting French *pas* at a stage in the development of French that *pas* carries emphasis, without mentioning new information focus.

Finally, since I assume that all different modal and aspectual projections come with a vP-shell in line with proposals by Kayne (1993), Iatridou et al. (2001), Deal (2009), Harwood (2014), a couple of different vPs are possible within one clausal spine. If a FocP comes above a vP-shell with perfective aspect (which is considered the highest aspectual position in the functional sequence), then this negation position overlaps with what is in many accounts of English – or other languages where the sentential negative marker surfaces in a position below TP-treated as the regular position for sentential negation and hence therefore often referred to as NegP (Pollock 1989, Ouhalla 1991, Laka 1990, 1994) or Pol[Neg] (Cormack & Smith 2002). It also coincides with what Zanuttini (1997) refers to as NegP$_2$ and Poletto (2008) calls MinimizerP, i. e. a position dominating perfective aspect.[26] However, within the confines of this book, I want to abstract away from aspect and how it interacts with both T^{NEG}- and Foc^{NEG}-markers. In this book I focus on predicative declarative main clauses with copular verbs in the simple present tense: different aspectual shells or layers for tense will not be further considered.[27]

Crucially, the idea that I want to develop in this book is that the negator languages use in adverbial modification, (77), is the same negator used to negate the untensed predicate, as well as the one used in preposed (left peripheral) constituents that are hosted by a left peripheral FocP, as discussed in 3.3. However, the focus in this book is on its appearance as an adverbial modifier and a low scope negator of the main predicate.

3.3.3 Class^{NEG}-markers

Class^{NEG}-markers, like *non-* in English,[28] take scope in a Classifier Phrase (ClassP) (cf. Borer (2005)), a projection that is usually considered to be part of the extended projection line of the nominal phrase and that turns mass into countable material. Considering the fact that we are dealing with copular clauses with adjectival predicates, the concomitant claim here is that I argue that also in the extended projection line of APs ClassP can be present, more in particular when adjectives are derived from nominals.

De Clercq (2013) used to label this group Deg^{NEG}-markers, in line with the functional projection Degree Phrase, for which Corver (1997a) argued it is one of the two functional projections in the extended projection line of gradable APs, (88).

---

[26] In line with Rizzi's (1997) proposal for the left peripheral FocP, I assume that also low FocPs and TopPs are only activated when needed.
[27] I tentatively assume that the structure of aspectual projections and associated vP-shells is only present in the derivation when needed (Harwood 2014).
[28] *Non-* is very productive and combines with all possible adjectives (and nominals) from all possible origins: *non-Turkish, nonintuitive, nonpsychiatric, non-colored, nonwhite, …*, though often it rather combines with derived adjectives than simplex adjectives.

(88)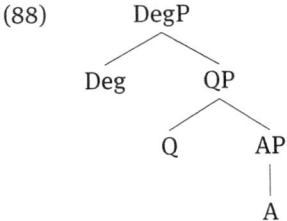

According to Corver DegP hosts degree items like *so, that* and *how*, as in (89), which are deictic and have determiner-like properties and therefore point to a specific degree on the scale of tallness.

(89)   That boy is so tall!

De Clercq (2013) argued that negative markers like *non* share this determiner-like property with degree-elements like *so* and hence labelled them Deg^{NEG}-markers. However, in spite of keeping the determiner-like/deitic intuition I had then, I want to argue in addition that negative markers like *non-* create two classes: P and non-P. The example in (90) illustrates what I mean with the notion Classifier within the extended projection line of the adjective. The adjective *professional* is derived from the noun *profession* and is hence a denominal adjective. The denominal adjective, *(non)professional*, can be predicated of the subject, denoting that the subject is either an amateur or not. The denominal adjective hence necessarily denotes a countable set, which *non-* divides into two groups or classes. Therefore, I argue that negative markers like *non* take scope in a position NegP above ClassP.

(90)   Clara and John both love acting. She is professional and he is nonprofessional.

In Aristotelian terms Class^{NEG}-markers express predicate term negation, i. e. negation which only scopes over the predicate term, not over the entire predicate, as illustrated by (91).

(91)   She is very professional and he is nonprofessional.
       = She is [very [¬ professional]].
       ≠ She is [¬ [very professional]].

3.3.4 Q^{NEG}-markers

Q^{NEG}-markers take scope over a QP, a functional projection that contributes gradability. The label is adopted from work by Bresnan (1973), Jackendoff (1974), Corver (1997b,a). QP is one of the functional projections which they propose dominates AP:

(92)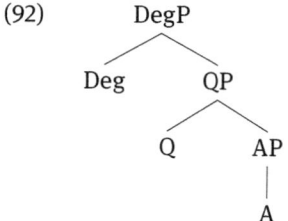

According to Corver Q° hosts quantity words like *much, more, less, enough*, (93), and contributes – to put it simply – gradibility.

(93)   John will never be more$_i$ intelligent than his sister.   (Corver 1997a:132)

I want to argue that Q^{NEG}-markers, like productive *un-* and unproductive *in-* (and its allomorphs *il-/im-/ir-*) and *dis-* (Zimmer 1964), contribute gradability like Corver's Q-elements do.

Support for the fact that Q^{NEG}-markers contribute gradability or scalar quantity comes from considering how they behave in comparison to Class^{NEG}-markers. This contrast is illustrated in (94). Whereas the Class^{NEG}-marker *non* does not trigger a scalar reading of the adjective *christian*, the Q^{NEG}-marker does (Zimmer 1964:33).

(94) a. non-christian: '(not) related to, pertaining to, characteristic of certain religious doctrines'
      b. un-christian: 'a scale of conformity or opposition to certain norms'

Another piece of support comes from the pair in (95). Since only gradable adjectives can undergo degree comparison, it follows that *un-* must contribute gradability in (95a), as opposed to *non*, which is ungrammatical in combination with degree comparison, (95b):

(95) a. This sentence is more ungrammatical than that one.
      b. *This sentence is more nongrammatical than that one.

Whereas *un-* can safely be considered the most productive Q^{NEG}-marker, *iN-* and *dis-* combine with words of foreign origin (Zimmer 1964) and they are less productive than *un-*. *iN-* is a Latin-based prefix and it combines with words from mainly Latin origin: *inhuman, impeccable, immaculate*, etc. *Dis-* usually combines with words from French (and hence mostly Latin origin): *disadventageous, discourteous, disharmonious*, etc. The unproductive prefixes, (96), are in complementary distribution with *un-*, (97), which is used for native English words and is – probably because of this – much more productive.[29]

(96) a. He is rational.
 b. He is irrational
 c. He is *un-rational.

(97) a. He is American.
 b. His behavior is un-American.
 c. *His behavior is in-American.
 d. *His behavior is dis-American.

Like Class^{NEG}-markers also Q^{NEG}-markers scope over the predicate term and not over the entire untensed predicate, as illustrated in (98). They thus express predicate term negation in Aristotelian terms.

(98) She is very unhappy.
 = She is [very [¬ happy]].
 ≠ She is [¬ [very happy]].

The Aristotelean terminology used to describe negative markers like *non* and *un-* is thus the same: both are described as being predicate term negators. Also Jespersen (1917) and Klima (1964) use the same labels: *special negation* and *constituent negation* respectively. However, there is reason to separate them out. Q^{NEG}-markers surface even closer to the adjectival stem than Class^{NEG}-markers do. This claim is not only based on the parallel with the two projections proposed by Corver (1997a), but also follows from the morphophonological behavior of some Q^{NEG}-markers. Some Q^{NEG}-markers in English, like the Q^{NEG}-marker *iN-*, have allomorphs, i. e. they undergo morphophonological change due to the adjectival stem to which they attach, as illustrated in (99).

---

[29] I do not consider the highly unproductive *a-* (Zimmer 1964, Kjellmer 2005). *a-* is derived from the Greek privative marker *a-* and combines in the first place with words from Greek origin like *agnostic*. However, often the marker is also attached to Latin-based words as for instance in *amoral, arational*.

(99) inhuman, ir-relevant, im-mature, im-portant, il-logical, ... (based on Zimmer 1964:28–29)

This is a typical property of Level I-morphemes (Siegel 1974, Allen 1978, Williams 1981, Lieber 1981, Selkirk 1982, Kiparsky 1982, 1983, Pesetsky 1985 and Horn 2001b), a morpheme that is structurally very close to the root. Level II-morphemes, like for instance the Class^{NEG}-marker *non-* (Horn 2001b:273–286), never show this morphophonological change. Not surprisingly, it is Q^{NEG}-markers, not Class^{NEG}-markers, which give rise to lexicalized readings, a property also associated with Level I-morphemes (cf. section 3.4 and Horn (2001b:282)). Class^{NEG}-markers, Foc^{NEG}-marker and T^{NEG}-markers on the other hand usually give rise to contradictory negation and hardly ever yield lexicalized readings.

A slightly different type of Q^{NEG}-marker is *-less*. *-less* differs from the other Q^{NEG}-markers at least with respect to the category it combines with, i.e. it selects nominals and turns them into adjectives. However, *-less* is also similar in many ways to the other Q^{NEG}-markers, as shown by De Clercq & Vanden Wyngaerd (2017b, 2019a). Like other Q^{NEG}-markers *-less* is not combinable with Q-negated negative adjectives, (100)b, whereas the combination of a denominal adjective with *-less* and *not* is perfectly acceptable, (100)c.

(100) a. breathless   b. *unbreathless   c. not breathless
      senseless   *unsenseless   not senseless
      merciless   *unmerciless   not merciless
      useless   *unuseless   not useless
      cheerless   *uncheerless   not cheerless

A similar pattern can be observed in the combination of Q^{NEG}-markers and negative adjectives. (101) shows how negative adjectives cannot co-ocur with Q^{NEG}-markers, whereas they can co-occur with *not*.

(101) a. unhappy   b. *unsad   c. not sad
         unwise   *unfoolish   not foolish
         unclean   *undirty   not dirty
         unfriendly   *unhostile   not hostile

The same happens when Q^{NEG}-markers like *un-*, *iN-* and *dis-* co-occur, as illustrated in (102).

(102) *undishonest   not dishonest
       *undiscourteous   not discourteous
       *undisloyal   not disloyal
       *undiscomfortable   not discomfortable

3.3 Property 2: Scope position — 53

Based on these data De Clercq & Vanden Wyngaerd (2019a) propose that negative adjectives like *sad* contain a negative feature that has a similar scope as the negative feature in *un-*, *dis-*, *iN-* and *-less*. De Clercq & Vanden Wyngaerd (2019a) explain the pattern exemplified above as following from a *X-X constraint, which states that the functional sequence (FSEQ) should not contain two contiguous identical features. For instance a T-feature does not select another T-feature etc. More in particular with respect to the data discussed above, there is a constraint on *Neg-Neg (cf. also Collins (2018) for a similar idea related to another set of data; also see section 3.2).

Now crucial for De Clercq & Vanden Wyngaerd (2019a:157) is that the same restriction holds with the Dutch Q-word *weinig* 'little' (as in (103)), and French *peu* 'little' (as in (104)), and that hence the pattern exemplified with respect to the Q^{NEG}-markers cannot be considered a restriction only at the level of morphology (as claimed by Horn (2001b) and Siegel (1978)), but that it extends to syntax.

(103) weinig
- actief/*passief 'active/passive'
- correct/*verkeerd 'correct/wrong'
- interessant/*saai 'interesting/boring'
- duidelijk/*onduidelijk 'clear/unclear'
- geduldig/*ongeduldig 'patient/impatient'
- nuttig/*nutteloos 'useful/useless'
- zinnig/*zinloos 'sensible/senseless'

(104) peu
- actif/*passif 'active/passive'
- aimable/*hostile 'friendly/hostile'
- clair/*embrouillé 'clear/confused'
- tolérant/*intolérant 'tolerant/intolerant'
- patient/*impatient 'patient/impatient'
- content/*mécontent 'satisfied/dissatisfied'
- heureux/*malheureux 'happy/unhappy'

In chapter 9 I will come back to the data discussed here, when I consider the question what this accounts means for the semantics of negation. For now these data are put forward to illustrate why *un-*, *dis-*, *iN-* and *-less* are all treated as Q^{NEG}-markers. Within the present book I will only consider Q^{NEG}-markers like *-less* if a language does not have adjectives and relies on strategies with *-less* to give rise to Q^{NEG}-markers.[30]

---

[30] Some languages do not have a *-less* strategy and always need to use the preposition 'without + noun' to express the same meaning, as for instance in Moroccan Arabic:

3.4 Property 3: Contradiction and contrariety

An important semantic difference between negative markers is whether they express contradictory negation or contrary negation. In this section I first explain the difference between both concepts and frame them briefly within logic. Subsequently, I argue—in line with Horn (2001b:ch5)—that T-, Foc- and Class^{NEG}-markers, as in (105), are contradictory negative markers, and that Q^{NEG}-markers, as in (106), are contrary negative markers, at least at a descriptive level. In chapter 9 I will ultimately argue that semantically contrariety derives from contradiction.

(105) a. He is not happy.
　　　b. He is nonhappy.
　　　c. He is NOT happy.
(106) a. He is disloyal.
　　　b. He is unhappy.

Two sentences, like in (107), are each other's contradictories since they cannot be true or false at the same time.

(107) a. Leila is not married.
　　　b. Leila is married.

Two sentences as in (108a) and (108b) are each other's contraries, since they cannot be true together, but they can be false together, as illustrated by (108c).

(108) a. She is happy.
　　　b. She is unhappy.
　　　c. She is neither happy, nor unhappy.

Following Jespersen (1917:144), Zimmer (1964:21–45), Horn (2001b:273–286) and Horn (2005:331–337), I assume that the contrariness of (108a) and (108b) is invoked (at least partically) by the low scope predicate term negator *un-*. When *un-*

(i) 　Elaf?aal djalu bla　akhlaaq.
　　　behavior of-him without moral
　　　'His behavior is immoral.'

This raises the question whether *without* consists of negation and more in particular whether the preposition *out* realizes the features Neg and Q^{NEG} in addition to some categorial P feature. However, I will not consider this issue further in this book.

combines with a gradable adjectival predicates it invokes a middle ground between two predicates, which does not happen in the same way by a negative like *not*, *n't* or *non*. Moreover, there are also triplets, illustrated in (109), that show that *un-* selects the gradable component of the predicate to which it attaches and gives rise to a characterizing reading, unlike *non*.

(109) a. inhuman   unhuman   nonhuman
       b. irreligious unreligious nonreligious
       c. impious   unpious   nonpious

Also the following doublet illustrates the contrast between contradictory inducing *non-* and contrary inducing *un-* nicely.

(110) a. being non-American by birth.
           ≠ inappropriate for an American
           = not American.
       b. His behavior is un-American.
           = inappropriate for an American.
           ≠ not American

However, the status of *un-* is more complicated. In combination with certain predicates, especially predicates ending in *-able*, *un-* behaves more like *non-* and gives rise to contradictory readings. As such, it seems that *un-* can sometimes function as a Class^{NEG}-marker, in combination with a non-gradable stem. As discussed in Horn (2001b:273–286), *un-* seems to have two faces: an *un-* that behaves like a Level I prefix (with the associated closeness to the root and lexicalized meanings), as in *unhappy*, and *un-* that behaves like a 'a word-level, neutral, Level II affix' with deverbal adjectives in *-able* and *-ible* and participles, like *unabsorbable, unadaptable, unabbreviated, unadapted, unavailing, and unbefitting* (examples from Jespersen 1917:144).[31]

The following figures in 3.1–3.2, based on Horn (2001b:270), illustrate the concepts contradictory and contrary opposition visually. The concepts are applied here to predicate terms and not to propositions as in the sentences in (107).[32] The

---

[31] For more discussion of Level-ordering see Siegel (1974), Allen (1978), Williams (1981), Lieber (1981), Selkirk (1982), Kiparsky (1982, 1983), Pesetsky (1985) and Horn (2001b).

[32] Strictly speaking the notion *contradiction* is applicable only to propositions. However, predicate terms can be each other's immediate (also called logical or strong) contraries and this can be viewed as contradiction. I follow Horn (2001b) in viewing immediate opposition within the domain of predicates as contradiction.

well	ill
bald	nonbald
even	odd

Figure 3.1: Contradictory predicates F and G.

predicates F and G, whether they consist of an overt negation like *non-* as in *nonblack* or not (as in *odd/even* or *male/female*) are each other's contradictories, because they cannot be true nor false at the same time.

When these predicates are compared to the predicates in 3.2, then it is clear that for the predicates P and Q a middle ground can be invoked such that both predicates can be false together, inducing a contrary interpretation. One negative prefix that is capable of invoking that middle ground is *un-*. Figure 3.2 (based on Horn (2001b:270)) shows this schematically.

Contrary opposition

P		Q
black	neither P nor Q	white
bad		good
sad		happy
unhappy		

Figure 3.2: Contrary predicates P and Q.

Based on the contrasts that we see in doublets and triplets, (110)–(109), I will mainly treat *un-* as a Q^{NEG}-marker that gives rise to contrary negation, just like the unproductive prefixes *iN-* and *dis-*. The negative markers *not*, *n't* and *non* will be treated as giving rise to contradictory negation. In chapter 9 I discuss the semantics of Q in more detail and its impact on adjectives and the semantics of *un-*. The semantics proposed there will explain why *un-* does not always give rise to contrariety. It is only in the presence of a contextual average that contrariety can arise.

3.5 Property 4: Function

The fourth criterion to distinguish negative markers from each other is their function. T^{NEG}-markers deny, Foc^{NEG}-markers contrast, emphasize or modify, $Class^{NEG}$-markers classify and Q^{NEG}-markers characterize.

Negative markers that scope over tensed predicates, our so-called T^{NEG}-markers, like English *n't* or *not*, predominantly have the function of denying an utterance spoken earlier in the discourse context. Horn (2001b:203) states that: 'the prototypic use (...) of negation is indeed as a denial of a proposition previously asserted, or subscribed to, or held as plausible by, or at least mentioned by, someone relevant in the discourse context.'[33]

The function of a Foc^{NEG}-marker, like English *not*, is ambiguous. It either has a modifying function, as in (111a), or it functions as a contrastive negative marker, introducing new or correct information, (111b). In the latter case the negative marker is usually stressed.

(111)   a.   a not very happy man, not long ago,
           b.   John was not happy, but sad.

The function of $Class^{NEG}$-markers like English *non-* is classifying (Warren 1984:101, Kjellmer 2005), whereas the function of Q^{NEG}-markers like English *un-, iN-, dis-* is characterizing (Funk 1971, Kjellmer 2005). The function of these negative markers is directly related to their semantics: negative markers, like $Class^{NEG}$-markers, that give rise to contradictory predicates can be classifying because they create

---

[33] Horn (2001b) distinguishes another function of sentence (and contrastive) negators (my T- and Foc^{NEG}-marker), namely the expression of metalinguistic negation. Examples of metalinguistic negation are in (ia)–(ib):

(i)   a.   Chris didn't MANage to solve the problem–it was quite easy for him.
        (Horn 2001b:368)
    b.   He didn't call the POLis, he called the poLIS.   (Horn 2001b:371).

In (ia) the speaker is not disputing the fact that Chris solved the problem. The speaker refers to how this happened. In (ib) the speaker is correcting the pronunciation of the word *police* of an interlocutor. Metalinguistic negation is not so much concerned with changing the truth value of the proposition, but with refuting the interpretation or pronunciation of a particular word or phrase in the discourse, as in (ia)–(ib). To put it in McCawley (1991:189)'s words: "In "metalinguistic negation" (more accurately, in a metalinguistic use of negation), a negative sentence is interpreted not as the negation of the proposition expressed by the negated sentence but rather as a rejection of the way that the content of that sentence is expressed." The properties of metalinguistic negation are clearly discourse related and will not be investigated in this book. I refer the reader to Horn (2001b:chapter 6), Horn (1985) and McCawley (1991) for discussion and references.

immediate opposites, whereas negative markers that give rise to mediate contraries, like Q^{NEG}-markers, can be characterizing because they invoke a middle ground between two opposed predicates. Kjellmer's (2005) corpus-based study of English provides support for this functional distinction. He shows that the English Class^{NEG}-marker *non-* is usually used as a classifying negative marker, as in (112), and the English Q^{NEG}-markers *un-, dis-, iN-* are usually characterizing, (113).

(112) a. Nicola believes herself to be a non-angry person and, indeed, she never loses her temper. (Corpus:ukbooks/08.)
b. Use non-fat milk instead of whole milk. (Corpus npr/07.)
c. I am an oddity in my family, having artfully asserted the dominance of my non-red gene. (Corpus:oznews/01.) (Kjellmer 2005:162)

(113) a. ... President Clinton, a man whose liberalism and personal lapses arouse distinctly unchristian hatred at First Federated. (Corpus: times/10.)
b. Lainey had a terrible voice, unmusical and sharp, and she usually pitched herself an octave below the sopranos to submerge it. (Corpus: usbooks/09.)
c. Germans are great if you're a little vague, indecisive and like to be told what to do in short, clear sentences. (Corpus: times/10.)
d. Some parents say children in Sarajevo have become increasingly disobedient and difficult to control during this wartime. (Corpus: npr/07.) (Kjellmer 2005:162–163)

The difference between Q- and Class^{NEG}-markers in terms of their function is also illustrated by the examples (114) and (115). The Q-negated adjective is appropriate in (114), but not the Class-negated predicate, because *un-* is a characterizing marker and what the teacher is doing is making a *qualitative* remark about the boy's behaviour. However, for a context like (115), only the Class-negated predicate is correct, because we are simply talking about whether someone is a professional actress or an amateur, i. e. whether someone belongs to one class/group or to another. If *unprofessional* were used, we'd be qualitatively judging Amie's behaviour as an actress (whether professional or not).

(114) a. Context: An American boy is spitting on the American flag. A teacher says:
b. His behavior is un-American. (= inappropriate for an American)
c. #His behavior is non-American.

(115) a. Context: Amie is an actress. However, she never obtained a degree for acting. Her friend says:

    b. She is non-professional.
    c. #She is unprofessional.

Sometimes, Q^{NEG}-markers, like *un-*, have a classifying function. This is mostly the case when they combine with adjectives ending in *-able* (Kjellmer 2005, Horn 2001b, Zimmer 1964). In this case they gave rise to contradictory readings, as discussed in section 3.4.

Summarising, T^{NEG}-markers deny, Foc^{NEG}-marker contrast, $Class^{NEG}$-markers classify and Q^{NEG}-markers characterize.

3.6 Conclusion

The criteria on which the classification of negative markers is based are 1) stacking properties and related to this 2) scopal properties, 3) semantic properties (contradictory or contrary) and finally, 4) functional properties. In the following section we broaden the sample and we look at 23 languages with respect to these properties.

In table 3.1 I provide an overview of the different types of negative markers with their distinctive properties.

Table 3.1: Classification of negative markers.

	T^{NEG}-markers	Foc^{NEG}-marker	$Class^{NEG}$-markers	Q^{NEG}-markers
	Predicate denial	*Predicate negation*	*Predicate term negation*	
scope over	tensed predicate	untensed predicate	predicate term	predicate term
stack	on Foc, Class, Q	on Class, Q	on Q	–
semantic	contradiction	contradiction	contradiction	contrariety
function	denying	contrasting/modifying	classifying	characterizing

In this chapter I illustrated these properties by means of data from English. The summary of negative markers in English is in table 3.2.

Table 3.2: English.

	T^{NEG}-marker	Foc^{NEG}-marker	$Class^{NEG}$-marker	Q^{NEG}-marker
Written English	not	not	non-	un, (iN-, dis-)
Spoken English	n't	not	non-	un, (iN-, dis-)

The different shades of grey between the two rows in the table show that the syncretism patterns between formal written English and informal spoken English are different. In written English, there is a syncretism between the T^{NEG}-marker and the Foc^{NEG}-marker. Spoken English is completely non-syncretic.

Summarizing, the four different groups of negative markers that we distinguish are the Q^{NEG}-markers, illustrated by *un-*, *iN-* and *dis-*, the Class^{NEG}-markers, with the example *non-* from English and the T^{NEG}- and Foc^{NEG}-markers which are syncretic in written English and instantiated by *not* and non-syncretic in spoken English, with *n't* realizing the T^{NEG}-marker and *not* the Foc^{NEG}-marker.

4 The crosslinguistic morphosyntax of negative markers

4.1 Some notes on the methodology

In this chapter I discuss the results of an examination of negative markers in 23 different languages in terms of the classification discussed above. The examples used in the discussion were either constructed with the help of an informant or are taken from the literature. If possible, I use examples from the literature and from informants. Of course, as always, there are never enough data. The same goes for some of the languages discussed in this book. For some languages it was not possible to discuss the data with an informant, which means that I could not get hold of any stacking data, since these data are usually not described in the literature or in grammars. If it was discussed, I mention it in the discussion of all separate languages. In spite of this, many languages studied in this book are well-documented enough to strongly believe that the hypothesis put forward in this book has serious foundations in language typology.

The examples that contain stacked negative markers are in many cases pragmatically odd. However, it seems that informants have strong intuitions on when something is completely ungrammatical or when it is just hard to process. These intuitions have been crucial for the stacking data. Also, many instances of Foc^{NEG}-markers are in spoken language often expressed by a wide scope sentential negation. When low scope negation is used, the reader should keep in mind that often the sentence could be expressed with the regular T^{NEG}-marker in that language as well.[34]

For the purpose of this study I was interested in all negative markers a language has at its disposal with the limitation that they can be combined within one copular predicational clause and that they are not fused with other categories like complementizers, coordinators, frequency adverbs or indefinites. The scope of this book thus goes beyond a discussion of standard negators (Miestamo 2005, 2007),[35] since it discusses different scopal negators of a language, but is also more restricted in that it does not discuss in any detail temporal, aspectual or mood-

---

[34] This chapter would have been impossible to write without the help and patience of my informants. I mention them whenever I discuss a new language for which I consulted an informant and I refer the reader to the introduction to this book where I mention the names of all my informants, also those whose judgments on some African languages did not make it to the book for reasons explained below. It goes without saying that all errors are mine.
[35] For Miestamo (2007) the standard negator of a language is the negator used with indicative declarative verbal predicates. In quite some languages the T^{NEG}-marker in copular clauses differs

related distinctions that languages often make within the domain of T^{NEG}-markers (Dryer 2011). With respect to T^{NEG}-markers I only discuss in detail the strategy used in the simple present indicative in predicational copular clauses, but if this strategy differs at the sentential level from the standard negator used in verbal clauses, then I mention this. Important to mention is that I do not discuss in any detail existential constructions or their negated counterparts, as in (116), unless when the construction is syncretic with predicational copular clauses, which is a common situation, as also for instance in English where the verb *be* is used to express existence and predication/identification.

(116)   a.   There is a tree in the garden.
         b.   There isn't any tree in the garden.

In Turkish on the other hand, cf. section 4.2.2.3, the negated existential differs from the negated predicational copula verb. I will not dwell on the existentials in this case, but I refer the reader to Veselinova (2013) for elaborate discussion of these verbs from a typological point of view. Another issues concerns special TAM-induced negative allomorphs. The negative marker for the subjunctive in Modern Greek for instance, namely *min* (Willmott 2008) (cf. section 4.2.1.1), will be mentioned but is not discussed in detail nor taken up in the discussion of the syncretism patterns. The reasoning is that if a language has different markers within the finite domain, these markers tend to be in complementary distribution with the present tense indicative marker. I therefore assume that most tense, mood— and possibly—aspect-related markers belong to the same group, i. e. the group of T^{NEG}-markers. I leave TAM-induced negative allomorphs for future research (but see chapter 8 for discussion of the literature and how the multiple NegPs in Zanuttini (1997) may relate to this point).

As I already mentioned in section 3.3.4, in languages where -*less* is the only available Q^{NEG}-marker in copular clauses, I will discuss it. This could for instance be the case in languages, that have been classified as not having adjectives. When languages have traditional adjectives and a Q^{NEG}-marker dedicated to negate that real adjective, I will not pay much attention to markers like -*less*.[36]

---

from the T^{NEG}-marker in verbal clauses. In this case it could be so that the standard negator as in Miestamo's terminology is not part of the typology presented for a particular language. If this is the case, I always discuss this.

36 I do not discuss affixes that are derived from the word 'bad', unless this were the only possible negative affix a language has at its disposal (but none of the languages is like this). An example with *bad* as an affix comes for instance from French, i. e. *mal-heureux*, and Greek *dhis-tixis*, both meaning 'unhappy'. It seems that quite some languages use *bad* as a Q^{NEG}-marker. However, as

As a final restriction, mentioned in the general introduction, I need to add that the study of n-words, negative quantifiers, NPIs, neg-raising or negative concord fall outside the scope of the present study. The aim of this book is to study the morphology of scopally different negative markers to get a better understanding of what it means to be negative across the syntax-morphology divide. Bipartite negation, i. e. the case of French *ne…pas* will be dealt with in chapter 7, since, as we will discuss extensively, these data follow naturally from the proposal formulated on the basis of the syncretism patterns.

For the present study I looked at 23 languages, of which 9 are Indo-European languages (English, Swedish, Dutch, French, Greek, Czech, Macedonian, Russian, Persian), 1 Sino-Tibetan language (Chinese), 1 Austronesian language (Malagasy), 3 Semitic languages (Hebrew, MS Arabic, Moroccan Arabic), 1 Finno-Ugric languages (Hungarian), 2 Turkic language (Turkish, Azerbaijani), Korean (for which the family is debated), Japanese (for which the family is also debated), 1 Khoe-language (Khwe), 1 Carib language (Hixkaryana), 1 Uto-Aztecan language (Tümpisa Shoshone) and 1 Dravidian language (Malayalam).

Even though this sample is small, it is relatively diverse and more languages are studied than typical in a generative study. The sample instantiates what Baker & McCloskey (2007:294) call a 'Middle Way' sample, i.e a sample that aims for an empirical coverage that is as wide as possible (a strength of typological research) and still allows for theoretical abstraction (a strength of generative syntax). Widening the sample is not as straightforward as it may seem. For many languages only the most dominant negator, i. e. the sentential negator, is mentioned in grammars or dictionaries. Moreover, ideally one gets native speaker judgements on stacking data, which cannot be obtained from grammars or dictionaries.

An important issue related to the sample is whether this study makes universal predictions with respect to the internal structure of negative markers in copular clauses (with property-expressing (adjectival) predicates). I want to argue, in line with ideas put forward in Haspelmath (1997), that the classification and syncretism patterns discussed in this book unveil an implicational universal (Haspelmath 1997:8). This means that when languages have adjectives and negative markers in at least two different scopal positions, even if the marker is morphologically the same, the analysis and classification presented in this book are relevant. However, quite some languages do not have pure adjectives, which means that one needs to be careful then. Following an idea by Starke (p. c.), I as-

---

far as I know, it is rarely the most productive Q^{NEG}-marker and hence I will usually not discuss it, though building on work by De Clercq & Vanden Wyngaerd (2017b, 2019a) the badness-strategy contains a Q^{NEG}-feature just like other negative Q^{NEG}- prefixes.

sume that in such languages the adverb, verb or nominal used in predicational constructions is syncretic with adjectives. In the present sample this issue was especially relevant when I was dealing with the African language Khwe and the Carib language Hixkaryana. Neither of those languages have 'pure' adjectives.

Since I argue in this book for an implicational universal, it is by no means my intention to claim that all languages have more than one scopal position for predicate (term) negation. Within the sample of languages I looked at, I noticed that there are languages that make use of only one strategy to negate a predicate and radically do not allow negation stacking. Negation stacking is in these languages only possible if clauses are stacked. Kimeru, a language spoken in the Democratic Republic of Congo, is such a language. As far as the native speaker that I contacted concerns, it seems that in Kimeru there is only one negative verbal marker, which cannot take scope in any other position than what I have labelled T^{NEG}-negation and no stacking is allowed.[37] My informant for Swahili also emphasizes that negation stacking is not possible in his language.[38] The same goes for Gungbe, a language spoken in Benin.[39] More research on Kimeru, Swahili and Gungbe from the perspective of negation is necessary to be sure that these languages indeed deviate from other languages with respect to the scopal properties of negative markers. The reason for this difference may lie in the internal structure of the predicate (verbal or nominal). However, I postpone a discussion of languages that do not allow stacking of negative markers to future research. The pattern discussed in this book is hence only an implicative universal: if languages allow stacking of negative markers of some sort in copular clauses, then the classification (see section 3) and generalisations discussed in this book become relevant.

Finally, the method used to uncover the inner structure of negative markers discussed in this book is presumably transferrable to negative markers with verbal predicates. However, it is not the aim of this book to elaborate on that. I postpone this to future work and focus for now on copular clauses with adjectival predicates.

In the sections that follow I present the data from my typological study, discussing for each language the four different types of negative markers distinguished in chapter 3. For the presentation of the results I focus on which languages show syncretisms between the four different groups and which do not show syncretisms. The seven detected patterns are visualised in table 4.1. For some patterns the sample contains several examples. For every language under

---

[37] I want to thank Joseph Koni Muluwa for discussion of Kimeru.
[38] I want to thank Anselm Theodos Ngetwa for his help with Swahili.
[39] Thanks to Enoch Aboh for helping me with Gungbe.

Table 4.1: Syncretism patterns.

	T^{NEG}-marker	Foc^{NEG}-marker	Class^{NEG}-marker	Q^{NEG}-marker
Pattern 1				
Pattern 2				
Pattern 3				
Pattern 4				
Pattern 5				
Pattern 6				
Pattern 7				

discussion the negative markers are ordered from wide to narrow scope or from narrow to wide scope, depending on how one reads the table.

4.2 Crosslinguistic sample

4.2.1 Pattern 1

Languages that are fully non-syncretic with respect to the types of negative markers distinguished in chapter 3 are Greek, Korean, informal English and le *bon usage* or formal French. I discuss Greek and Korean in this section in detail. I discussed informal English largely in section 3, and I will discuss colloquial French in detail in section 4.2.2.2. Moreover, I will come back to le bon usage French and a comparison with colloquial French in chapter 7.

4.2.1.1 Greek

Modern Greek[40] has four different negative markers for the four different types of negative markers we distinguished in section 3. The markers are illustrated in table 4.2.

Table 4.2: Greek negative markers.

	T^{NEG}-marker	Foc^{NEG}-marker	Class^{NEG}-marker	Q^{NEG}-marker
Pattern 1	dhen	oxi	mi(-)	a-

---

[40] Many thanks to Metin Bağriaçik and Marika Lekakou for help with the data.

The Q[NEG]-marker is *a-*.[41] *A-* gives rise to contrariety and has a characterising function, as illustrated by the examples in (117).[42]

(117) a. Ine an-endimi.
      be.PRS.3SG NEG-honest.NOM.F
      'She is dishonest.'
   b. Ine an-ithikos
      be.PRS.3SG NEG-moral.NOM.M
      'He is amoral.'
   c. Ine a-pistos
      be.PRS.3SG NEG-loyal.NOM.M
      'He is disloyal.'
   d. I methodhos tu ine a-katalili
      Det method his be.PRS.3SG NEG-suitable.NOM.F
      'His method is unsuitable.'
   e. Ine a-thriskos
      be.PRS.3SG NEG-religious.NOM.M
      'He is unreligious/irreligious.'

The scope of *a-* is restricted to the adjective to which it attaches and it cannot stack on other negative markers, (118).

(118) *a-mi-thriskos
      NEG-NEG-religious.NOM.ACC

The Class[NEG]-marker in Modern Greek is *mi(-)*. *Mi(-)* was the marker for standard negation in Old Greek.[43] *Mi(-)* expresses contradiction and has a classifying func-

---

41 *a-* attaches to the adjectival stem without a hyphen in the spelling. In order to gloss the examples and indicate the negative marker I separate *a-* from the stem. I do this for all languages I discuss in this chapter. When a hyphen is used in writing I mention it.

42 The Greek privative marker *a-* influenced the vocabulary of many other Indo-European languages like English, French, Czech, etc. Even Hungarian has words that combine with *a-*. However, I will not discuss *a-* in my overview of these languages, because it is in all these languages a very unproductive negative marker, restricted to words related to medicine or philosophy. Nevertheless, it could be considered part of the unproductive markers within the Q-group.

43 *Min* is a negative marker that is prototypically related to the subjunctive, (ia), though this is far from the only environment in which it occurs. Holton et al. (2004) and Mackridge (1985) also mention its usage in gerunds, (ib), after verbs of fearing and in (periphrastic) negative imperatives, (ic).

(i) a. Ithela na **min** ime ef-tixismeni.
       wanted.1SG SBJV NEG be.1.SG good-happy.NOM.F

tion, as illustrated by the examples in (119).⁴⁴ When nothing intervenes between *mi* and the adjectival predicate, it attaches to the adjective.

(119) a. Ine   mi-thriskos.
         be.PRS.3SG NEG-religous.NOM.M
         'He is non-religious.'
     b. Ta   mi-emborika   proionda.
         the NEG-commercial products
         'the noncommercial products.'
     c. Ine   mi-elinas
         be.PRS.3SG NEG-Greek.NOM.M
         'He is non-Greek.'
         'He is a foreigner.'

Although rare in Greek, *mi* can stack on an already negative adjective, i. e. one that already consists of a Q-marker, as in (120). In this case *mi* does not attach to the negated predicate. The fact that *mi* can do this – even though it is often pragmatically rare – whereas *a*- cannot, is support for the present classification of *mi*- as a Class^{NEG}-marker, which thus takes scope in a position that is higher than the position in which *a*- takes scope.⁴⁵

(120) a. Ine   mi   a-theos.
         be.PRS.3SG NEG NEG-theist.NOM.M

         'I wanted to not be happy' (ok when continued with *I wanted to be happy!*)
     b. Min   xerontas   poios ine, tou   milise   kapos   apotoma
         NEG knowing   who is,   him spoke.3SG somehow abruptly
         'Not knowing who it was, (s)he spoke to him rather abruptly.' Mackridge (1985:211)
     c. mi   féris   ton Jáni.
         NEG bring.SBJV.2SG the John
         'Don't bring John.'

Giannakidou (1998) and Chatzopoulou (2011) call the environments in which *min* occurs non-veridical environments. *Min* has always been the polarity marker for the subjunctive throughout the history of Greek (Chatzopoulou 2013, 2011), whereas *dhen* became the negative marker of the indicative after a process that Chatzopoulou (2013) describes as bleaching of the emphatic predicate negative marker. *Dhen* can only be stacked on *min* if both belong to different clauses, i. e. main clause and subclause. However, they cannot co-occur within the same clause. I consider *min* therefore to be in complementary distribution with *dhen*. As I said in section 4.1, I keep the interaction between negative indicative T^{NEG}-markers and mood-related T^{NEG}-markers for future research.

44 When I put hyphens in between brackets I want to indicate that the hyphen is not always necessary. I do this throughout the presentation of the syncretism patterns.
45 Thanks to George Tsoulas for these judgments.

'He is non-atheist.'
b. mi a-theoretiki psychiatriki
NEG NEG-theoretical psychiatry
'non atheoretical psychiatry'
c. Ine mi a-thriskos.
be.PRS.3SG NEG NEG-religious.NOM.M
'He is non ir-religious.'
d. Ine mi an-ithikos.
be.PRS.3SG NEG NEG-moral
'He is non immoral.'

The Foc^{NEG}-marker is *oxi*. It expresses contradictory negation and it functions either as an adverbial modifier, as in (121), or as a negative marker in contrastive contexts, like (122a), (122b). In contrastive contexts *oxi* can also give rise to metalinguistic negation, (123)–(124). The ungrammatical example in (123) shows that *oxi* cannot be used in a contrastive context if no correction is added. However, when there is a corrective statement added, the use of *oxi* is grammatical, (123b).[46]

(121) I Roxanni metakomise oxi poli kero prin.
The Roxanne moved.3SG NEG much time ago
'Roxanne moved not long ago.' (Giannakidou 1998:50)

(122) a. Podhosferistis ine oxi ithopios.
Football.player be.PRS.3SG no actor
'He is a football player and not an actor'
b. (Aftos) ine Elinas ke oxi fliaros? Adhinato.
He be.PRS.3SG Greek and no chatty impossible
'He is Greek, and (he is) not chatty? Impossible'

(123) a. *Oxi poli fitites irthan.
not many students came.3PL
b. Irthan, oxi poli fitites ala liji.
Came.3PL not many students but few
'Not many students came; only a few did.' (Giannakidou 1998:50)

---

46 Unlike in English metalinguistic negation in Greek is only possible with the Foc^{NEG}-marker, not with the T^{NEG}-marker. This leads Giannakidou (1998) to claim that Greek has a special negative marker for metalinguistic negation. Even though it is an option to consider the expression of metalinguistic negation as one of the functions of the Foc^{NEG}-marker, Greek *oxi* fulfills other functions, like that of an adverbial modifier, a constituent negator, a negator in small clauses and a polarity marker similar to English 'no'. Hence, if it is a metalinguistic negator, it is not exclusively so.

(124) De tha su to doso, oxi apo tsigunia, ala apo endiaferon.
NEG will you.GEN it.ACC give.1SG, NEG from stinginess but from interest
'I won't give it to you, not because I'm stingy, but because I'm concerned.'

Support for the classification of *oxi* as a Foc^{NEG}-marker above vP also comes from stacking: *oxi* can be stacked on top of *mi*, i. e. on the main clausal predicate, as in (125a)–(125b).

(125) a. A: aftos dhen ine katholu kalos stin dhulia tu.
A: He NEG be.PRS.3SG. NEG.at.all good in.the work his
'He is not good at all at his work.'
b. B: ... e, oxi mi-epangelmatikos omos.
B: PRT, NEG NEG-professional though
'... but not unprofessional though.'

More support for the fact that *oxi* must be a Foc^{NEG}-marker comes from the fact that if negation is used in a small clause, it is *oxi* that is used, (126)–(128). However, more naturally in Greek the negation will take scope at the level of the main clause predicate and not at the level of the small clause, (129).

(126) To theoro oxi apithano.
it consider.1SG NEG impossible
'I consider it not impossible.'

(127) To theori oxi aparetito.
it consider.3SG NEG essential
'S/he considers it not essential.'

(128) To theoro oxi to pio simadiko erotima.
it consider.1SG NEG the most important question
'I consider it not the most important question.'

(129) Dhen to theoro aparetito.
NEG it consider.1SG essential
'I do not consider it essential'

The T^{NEG}-marker is *dhen*. *Dhen* gives rise to contradictory negation and is used to express speaker denial. *Dhen* precedes finite verbs and takes overt scope over the tensed predicate. It can be stacked on other negative markers: within a clause with one main lexical predicate it can co-occur with Q^{NEG}, (130a), Class^{NEG}, (130b) and Foc^{NEG}-markers, (131), giving rise to double negation. For the example in (131) focal stress is needed on both *dhen* and *oxi*. I indicate this in capitals.

(130) a. Dhen ine an-endimi.
NEG is NEG-honest.NOM.F
'She is not dishonest'
b. Dhen ine mi-thriskos.
NEG is NEG-religous.NOM.M
'He is not non-religious.'

(131) a. A: Ine OXI eksipnos ala ergatikos.
is NEG clever but hardworking
'He is not clever, but hardworking.'
b. B: DHEN ine OXI eksipnos ala ergatikos.
NEG is NEG clever but hardworking
'It is not the case that he is not clever, but hardworking.'

Summarizing, there are no syncretic negative markers in Greek for the four types discussed in chapter 3. *A-* is the Q^{NEG}-marker in Greek, *mi-* the Class^{NEG}-marker, *oxi* the Foc^{NEG}-marker and *dhen* the T^{NEG}-marker.

4.2.1.2 Le bon usage French

The pattern in *le bon usage* French (Grevisse & Goosse [1936] 1993, Rooryck 2017),[47] i.e. the French used in formal written register, is as in table 4.3.[48] We propose that for each of the four types discussed in chapter 3, BUF has a dedicated negative marker. However, as we will discuss in this section, the T^{NEG}-marker in BUF consists of the Foc^{NEG}-marker, *pas*, with an additional element, i.e. *ne*.

Table 4.3: *Le bon Usage* French.

	T^{NEG}-marker	Foc^{NEG}-marker	Class^{NEG}-marker	Q^{NEG}-marker
bon usage French	ne...pas	pas	non	iN-

We start our discussion with the Q^{NEG}-marker. The most productive Q^{NEG}-marker in French is *iN-*, (132a)–(132b) (Zimmer 1964:48–51).[49] A more unproductive marker

---

47 Rooryck (2017:2) describes this variety of French as the French spoken by the upper class between 1830 and 1960. It is nowadays only used in writing.
48 Many thanks to Amélie Rocquet for careful help with the data.
49 *iN-* can also give rise to allomorphy, a property typical of Level I morphemes (Zimmer 1964, Siegel 1974, Allen 1978, Horn 2001b), i.e. prefixes that are very close to the root. The rules for the phonological change are:

is *dé(s)-*,(133) (Zimmer 1964:47–48).⁵⁰ Both negative markers are of Latin origin.⁵¹ Both *iN-* and *dé(s)-* give rise to contrary readings and have a characterising function.

(132) a. Il est in-tolérant.
        he is NEG-tolerant.
        'He is intolerant.'
    b. Il est im-moral.
        He is NEG-moral
        'He is immoral.'
        = He violates the rules of morality.
        = qualifies what goes against morality and is done with a certain awareness of the immorality of the act.   (ATILF 2003).

(133) Il est dé-loyal.
      he is NEG-loyal
      'He is disloyal.'   (Zimmer 1964:47)

Sometimes these Q^{NEG}-markers even have a lexicalized meaning, a property typical of Level I-prefixes, as explained in section 3.3.4. An example of *iN-* with its lexicalized and non-lexicalized meaning is illustrated in (134).⁵²

(i) a. in+ V → in-
    b. in+m → im-
    c. in+l → il-
    d. in+r → ir-
    e. in- or im- before p/b (relic of earlier phonetic assimilation).   (Zimmer 1964:50)

In the rest of this study I will refer to these alternations with capital N- in *iN-*.
50 Note that *dé(s)* is synchronically quite productively used as a reversative verbal prefix. (Zimmer 1964:48).
51 I am again not taking the prefix *a-* into account, (ia).

(i) a. C'est a-grammatical.
      it-is NEG-grammatical
      'It is ungrammatical.' .

According to Grevisse & Goosse ([1936] 1993) *a-* came via Latin into French, but according to ATILF (2003) the marker came almost aways directly via Ancient Greek into French. Since the marker is so unproductive, I do not take it into account.
52 Like English *un-*, French *iN-* also sometimes does not give rise to a contrary interpretation. This is the case in combination with adjectives that are participles or end – as in English – in *-ible* or *-able*. Moreover, in this case, *iN-* does not usually show phonological change, as illustrated by (i).

(134) a. Il est in-conscient.
he is NEG-conscious
b. = 'having lost conscience, being deprived of conscience, the opposite
of lucid' (ATILF 2003) (non-lexicalized)
c. = He is crazy. (lexicalized)

The markers *iN-* and *dé(s)-* discussed here cannot be stacked on each other. I consider this support to put them in the same group, i. e. to consider them Q^{NEG}-markers.

The Class^{NEG}-marker is *non(-)*. It gives rise to contradictory readings and functions as a classifying negative marker, (135a)–(135b), with a slightly wider scope than the regular negative prefixes (Muller 1991:170–171).[53]

(135) a. Le but de cette organisation est non-lucratif.
the goal of this organisation is NEG-profit
'The of this organisation is non-profit.'
b. Les déchets sont non-dangereux.
the trash-es are NEG-dangerous
'The trash is non-dangerous.'

Even though it is rare and pragmatically odd, it is possible to stack Class^{NEG}-marker *non* on a Q^{NEG}-marker, as in (136).

(i) in-racontable.
NEG-tellable
'too complicated to tell'

Horn (2001b:293) discusses how this could be attributed to the fact that *iN-* is ambiguous (or syncretic) between a Level I and a Level II-affix. Within the present account this means that both English *un-* and French *iN-* can sometimes also be a Class^{NEG}-marker.

[53] *Non* is usually a free morpheme, though it might have a closer connection to the adjectival root in some fixed expressions, in combination with nominals or denominal adjectives, often in *-ible* or *-able*, or adjectival participles in attributive position, as in (ic)–(ib) (Zimmer 1964).

(i) a. une pacte de non-agression
a pact of NEG-agression
'a non-agression pact'
b. L'Oréal est le 7ième groupe non-américain le plus admiré.
L'Oréal is the 7th group NEG-American the most admired
'L'Oréal is the 7th non-American group that is most admired.' (ATILF 2003)
c. une activité à but non-lucratif.
an activity to goal NEG-lucrative
'a non-commerical activity'

(136) Son comportement était plutôt non im-moral.
       his behavior   was rather NEG NEG-moral
       'His behavior was rather non im-moral.'

Non can also be used as a Foc^{NEG}-marker, (137a)–(137b). Contrastive *non* does not give rise to lexicalized meanings, only to contradiction.

(137) a. Il est non arrogant, mais froid.
           he is NEG arrogant, but cold
           'He is not arrogant, but cold.'
       b. Il est froid, non arrogant.
           He is cold, NEG arrogant
           'He is cold, not arrogant.'

The Foc^{NEG}-marker *non* can be stacked on adjectives that are already morphologically marked with a Q- marker, as (138a) and (138b) show, and with a Class^{NEG}-marker (see (139) and (140b)). Its stacking properties provide evidence to consider it also a Foc^{NEG}-marker.[54]

(138) a. Ses idées sont non im-morales, juste un peu bizarres.
           his ideas are NEG NEG-moral, just a bit weird
           'His ideas are not immoral, just a bit weird.'
       b. La maladie est non in-curable, mais douloureuse.
           the disease is NEG NEG-curable, but painful.
           'The disease is not incurable, but painful.'

(139) a. A: Le but de cette organisation est non-lucratif.
              the goal of this organisation is NEG-lucrative
              'The goal of this organisation is non-profit.'
       b. B: Au contraire, le but de cette organisation est non
              to.the contrary, the goal of this organisation is NEG
              non-lucratif, mais vraiment commercial.
              NEG-lucrative, but really commercial.
              'To the contrary, the goal of this organisation is not non-profit, but really commercial.'

(140) a. A: Les déchets sont non-dangereux
              the trashes are NEG-dangerous
              'This trash is non-dangerous.'

---

[54] Like other Foc^{NEG}-markers *non* can also be used in the C-domain, amongst others as a polarity marker and negative counterpart to *oui* 'yes'. For more ways to use *non* I refer the reader to Muller (1991:156).

b. B: Au contraire, les déchets sont non non-dangereux, mais
to.the contrary, the trashes are NEG NEG-dangerous, but
vraiment mortels si on les touche.
really mortal if one them touches.
'To the contrary, this trash is not non-dangerous, but really life-threatening if you touch it.'

However, there is another Foc^{NEG}-marker, *pas*, (141)–(142b). It expresses contradictory negation and functions as an adverbial modifier, (141), as well as as a contrastive negation, (142a)–(142b).

(141) Il s'est arrêté pas loin de là.
he REFL.is stopped NEG far of there
'He stopped not far from there.'

(142) a. La réunion est, je trouve, pas longue, mais ennuyeuse.
the reunion is, I think, NEG long, but boring
'The reunion is, I find, not long, but boring.'
b. La maladie est curable, mais pas supportable.
the disease is curable, but NEG bearable
The is curable, but not bearable.'

It shows the same stacking properties as the other Foc^{NEG}-marker *non*. In the examples in (138a) and (138b) and (139) and (140b) *non* can be replaced by *pas*. The table in 4.3 above presents the syncretism pattern with *pas* as Foc^{NEG}-marker. However, if we zoom in on the fact that *non* is syncretic for two different types of negative markers, then we can see that there is another pattern emerging, one which will become more relevant in the discussion in section 4.3 and which is illustrated here in table 4.4.

Table 4.4: *Le bon Usage: formal* French.

T^{NEG}-marker	Foc^{NEG}-marker	Class^{NEG}-marker	Q^{NEG}-marker
ne pas	non	non(-)	iN-, (dé(s)-)

For now I abstract away from the pattern that *non-* gives rise to and I will stick to *pas* as the relevant Foc^{NEG}-marker in the current discussion. However, I will get back to *non* in section 4.3.

Pas is also one of the two parts that constitutes the T^{NEG}-marker in BUF as mentioned at the beginning of this section. The other element is *ne*, (143). Both elements are required in BUF to give rise to sentential negation and hence both elements together will spell out T-negation. This is called bipartite negation or embracing negation and sometimes also negative doubling, a term not to be confused with double negation. Whilst double negation leads to two semantically interpretable negative markers, negative doubling expresses one semantic negation by means of two (in the case of bipartite negation), sometimes even three different negative markers. Negative doubling is a type of concord, though usually the term negative concord is reserved for the concord reading that can arise between negative indefinites (*rien/jamais/ personne* and/or a negative markers.[55]

One part of the bipartite negation, *pas*, will spell out one group of the features that we will argue constitutes a part of the negative nanospine. The other part, *ne*, will spell out the remaining features that belong to the negative nanospine, together giving rise to sentence negation, i. e. to a T^{NEG}-marker. The exact technical execution will be the focus of chapter 7.[56]

(143)   Francois ne doit pas embrasser Valérie.
           Francois NE must NEG kiss   Valérie.
           Francois doesn't have to kiss Valérie.   (Rowlett 1998b:15)

---

[55] The examples in (i)–(ii) illustrate concord patterns in French.

(i)   a.   Personne (n') a rien dit.
          nobody NE has nothing said
          'Noone said anything.' (NC)
          'Nobody said nothing.' (DN)
    b.   Personne (n') est le fils de personne.
          Nobody NE is the son of nobody.
          'No-one is the son of anybody' (NC)
          'Nobody is the son of nobody' (DN)
          (De Swart 2010:156–157)

(ii)   a.   Personne (ne) mange pas (rien)
          Nobody NEG eats   NEG nothing
          'Nobody doesn't eat anything.'
    b.   J'ai pas rien dit.   (Zeijlstra 2009)
          I have NEG nothing said
          ≠ 'I didn't say anything' (NC)
          = 'I didn't say nothing.'(DN)
          (De Swart 2010:156)

What these data also show is that concord is not the only possible reading in French: a double negation reading is sometimes also possible. However, neither the concord reading with negative indefinites nor the double negation reading will be the topic of this book. I refer the reader to De Clercq (2019a) for an analysis of these data from a nano perspective.

[56] According to Grevisse & Goosse ([1936] 1993) the more formal *point* behaves fairly similar to *pas*, (i).

The bipartite pattern in BUF is known as a stage in Jespersen's Cycle (Jespersen 1917, Horn 2001b, Van der Auwera & Neuckermans 2004, Zeijlstra 2004a, Breitbarth 2009, Breitbarth & Haegeman 2010, De Swart 2010, Chatzopoulou & Giannakidou 2011, Breitbarth & Haegeman 2014, Willis et al. 2013), a cycle which describes the development of sentential negative markers. The term Jespersen's Cycle was coined by Dahl (1979) to refer to the evolution described by Jespersen (1917:4):

> The history of negative expressions in various languages makes us witness the following curious fluctuation: the original negative adverb is first weakened, then found insufficient and therefore strengthened, generally through some additional word, and this in its turn may be felt as the negative proper and may then in course of time be subject to the same development as the original word.

The evolution of negative markers can be represented in a simplified way by means of three stages, of which BUF represents stage II:

(144)   a.   Stage I: Preverbal expression of sentential negation.
           b.   Stage II: Discontinuous expression of sentential negation.
           c.   Stage III: Postverbal expression of sentential negation. (De Swart 2010:114)

In general we can say that the preverbal negator in Stage I gets strengthened at some point by an emphatic element, which leads to the development of bipartite negation or Stage II once the emphasizer gets semantically bleached and becomes a negator. The preverbal element then disappears due to the presence of this new negator and gets lost, thus entering Stage III (Willis et al. 2013:6–7). The three-way split is a simplification for French and it has been argued that this picture should be enriched with intermediate stages in the development of negation in French (Rowlett 1998b:96, Zeijlstra 2004a:56, Van der Auwera 2009, Breitbarth & Haegeman 2010). During these intermediate stages one of the two elements is

---

(i)   Il n'est point nécessaire d'espérer pour entreprendre ni de réussir pour
       it NE.is NEG necessary of-to.hope for to.act nor of to.succeed for
       persévérer. (William of Orange)
       to.persevere
       'It is not necessary to hope in order to act, nor to succeed in order to persevere.'

Point expresses a more vigorous negation than *pas* and its usage is regional (Grevisse & Goosse [1936] 1993:144X). It is one of the many items that at some point – precisely like *pas* – were used to reinforce *ne* when the latter negative marker was losing its negative force, i. e. as a typical stage in Jespersen's Cycle.

optional. As such, the more complicated picture for French consists of five or more stages (cf. Van der Auwera 2009 for an overview). In (145) this more complicated picture is illustrated for French, with optionality indicated by brackets.

(145)   a. jeo ne di. (1600)
       b. je ne dis (pas). (1600–1700)
       c. je ne dis pas. (Standard written French = BUF)
       d. je (ne) dis pas. (Standard spoken French)
       e. je dis pas. (Colloquial French = CF)
          I say NEG
          'I don't say.'   (Jespersen 1924:335–336, Rowlett 1998b:90)

Willis (2011:94) labels the stage in which *pas* is optional as Stage IIa, and the period in which the postverbal negator becomes compulsory as Stage IIb. The transition from stage II to stage III can also be treated as involving periods in which the preverbal element seems optional or the two stages co-exist. In Standard spoken French, the marker *ne* has not yet fully disappeared, even though it is not obligatory anymore.

The role of the two negative components in Stage II of Jespersen's Cycle, i. e. in BUF, is not easily captured within a formal system, but this precisely will be the focus of discussion in chapter 7.

Summarizing, formal written French, the so-called *bon usage* French, is fully non-syncretic, with the caveat that the T^{NEG}-marker, *ne ... pas* shares one of its two elements with the Foc^{NEG}-marker, *pas*. The $Class^{NEG}$-marker- is *non* and the Q^{NEG}-marker is *iN-*.

4.2.1.3 Korean
Korean borrowed and adapted many words from Chinese in many different periods over time.[57] Also within the domain of negative markers important Sino-Korean borrowings took place, which enriched the vocabulary system considerably. According to Sohn (1999:13) Korean vocabulary consists of about 60 % Sino-Korean words and 35 % native Korean words. 5 % are borrowings from English and Japanese. Due to the fact that the language contains these two dominant strata, i. e. Sino-Korean and native Korean, we hypothesize that two different syncretism

---

[57] In spite of the cultural and geographical closeness with China, Korean belongs to a totally different language group. Korean is a language that like Japanese, cf. section 4.2.2.1, presumably belongs to the group of Altaic languages (Sohn 1999:11), though its origin is debated. I want to thank Minjeong Son and Jaehoon Choi for help with the data. All errors and interpretations are mine.

patterns can be detected. One pattern for Sino-Korean predicates and one for native Korean predicates.

The syncretism pattern for Sino-Korean negators is summarized in table 4.5. For all different types of negative markers that we discussed in chapter 3 Korean has a morphologically different negator, at least if we consider the bipartite T^{NEG}-marker a different one from the Foc^{NEG}-marker. To form a T^{NEG}-marker there are two elements added to the regular negator *an(i)*: a nominalizing element *-ci* that attaches to the lexical verb and the light verb *hata* 'do' that takes the inflection. Korean also has a well-known modal negator, *mos*, that can also take sentential scope and that is taken up in the table as well and illustrated in the second row. I will come back to this modal negator later in this section.

Table 4.5: Korean: Sino-Korean stratum.

	T^{NEG}-marker	Foc^{NEG}-marker	$Class^{NEG}$-marker	Q^{NEG}-marker
Pattern 1	(-ci) an(i) (ha-)	an(i)	pi-	pul-/pu-
	(-ci) mos (ha-)	mos	mol-	mol-

If we were to consider the stratum of native Korean words, i.e. (35%) of the lexicon, and how negation interacts with it, i.e. the fact that native Korean words do not usually take morphologically specialized Q^{NEG}- and $Class^{NEG}$-markers, then either the pattern in 4.5 is not correct for this substratum or we could adopt the idea that there is another pattern for these predicates, illustrated in 4.6.

Table 4.6: Korean: native Korean stratum.

	T^{NEG}-marker	Foc^{NEG}-marker	$Class^{NEG}$-marker	Q^{NEG}-marker
Pattern 1	(-ci) an(i) (ha-)	an(i)	ani	ani
	(-ci) mos (ha-)	mos	mos	mos

If speakers of Korean indeed have both patterns, then this would suggest that speakers of languages with several lexical strata could be considered bilingual speakers that make use of different grammars. For languages where the non-native stratum is small, it is usually argued that the non-native derivational morphology is a consequence of some type of listing in the lexicon. However, in this particular case both the native and non-native stratum form a substantial part of the lexicon, so one wonders whether this could be the right approach. It has been proposed for Korean that speakers of the same language have different underlying grammars, for instance when it comes to V-raising (Han et al. 2007), but as far as I know it has not been proposed that speakers use two different grammars depending on the lexical predicate involved. The idea of bilingualism has been proposed though in relation to the human capacity to deal with different types of genres/registers within one language. An example is subject omission in English, which is considered ungrammatical in main clauses in most registers, but totally acceptable in some registers, like diary language (Haegeman & Ihsane 1999, Haegeman 2002, Weir 2012). The same goes for the omission of articles in headlinese and the omission of objects in recipes or other types of instructional writing (Haegeman 1987b,a, Massam & Roberge 1989, Weir 2009, 2017). Therefore, it has been proposed that human beings are endowed with a core grammar and a peripheral grammar (Haegeman 2006) or a sentential and non-sentential grammar (Progovac 2006) to handle the grammatical differences that are associated with different registers, in line with Roeper (1999)'s proposal that there is something like Universal Bilingualism, i.e. human beings are endowed with a proto-grammar and a full fledged grammar. If human beings can deal with different grammars for different registers, then it is not a far leap to hypothesize that within the same register different grammars can be active to deal with different types of predicates, in this particular case predicates stemming from different origins. Even though this could be a possible way to deal with these different patterns for different strata in Korean, in section 4.3 we will suggest another – more economic – way to deal with this issue, i.e. one without adopting an extra syncretism pattern. In what follows I focus on the Sino-Korean pattern, since I will argue 4.3 that this patterns is the only pattern we need to account for both strata.

Kim-Renaud (2009:132) distinguishes between different negative prefixes in Korean, all with a slightly different meaning. It is clear that these prefixes belong to the group of Q^{NEG}-markers and $Class^{NEG}$-markers. However, deciding which is which, is a hard task. Korean can use these prefixes to express negation with Sino-Korean words, but not with native Korean words.

Table 4.7: Sino-Korean negative prefixes (after Kim-Renaud (2009:132)).

prefix	meaning	example	gloss
mu	absence	musosok	independent
mi	unattaining	miwansŏng	unfinished
mol	demise	molsangsik	ignorance
pi	counter	pijongsăng	abnormality
pul/pu	absence	pujayu	lack of freedom

As can be noticed in table 4.7 the list of possible negative prefixes is bigger than the two categories we distinguished. Hence, some explanation is in order with respect to how I have divided the prefixes over the Q^{NEG}- and Class^{NEG}-groups in table 4.5. Strictly speaking there are three options to treat these prefixes: either 1) we put all these negative markers in one group and conclude that in Korean the Q- and Class-group conflate, or 2) we split the prefixes over the two groups we detected before; or 3) we increase the number of different of different groups. I will argue for option 2.

Chung (2007:100) argues that neither of the markers in 4.7 can be stacked. This could be considered an argument for option 1. However, given that at least in some languages Class^{NEG}- and Q^{NEG}-markers can be stacked, I am not willing to touch the classification as it stands immediately. We saw that also in other languages, like Greek and English, the stacking of these types of markers is a rare phenomenon. One argument in favour of solution 2 is phonological in nature. Chung (2007:99) and Kim-Renaud (2009:132) note that *pul* and *pu* can be traced back to the same Chinese character, but that in the presence of a coronal stop or affricate *pul* becomes *pu*. Therefore, it makes sense to consider *pul* and *pu* the same negative marker, which depending on the phonological context alters its appearance. This ability to give rise to allophonic variation under the influence of the root we considered a sign of level I-affixes and of a closer association with the root (cf. section 3.3.4 and Horn (2001b) and references cited there).

(146) a. pul-kanungha
          NEG-possible
       b. pul-chincelha
          NEG-kind
       c. pul-myenghwakha
          NEG-distinct

(147) a. pu-cekhapha
          NEG-congruous
       b. pu-totekha
          NEG-moral
       c. pu-cayensurep
          un-natural
                                                        Chung (2007:99)

Therefore, I want to suggest that *pul-/pu-* are Q^{NEG}-markers. This is supported by the different meanings assigned to these prefixes: 'non-, in-, un-, ir-' (Sohn 1999:221), which clearly involve the level I affixes in English. *Pi-*, (148) , on the other hand, does not show this phonological alternation. Hence, it is an option to consider *pi-* a Class-^{NEG}-marker. Moreover, if we look at the translations given by Sohn (1999:221) for the different negative markers, then the meanings of *pi-* involve (mainly) contradictory meanings translated in English by *non-, un-, anti-*.

(148)   a. pi-kyoywukcek-i
            NEG-educational
        b. pi-kwahakcek-i
            NEG-scientific
        c. pi-sinsacek-i
            NEG-gentlemanly   Chung (2007:99)

Taking into account the translation provided by Chang (1996:100) for *mwu* as 'non-' or 'un-', the prefix *m(w)u*, is probably also a Class^{NEG}-marker. The prefix *mi*, characterised as 'yet', attaches to an event in that it expresses that a certain event is not yet complete. Given that the adjectives under scrutiny denote properties here, rather than events I subsume *mi-* under the group of prefixes which attaches to verbal or nominal constituents and hence leave it out of consideration for now.

The negative prefix *mol-* is translated by Sohn (1999:221) as *non-* and *less-*, which suggests that the prefix belongs to both the Q- and Class-group within the present system.

(149)   mol-sangsik
        NEG-common.sense
        'ignorance'   (Sohn 1999:221)

I would like to argue that *mol* is special in that it seems to be partially syncretic with one of the sentential negators, i. e. *mos*, which expresses a modal meaning 'impossibility, inability' in addition to the main negation *an(i)* (De Clercq 2016). Before I continue with how *mol* and *mos* could be regarded as partially syncretic, I first need to say something about the regular sentential negators, i. e. *ani* and *mos*.

Both *an(i)* and *mos* can be used in long and short form negation in Korean. (150b) exemplifies short form negation (SN) with *ani* and *mos*: the negative marker is before the verbal predicate. With long form negation (LN) the negator is preceded by the verbal predicate that needs to be nominalized by the morpheme *-ci*, and followed by a light verb, *hata*.

(150)   a. eysute-ka   an(i) ca-n-ta.
            Esther-NOM NEG   sleep-PRES-DECL
            'Esther doesn't sleep/isn't sleeping.'

　　　　b.　eysute-ka　　mos ca-n-ta.
　　　　　　Esther-NOM NEG sleep-PRES-DECL
　　　　　　'Esther cannot/is not allowed to sleep.'
(151)　a.　eysute-ka　　ca-ci　　an(i) ha-n-ta.
　　　　　　Esther-NOM sleep-CI NEG do-PRES-DECL
　　　　　　'Esther doesn't sleep.' (Chung 2007:97)
　　　　b.　eysute-ka　　ca-ci　　mos ha-n-ta.
　　　　　　Esther-NOM sleep-CI NEG do-PRES-DECL
　　　　　　'Esther cannot/is not allowed to sleep.'
　　　　　　(Chung 2007:98)

I would like to propose that the -s in mo-s is derived from swu 'ability'. Support for the presence of swu 'ability' in mos 'cannot' comes from the fact that the usual construction to express negative modality given in (152), and involving the noun swu 'ability', can be replaced by mos 'cannot' without any change in meaning, as shown in (153).

(152)　Na-nub keki-ey ka-l　　swu　　eps-ta
　　　　I　　there-to go-ADNZ ability NEG.exist-DEC
　　　　'I can't go there.'　　　　　　　　　　　　　　　　(Kim 2010)
(153)　Na-nun keki-ey ka-ci　　mos-ha-ta
　　　　I　　there-to go-NMLZ can.NEG-do-DECL
　　　　'I can't go there.'

It should be noted that the idea that *mol-*, a Sino-Korean prefix, combines with a native Korean dependent noun *swu* is not uncontroversial. It is unusual that Sino-Korean prefixes combine with native Korean forms. Nevertheless, exceptions to this kind of compounding have been noted, as mentioned by Sohn (1999:222) with respect to suffixes of Sino-Korean origin.[58]

An added bonus of this analysis of *mos* is that it may explain why the combination of short form *mos* with adjectives is said to be ungrammatical, as exemplified in (154), whereas *ani* is possible with short and long form negation with adjectives.[59]

---

[58] I want to thank Jaehoon Choi for discussion of this proposal and for his critical remarks. All errors are mine of course.

[59] Interestingly, *mol-*, and if this analysis is on the right track, also *mos*, is partially syncretic with the frequently used verbal suppletive form, *molu*, i. e. 'not know'. Chung (2007) shows that *molu* licences NPIs and that it behaves scopally like short form *ani* and *mos*. Chung considers this a reason to call the suppletive negation with *molu* a syntactic negation. Now if *molu* is indeed syn-

(154) *eysute-nun mos sengsilha-ta.
  Esther-TOP can.NEG sincere-DECL
  'Esther is not sincere'. (Chung 2007:98)

If *mos* is derived from what used to be a nominal compound, similar to *unability*, then it is no surprise that an adjective cannot be immediately modified by it. However, it is not completely ungrammatical. Sohn (1999) mentions a few examples where the combination of *mos* and adjectives leads to an idiomatic reading, (155b).

(155) a. mos-hata
  NEG-X
  'be inferior'
 b. mos-matanghata
  NEG-be.satisfactory
  'be unsatisfactory'

A plausible representation of the Q^{NEG}-marker and $Class^{NEG}$-marker in the table based on this discussion is as in table 4.5, repeated here as in 4.8. The table separates the modal negator *mos* from the standard negator *ani* and makes the partial syncretism, as proposed in the present discussion, visible by putting *mol-* in a separate box. However, nothing crucially hinges on keeping the dividing line between the two series of negators.

Table 4.8: Korean.

	T^{NEG}-marker	Foc^{NEG}-marker	$Class^{NEG}$-marker	Q^{NEG}-marker
Pattern 1	(-ci) an(i) (ha-)	an(i)	pi-	pul-/pu-
	(-ci) mos (ha-)	mos	mol-	mol-

The negators *an(i)* and *mos* have to negate larger constituents than only the predicate term when it comes to Sino-Korean predicates. They can for instance take a negatively prefixed adjective in their scope, (156). Therefore, I consider the short form negators *an(i)* and *mos* Foc^{NEG}-markers.

(156) con-un an(i) pul-sengsilha-ta.
  John-TOP NEG NEG-sincere-DECL
  'John is not insincere.' (Chung 2007:100)

---

cretic with *mol-*, this would support the claim in this book that all negative markers need to be treated in syntax and the differences that arise between what is traditionally called morphological or syntactic negation is a consequence of their scope. See De Clercq (2016, 2019b) for a first analysis of the relation between *molu* and *mos*.

Long form negation, (157), i. e. the same negative markers *an(i)* and *mos* in combination with the light verb *ha* 'do, be in the state of' (often contracted to 'h') and the *ci*-nominalized main verb is to be considered a complex T^{NEG}-marker. In this particular case the situation is even more complex than what we get to see in French. Whereas *ani/mos* can be argued to spell out part of the spine that corresponds to the Foc^{NEG}-marker, the nominalizing element and the light verb together must be responsible for spelling out the features that give rise to T-negation. Long form negation in Korean is highly reminiscent of the requirement to get do-support under sentential negation in English. Within the confines of this book I will not present a full nanosyntactic analysis of the complex LF Korean negation. Crucial for the current enterprise are the stacking data in (158), which shows LF negation stacked on SF negation *an(i)* and *mos*.

(157) a. Yongho nun hakkyo ey ka-ci an-h-nun-ta
 Yongho TC school to go-NMLZ NEG-do-in-DECL
 'Yongho does not go to school.'
 b. Minca nun sengkyek i coh-ci an-h-ta
 Minca TC personality NM good-NMLZ NEG-do-DECL
 'Minca's personality is not good.' (Sohn 1999:391)
(158) Inho-nun amwu kes-to an masi-ci ani ha-yess-ta.
 Inho-TOP any thing-even NEG drink-NMLZ NEG do-PST-DECL
 'Inho didn't not drink anything.' (Han & Lee 2007:379)

Two SF negators cannot be combined with predicates from Sino-Korean origin: **ani ani* (159), **mos mos* or **mos ani*. According to Chung (2007:101) *an(i) mos* is marginally allowed.

(159) a. *con-un an(i) an(i) sengsilha-ta.
 John-TOP NEG NEG sincere-DECL
 b. *i an-un an(i) an(i) kanungha-yess-ta.
 this plan-TOP NEG NEG possible-PST-DECL
 c. *ku noli-nun an(i) an(i) kencenha-ta.
 the/that game-TOP NEG NEG sound-DECL
 (Chung 2007:100)

Based on the stacking data in (158) and (159), I consider the complex long form negation the T^{NEG}-marker. This proposal is in line with claims made by Hagstrom (2000, 1997) that long form negation has wider scope than short form negation. The short form negation thus seems to have the role of a Foc^{NEG}-marker.

An interesting fact, which has been largely ignored in the literature, is that in some cases the regular sentential negation is dispreferred compared to the negative prefix. When the Sino-Korean predicate is modified by *very* and negation needs to take very low scope, the construction with the Sino-Korean prefix (the Q-marker), (160a) has clear preference over a construction with sentential negation, (160b). This supports the enterprise of this book in the sense that these low scope negators which are often neglected in the literature on negation have a meaning, scope and/or function of their own, which needs to be distinguished from the dominant sentential negator.

(160) a. Kunye-nun acwu/maywu pwul.chincelha-ta.
           She-TOP   very   NEG.kind.DECL
           'She was very unkind.'
       b. ??Kunye-nun acwu/maywu chincelha-ci an-h-ta.
           She-TOP   very   kind-NMLZ   NEG-do-DECL
           'She was very unkind.'

Whereas short form negation *ani* in Korean cannot be considered a Q^{NEG}-marker or $Class^{NEG}$-marker when it comes to Sino-Korean words, it looks – at least at first sight – as if it can be when it comes to native Korean words. Native Korean words can incorporate *mos*, (161a), or *an*, (161b), and can occasionally be negated with what looks like another short form negation, as in (161a).

(161) a. an mos-sayngki-ess-ta
           NEG can.NEG-appear-PST-DECL
           'He is not ugly.'
       b. an-toyta
           NEG-become
           'be pitiful'
       c. ansim-ch-an-h-ta < ansim-ha-ci   ani ha-ta
                              feel.at.rest-do-NMLZ NEG do-DECL
           'be uneasy'   (Sohn 1999:393)

If we consider only the native Korean vocabulary items in Korean, which make up 35 % of the lexicon (Sohn 1999:13), then a substratum of Korean predicates seem subjected to syncretism pattern 5, illustrated in table 4.6.

However, it is unclear whether these data provide enough support to treat these negators as Q^{NEG} or $Class^{NEG}$-markers in a separate native Korean stratum. As already mentioned and described by Chung (2007), stacking of SF *ani* and *mos* is occasionally possible and this could also be what happens in examples like (161a). Moreover, as will be discussed in section 4.3 it is more likely that native Korean predicates differ structurally from Sino-Korean predicates, hence disallowing the presence of certain negative markers. This will be the option put forward in the discussion in section 4.3.

Summarizing, with respect to the Sino-Korean stratum in Korean, I have argued that *pul-/pu* and *mol* are Q^{NEG}-markers and *pi-/mu-* and *mol-* are $Class^{NEG}$-markers. *Ani* and *mos* are the short form negators, which I have argued can be labelled as Foc^{NEG}-markers. When these markers are combined with the light verb *hata* 'to do' and the nominalizing suffix *-ci* on the main verb, a complex T^{NEG}-marker is formed. For the native Korean stratum in the language it seems – at first sight – that another pattern needs to be considered, a pattern with a syncretic marker for Q^{NEG}, $Class^{NEG}$ and Foc^{NEG}-negation and a more elaborate construction with *-ci*, *ha* and the Foc^{NEG}-marker for the expression of T^{NEG}-negation. However, in section 4.3 we will see that another solution is to be preferred over postulating two different syncretism patterns.

4.2.1.4 Other language

Table 4.9: Informal English

	T^{NEG}-marker	Foc^{NEG}-marker	$Class^{NEG}$-marker	Q^{NEG}-marker
spoken English	n't	not	non	un-/iN-/dis-

Anther language that has syncretism pattern 1 is informal English, 4.9. I have discussed spoken (and written) English largely in section 3 and will therefore not discuss it here in detail anymore. However, the syncretism pattern is visualized in table 4.9.

4.2.2 Pattern 2

4.2.2.1 Japanese

As Shibatani (1990:94) notes Japanese[60] is the only major world language whose affiliation to any kind of phylum or language family is not clearly defined and still remains controversial. Many different hypotheses have been offered and one could say that Japanese has been assigned to almost every possible phylum, i. e. Altaic, Austronesian, Sino-Tibetan, Indo-European and Dravidian. I will not dwell on this issue here, but refer the reader to Shibatani (1990), Whaley (1997), Comrie

---

[60] Many thanks to Reiko Vermeulen, Yasuhira Iida and Makoto Ishii for help with Japanese at different points. All errors are mine.

(1989) and others for discussion of this topic. Japanese has three different negative markers that can be distributed across the four types of negative markers discussed in the classification in this book (Sansom 1928:129) and summarized in table 4.10.

Table 4.10: Japanese.

	T^{NEG}-marker	Foc^{NEG}-marker	Class^{NEG}-marker	Q^{NEG}-marker
Pattern 2	na	-na-	hi-	fu-

The T^{NEG}-marker in Japanese is what is usually referred to as the standard negator. It is formed by adding *na-i* to the verb. *-nai-* remains unaltered in the present tense, (162a)–(162b), but the *i-* is replaced by other morphemes in the past tense, (162c).

(162)   a.   tabe-ru
               eat-NPST
               'I/you/[...] eat(s).'
      b.   tabe-na-i
               eat-NEG-NPST
               'I/you/[...] do(es) not eat.'
      c.   tabe-na-katta
               eat-NEG-PST
               'I/you/[...] did not eat.'   (Nyberg 2012:19)

Japanese has two types of adjectives, the so-called *i*-adjectives, which are of Japanese origin, and *na*-adjectives, which are of Chinese origin and more recently also of English, German and French origin. The first type of adjectives are inflected like verbal predicates, (163a): the tense marking and the negative marker attach to the adjectival stem. The affirmative counterpart is in (163b), with *da*, the copula, between brackets. The latter can be added to enhance extra politeness. Japanese also has a special polite negation form, which is illustrated in (163c). The negated polite form is not very different from the affirmative polite form of the verb *aru* 'be', i.e. *arimasu*.[61]

---

[61] There is a subset of words in Japanese that use *-na(i)-* as a predicate negator to express 'undesirable qualities' (Nyberg 2012:43), i.e. expressing polar opposites like *tumaranai* 'boring' or *abunai* 'dangerous'. Nyberg (2012), following Martin (1975), argues that *-nai-* is an 'etymological negator' here and hence cannot be considered a real negation anymore. However, on the other hand he also mentions that it still follows the same conjugation pattern as negation does with i-adjectives. It thus seems that this negation is still fairly active. Moreover, an older grammar,

(163) a. Sora-ga ao-ku-na-i.
sky-NOM blue-ADV-NEG-NPST
'The sky is not blue.'
b. Sora-ga ao-i (da)
sky-NOM blue-NPST (COP)
'The sky is blue.'
c. Sora-ga ao-ku ar-i-mas-en
sky-NOM blue-ADV be-INF-T-NEG
'The sky is not blue.'

The second type has negation on the copula accompanying the adjective, (164b). The copula with the topic-marker is often contracted to *zya* in spoken Japanese. Also with these adjectives the polite negation strategy is an option, (164c). I have not listed the polite form in the table, since I consider the allomorph -*en* a suppletive negative form conditioned by honorification.

(164) a. Kore kirei da.
this pretty COP
'This is pretty.'
b. Kore wa kirei de-wa/zya na-i.
this TOP pretty COP-TOP/COP.TOP NEG-NPST
'This is not pretty.'
c. Kore kirei de-wa ar-i-mas-en.
this pretty COP-TOP be-INF-T-NEG
'This is not pretty.' (Nyberg 2012:28–29)

The same *na-i* is also used to express contrast. However, when contrast is expressed the constituent that is contrasted and focused is followed by the topic marker *wa-*. This construction is called *wa*-negation in Japanese (Storoshenko 2004).

(165) sanji ni wa jidoosha de tomodati to daigaku e ika-na-katta
3:00 at TOP car by friend with university to go-NEG-PST
'I didn't go to the university with friends at 3 by car.'
(from Hinds 1986:149–150, cited in Nyberg 2012:45)

Hoffmann (1876) mentions the same group of words that take -*na*- and refers to them as being negative. There are two options here. Either we argue that for a small subset of words the pattern of negative markers is fully syncretic and *na* is also a Q- and Class^{NEG}-marker. Another option is that in these words *na* is a Foc^{NEG}-marker, taking scope over the untensed predicate, and that the contrary reading is a consequence of pragmatic strengthening (cf. Horn 2001b).

Moreover, *na-* is also used as an adverbial modifier or adjunct negation, a typical property of a Foc^{NEG}-marker.

(166)   watasi de-wa/zya   na-ku,   Taroo ga   si-ta
        me   COP-TOP/COP.TOP   NEG-ADV,   Taro NOM   do-PST
        'It was not I, it was Taro who did it.'   (Nyberg 2012:46)

Based on these data I want to argue that *na-* is syncretic for two types of negation, i. e. depending on whether it combines with tense morphology or adverbial morphology is it a T^{NEG}-marker or Foc^{NEG}-marker respectively.

Hi-, I propose, is a Class^{NEG}-marker. As Kageyama & Kishimoto (2016:126–127) propose, it behaves like English *non-*.

(167)   a. hi-goohoo
            NEG-lawful
            'unlawful'
        b. hi-gunzika
            NEG-militarized
            'non-militarized'

(168)   Kareno setsumeiwa kyokutanni hi-cyokkanteki desu.
        his   explanation extremely NEG-intuitive it.is
        'His explanation is extremely non-intuitive.'

(169)   Kare-wa hi-kirisutokyooto-dewa arimasen.
        he-TOP NEG-Christian-be.INF   T.NEG
        'He isn't non-Christian.' (= He has another religion)

Fu (or *hu*) on the other hand behaves much like English *un-* in *unkind* or *in-* in *insignificant* and is used to negate a state or action (Taylor & Taylor 2014:307). It expresses contrary readings (Hoffmann 1876:128–129) and has a characterising function. I will refer to this marker as a Q^{NEG}-marker.

(170)   hu-kakuzitu
        NEG-certain
        'uncertain'

(171)   fu-kattenaru
        NEG-comfortable
        'uncomfortable'   (Hoffmann 1876:128)

Both the Q^{NEG}-marker *fu* and the Class^{NEG}-marker *hi-* can attach to nouns, adjectival nouns and verbs.[62]

Mu-, illustrated in (172), could be considered a Q^{NEG}-marker. Like English *-less*, it turns nouns/verbs into adjectives. It must thus also consist of adjectivizing features and hence, as explained in the introduction to this chapter, I will not dwell on it, since Japanese has other Q^{NEG}-markers and real adjectives.

(172)   mu-sinkei
        NEG-sensitive
        insensitive'

Summarizing, I have argued that the Japanese T^{NEG}- and Foc^{NEG}-marker is *na*, the Class^{NEG}-marker is *hi-* and the Q^{NEG}-marker is *fu*.

4.2.2.2 Colloquial French

Modern spoken French or Colloquial French (henceforth CF) (as opposed to *le bon usage* French, see section 4.2.1.2) has three different negative markers. *pas* is syncretic for T- and Foc-negation.[63] In spoken and informal French *ne* is not used for the expression of sentential negation. I compare the different status of *ne* and *pas* in spoken French and in *le bon usage* French (Grevisse & Goosse [1936] 1993), the written standard, in more detail in chapter 7. For the present discussion of spoken Modern French, I want to refer the reader to the section on BUF, 4.2.1.2, since most elements discussed there pertain also to CF, apart from *ne*, which is not present in this variety of the language, as illustrated in table 4.11, thus giving rise to a slightly different syncretism pattern for the two varieties of French.

Table 4.11: Spoken French.

	T^{NEG}-marker	Foc^{NEG}-marker	Class^{NEG}-marker	Q^{NEG}-marker
Pattern 2	pas	pas	non(-)	iN-, (dé(s)-)

Summarizing, apart from being a Foc^{NEG}-marker, *pas* is definitely also a T^{NEG}-marker. *Non* behaves like a Class^{NEG}-marker in CF, whilst *iN-* and *dés-* are Q^{NEG}-markers.

---

[62] Japanese also has the two literary negative forms *zu* and *nu* which attach to verbs; I will not deal with them here due to the fact that they do not combine with adjectives in the first place and seem quite unproductive. Another negative prefix is *mi-*, which attaches to verbal nouns and indicates that an action is not yet completed (cf. Korean). However, given that it clearly includes event-related features and does not attach to adjectives I do not further consider it here.

[63] Many thanks to Amélie Rocquet for careful help with the data.

4.2.2.3 Turkish

The syncretism pattern for Turkish as it will be discussed in this section is in table 4.12.

Table 4.12: Turkish.

	T^{NEG}-marker	Foc^{NEG}-marker	Class^{NEG}-marker	Q^{NEG}-marker
Pattern 2	değil	değil	(gayri)/-mE-	(gayri)/siz-

There are two main negators in Turkish:[64] one is the negator that occurs with verbal predicates, -mE-, and one is the negator that occurs with non-verbal predicates, i. e. değil (Kelepir 2001:16–17). Given that our investigation is on negation in combination with adjectival predicates, we will first discuss değil and come back to -mE- later in this section.

Değil is used to negate copular sentences with adjectival, (173a), and nominal predicates, (173b). In the cases in (173a) and (173b) değil takes overt agreement marking. I propose that değil functions as a T^{NEG}-marker here. However, an issue that is unclear from this example is whether the copula 'be' is spelled out by değil, i. e. whether değil is a negative copula, or whether the copula is a non-overt independent element. Kelepir (2001:50) argues that the latter is the case. This would imply that değil is itself not a negative copula.

(173) a. Hasta değil-ø-im.
       sick NEG-ø-1SG
       'I am not sick.'
   b. Artık   dgrenci değil-ø-im.
       anymore student NEG.COP-1SG
       'I am not a student anymore.' (Kelepir 2001:204)

Değil can also select participles or clauses with verbal predicates, which can themselves be negated by -mE-, (174a). In these cases değil seems to be part of a biclausal structure. In (174b) and (174c) respectively the same sentence is negated first with degil, which introduces a cleft here, and then with the regular negator -mE-. This type of sentences that introduce biclausal structures will not be discussed further.

(174) a. Sen-i   anla-m-ıyor   değil-ø-im.
         you-ACC understand-NEG-PROG NEG-COP.1SG

---

[64] Thanks to Metin Bağriaçik and Karsan Seyhun for help with the data.

'It's not that I don't understand you.'
b. Her yer-e taksi-yle gid-iyor değil-im.
every place-DAT taxi-INST go-PROG.3SG NEG.COP-1sg
'It's not the case that I go everywhere by taxi.'
c. Her yer-e taksi-yle git-m-iyor-um.
every place-DAT taxi-INST go-NEG-PROG-1SG
'I don't go everywhere by taxi.'

Support for the idea that *değil* is in itself not a copula comes from the fact that it can also be used as a real constituent negator with the agreement on *değil* missing.[65]

(175) a. Değil sinema-ya git-mek, televizyon bile seyred-ecek
NEG.COP.3SG cinema-DAT go-INF TV even watch-FUT.PRTCP
zaman-ım yok
time-POSS.1SG NEG.EXIST.3SG
'I don't even have time to watch TV, let alone go to the cinema.'
(Göksel & Kerslake 2005:275)
b. Kahya-yı değil şoför-ü tutukla-dı-lar.
butler-ACC NEG.COP.3SG driver-ACC arrest-PST-3PL
'They arrested not the butler but the driver.' (Kelepir 2001)

Supporting evidence for the fact that *değil* is both a T^{NEG}-marker and a Foc^{NEG}-marker, comes from the data in (176a), where it is clear that when there is no agreement on *değil* the scope of *değil* is that of a low scope negator, a

---

[65] Turkish has a negative existential form, *yok*, which I will not treat here. I consider it a suppletive form, in line with a proposal by Kelepir (2001:199–205) to treat it as the negative form of the participle *var*. *Var* in itself is the spellout of *ol-*, the verbal copula 'to be', with a locative feature.

(i) a. Evde bir tane bile fazla ampul yok.
'There isn't even one spare light bulb in the house.' (Göksel & Kerslake 2005:276)
b. Çorbanın tuzu yok.
'The soup doesn't have any salt [in it].' (Göksel & Kerslake 2005:276)

Yok and *değil* can be used in the same sentence:

(ii) Maaşımdan şikayetim yok değil ama idare ediyorum işte.
my.salary my.complaint NEG.exist NEG but administration would.1SG here
'I'm not without complaints about my salary, but I get by all the same.'
(Göksel & Kerslake 2005:276)

I will leave these kinds of stacking examples for future study, but I assume that there is a biclausal structure here, introducing two different T^{NEG}-markers.

Foc^{NEG}-marker, whilst *değil* with agreement takes the role of the T^{NEG}-marker. Interestingly, it is not possible to have the agreement on both instances of *değil*, as illustrated in (176b). What is possible on the other hand is a biclausal cleft-like structure with *değil* taking widest scope when it comes clause finally, taking the rest of the clause as its complement, (176c), comparable to the examples discussed in (174).

(176) a. Biz deli değil-Ø değil-iz
   We crazy NEG-3SG NEG-1PL
   'We are not not crazy'/*It is not the case that we are not crazy.'
 b. *Biz deli değil-iz değil-iz
   We crazy NEG-1PL NEG-1PL
   'We are not not crazy/it is not the case that we are not crazy.'
 c. Biz deli değil-iz değil-Ø
   We crazy NEG-1PL NEG-3SG
   '??We are not not crazy/It is not the case that we are not crazy.'

On the basis of these examples, I would like to conclude that *değil* functions both as a T^{NEG}- and Foc^{NEG}-marker.

There is also a complex phrase that seems to express lexical negation, i. e. it either belongs to the Class^{NEG}- or Q^{NEG}-group. *Olmayan* is such a negator. It is a negative participle, which consists of the copula *ol-* 'be' and the negative verbal negator *mE-*. It can be translated as 'lacking' or *non-*. Even though *mE-* needs a participle to express the meaning of a Class^{NEG}- or Q^{NEG}-marker on an adjective, this is how I would like to treat it. I thus want to treat *mE-*, which is also the standard negator in verbal clauses, as a Class^{NEG}-marker.

(177) a. Ticari   ol-ma-yan   ürün-ler.
   commercial be/become-NEG-SUB.REL product-PL
   'non-commercial products'
 b. Sıcak ama [bunaltıcı ol-ma-yan]   bir
   Hot but muggy   be/become-NEG-SUB.REL a
   hava-sı   var   Ankara'nın.
   weather-POSS.3SG EXIST.3SG Ankara-GEN.3SG
   'The weather in Ankara is hot but not suffocating.'
   (Göksel & Kerslake 2005:446)

Support for this idea comes also from Kelepir (2001), who treats the verbal negator *me-* as a negator with lower scope than *değil*. *Me-* merges with the verbal stem before the verb picks up aspectual or tense marking. A verb with *-me-* can be embedded under *değil* suggesting that *değil* takes wider scope than the base position of *-me-*.

(178) Program-da şu an-da akıl-da ol-ma-yan bazı
program-LOC this moment-LOC mind-LOC be/become-NEG-SUB.REL some
değişiklik-ler(-i) yap-ma-mız gerek-ebil-ir.
change-PL(-ACC) make-NFNOM-1PL be.necessary-POSS-AOR.3SG
'It may be necessary for us to make some changes to the programme that are currently unpredictable.' (Göksel & Kerslake 2005:327)

A suffix, borrowed from Classical Arabic, which is mainly part of literary Turkish and which can be classified as a Class^{NEG}-marker and a Q^{NEG}-marker is *gayri*. The example in (179) shows that *gayri* can be used to classify, whilst the example in (180) shows it can also give rise to contrary characterising readings. (179) also shows that stacking is possible with this type of marker, so it seems to comply with the requirements to be taken up in this overview.

(179) (O) gayri-müslim/gayri-müslüman değil-ø.
he.NOM NEG-muslim/NEG-muslim NEG-3SG
'He isn't non-Muslim.'

(180) Davranış-ı çok (da) gayri-müslüman-vari değil-ø
behavior-POSS.3SG very PART NEG-Muslim-esque NOM.NEG-3SG
'His behaviour is not very unchristian.'

However, *gayri* got out of use and is no longer a productive marker. A productive suffix that functions as a characterising marker and that can give rise to contrary interpretations is *-siz*. *-siz* turns a noun into an adjective, comparable to English *-less*. I consider it a productive Q^{NEG}-marker in Turkish, but since it also incorporates a feature that derives adjectives from nominals, it cannot be fully equated with negative markers like *un-*. Nevertheless I take it up in the overview here, because of the fact that it is semantically and in terms of its productivity the best match for what we described as Q^{NEG}-markers, as illustrated by the example in (181).

(181) (O) mut-lu değil-ø fakat mut-suz da değil-ø
s/he.NOM hope-REL NOM.NEG-3SG but hope-NEG PART NOM.NEG-3SG
'He isn't happy, but he isn't unhappy either.'

The data in (182) show *değil* can be stacked on predicates ending in *-sız* and even three negations can be stacked, as illustrated in (183).

(182) a. Görev imkan-sız değil.
　　　　the.task facility-NEG NEG
　　　　'The task is not impossible.'
　　b. O inanç-sız biri değil.
　　　　he believer-NEG one NEG
　　　　'He is not unreligious.'

(183) 　(O) mut-suz değil-ø değil-ø
　　　　s/he.NOM hope-NEG NEG-3SG NEG-3SG
　　　　'lit: it is not the case that he isn't unhappy'

Summarizing, a Q^{NEG}-marker in Turkish is *siz-*, two $Class^{NEG}$-markers are *gayri* and *olmayan* with the latter being a complex construction consisting of the negative particle *-mE-* and then *değil* as the Foc^{NEG} and T^{NEG}-marker.

4.2.2.4 Other languages

In what follows I will discuss the languages, Swedish and Azerbaijani, a bit briefer, because they do not illustrate a new pattern and belong to the same language families as English and Turkish respectively.

Swedish[66] also has pattern 2, as illustrated by the table in 4.13.

Table 4.13: Swedish.

	T^{NEG}-marker	Foc^{NEG}-marker	$Class^{NEG}$-marker	Q^{NEG}-marker
Pattern 2	inte	inte	icke-	o-

The Q^{NEG}-marker in Swedish is *o-*. It is a characterising marker, (184), and can give rise to contrary readings, as illustrated in (185).

(184) 　Hans beteende är väldigt o-amerikanskt.
　　　　his behaviour is very NEG-american
　　　　'His behaviour is very unAmerican.'

(185) 　Han är inte lycklig, men han är inte o-lycklig heller.
　　　　he is NEG happy, but he is NEG NEG-happy either.
　　　　'He is not happy but he is not unhappy either.'

The $Class^{NEG}$-marker is *icke*. It has a classifying function, illustrated by the example in (186), and can be stacked on the Q^{NEG}-marker, (187).

---

66 Thanks to Johan Brandtler for help with the data.

(186) Han är icke-kristen.
he is NEG-Christian
'He is non-Christian.'

(187) Hans icke-o-moraliska beteende
his NEG-NEG behaviour
'His non-immoral behaviour.'

The Foc^{NEG}-marker and T^{NEG}-marker is *inte*. The reason that I consider it both a Foc^{NEG}-marker and a T^{NEG}-marker is that it can on the one hand be used as an adverbial modifier, (188a), and contrastive negator giving rise to so-called constituent negation, (188b), and on the other hand as the regular sentential negator taking scope over the tensed predicate, (189). For more discussion of negation in Swedish I refer the reader to Holmes & Hinchliffe (2008 [1997]), Sells (2000), Christensen (2005), Brandtler (2006).

(188) a. för inte så länge sedan
for NEG so long ago
'not so long ago'
b. Inte Sven, utan Bertil, kom till festen igår
NEG Sven but Bertil came to party-the yesterday
Not Sven, but Bertil came to the party yesterday. Brandtler 2006:185

(189) Sven är inte vänlig
Sven is NEG friendly
'Sven is not friendly.'

Support for the fact that *inte* can play the role of constituent negator (Foc^{NEG}-marker) and sentential negator (T^{NEG}-marker) within one clause comes from the stacking data in (190) and (191b).

(190) ?Han är inte INTE lycklig. (only with stress on second *inte*)
he is NEG NEG happy
'He isn't not happy.'

(191) a. [Context: A says: 'He is not unhappy.' B constradicts this and says:]
b. ?Han är visst inte inte o-lycklig.
he is definitely NEG NEG NEG-happy.
'He is definitely not not unhappy.'

Azerbaijani[67] could be looked at as having Pattern 2 as well, as illustrated in the first row in table 4.15. However, unlike in Turkish, *qeyri-*, also derived from Classical Arabic and similar to Turkish *gayri-*, is productively used both to express the corresponding English *non-* and *un-* (p. c. Sevda Selayeva), i. e. it can be used as a Class^{NEG}-marker and a Q^{NEG}-marker, as illustrated by the words in table 4.14 and the sentences in (192). The example (192b) also provides us with a nice case of stacking a T^{NEG}- and Q^{NEG}-marker within the same clause.

(192) a. O   qeyri-nəsrani deyil.
        s/he.NOM NEG-Christian NEG-3SG
        'He isn't non-Christian.'
    b. Onun hərəkəti o   qədər də   qeyri-nəsrani deyil
        his   actions that up.to much NEG-Christian NEG
        'His behaviour is so not un-Christian.'

Table 4.14: Azerbaijani: qeyri.

POS	NEG	TRANSLATION
müəyyən	qeyri-müəyyən	(in)definite
dəqiq	qeyri-dəqiq	(in)accurate
etik	qeyri-etik	(im)moral
standart	qeyri-standart	(non-)standard

Table 4.15: Azerbaijani.

	T^{NEG}-marker	Foc^{NEG}-marker	Class^{NEG}-marker	Q^{NEG}-marker
Pattern 2	deyil	deyil	-ma-	qeyri-
Pattern 3	deyil	deyil	qeyri	qeyri-

Nevertheless, also the construction with *olmayan*, for which we argued for Turkish that it consists of a Class^{NEG}-marker, is available in Azerbaijani, as illustrated in the stacking example in (193).

(193)   Onun qeyri-etik olmayan davaranışı
          (s)he NEG-moral NEG   behaviour
          His non-immoral behaviour.'

---

[67] Thanks to Sevda Salayeva for help with these data. Her judgments are vital for this paragraph on Azerbaijani, since there is extremely little research on Azerbaijani negation accessible in English. Errors in presentation are of course mine.

As such, depending on how we cut the cake and which of the Class^{NEG}-markers we consider most productive, Azerbaijani could be grouped with pattern 2 or 3. More study on the frequency of negative markers is necessary to determine how to best represent the syncretism pattern in Azerbaijani.

4.2.3 Pattern 3

4.2.3.1 Mandarin Chinese

Chinese has a syncretic marker *bù* for T- and Foc-negation and another marker *fēi(-)* which functions as a Class^{NEG}- and Q^{NEG}-marker, table 4.16.[68]

Table 4.16: Mandarin Chinese.

	T^{NEG}-marker	Foc^{NEG}-marker	Class^{NEG}-marker	Q^{NEG}-marker
Pattern 3	bù	bù	fēi(-)	fēi(-)

Fēi(-) is used as a Q- and Class^{NEG}-marker. On the one hand it gives rise to lexicalized readings, as in (194), which is a property of Q^{NEG}-markers. On the other hand, it functions as a classifying negative marker, yielding low scope contradictory readings, as in (195a)–(195b).

(194) a. Tā fēi- rén
he NEG- human
'He is inhuman/cruel.'
≠ 'He is not human.'
b. fēi-cháng
NEG-daily
'extra-ordinary, unusual.'
≠ 'not daily.'

(195) a. fēi-shāngyè chǎnpǐn.
NEG-commercial products
'the noncommercial products.
b. Tā de fāngfǎ shì fēi zhuānyè de.
he of method is NEG profession of
'His method is nonprofessional.'

---

68 Many thanks to Li Man for help with the data.

The use of *fēi(-)* goes back to Old Chinese. In isolation it means 'to be wrong' and it was the opposite of *shì* to be right'. *Fēi-* is nowadays often associated with literary style.[69]

The Foc^{NEG}- and T^{NEG}-marker are also morphologically syncretic in Chinese: *bù*. When *bù* precedes the finite verb, as in (196a), it has sentential scope. When it follows the verb on the other hand, it does not take scope over the tensed predicate and it triggers a low scope contradictory reading. It can even trigger a contrary reading, as illustrated by the two readings in (196b).[70]

(196) a. Tā bú shì kuàilé.
       (s)he NEG is happy.
       'She is not happy.'
   b. Tā shì bú kuàilé.
       (s)he is NEG happy.
       'She is NOT happy.'
       'She is unhappy.'

With adjectival predicates, the copular verb is usually not overt. Hence, the same sentence can give rise to a low scope contradictory negation or sentential negation on the one hand and a contrary negation, as illustrated by the examples in (197a)–(197e). There are two options here. Under the first option we assume that these contrary readings are a consequence of pragmatic strengthening of the contradictory negation, a phenomenon discussed by Horn (2001b). As we will see, once we provide a nanosyntactic formal analysis of negative markers, the features related to Q- and Class^{NEG}-markers, will turn out to be contained in Foc- and T^{NEG}-markers and hence it is not surprising that Foc- and T^{NEG}-markers can give rise to contrary readings, i. e. what is referred to as pragmatic strengthening could be argued to follow from the syntax of the negative marker combined with the syntax of the predicate it combines with. Under the second option, it could be assumed that *bù* is not only a Foc- and T^{NEG}-marker, but that it can also be a Q- and Class^{NEG}-marker. The contrary readings are then a consequence of the fact that *bù* is syncretic throughout and thus also a Q^{NEG}-marker. If the latter option is on the right track, this would bring us again to a situation similar as the one that we also discussed for Korean. However, in this particular case the different grammars (i. e.

---

[69] The marker *wù* is also frequently used to create adjectival-like negative predicates. Its meaning is reminiscent of English *-less* and Hungarian *-tElEn*. It always combines with a nominal predicate expressing a concrete thing which then gives rise to an adjective expressing 'the property of being deprived of a certain thing'.
[70] The tone on *bù* changes from fourth tone to second tone (bú) when *bù* precedes a word with fourth tone, as in (196a)–(196b).

syncretism patterns for negation) would not depend on the linguistic origin of the predicate, but rather on whether a predicate belongs to a more formal/literary register or not. The more formal/literary register would have the grammar as discussed in this section and the more colloquial grammar would be the one where *bù* is fully syncretic. As we will see in section 4.3 there is another option which combines option 1 (pragmatic strengthening) with the fact that different types of predicates may come in different sizes and therefore allow or disallow to be combined with particular negative markers. I will come back to this option in section 4.3. In what follows I treat Chinese as adhering to pattern 3.

(197) a. Tā   bù   kuàilé.
         (s)he/he NEG happy.
         'She is not happy.'
         'She is unhappy.'
      b. Tā   bù   zhōngchéng
         (s)he NEG honest
         'She is not honest.'
         'She is dishonest.'
      c. Tā   bù   zhōngchéng
         (s)he NEG loyal
         'He is not loyal.'
         'He is disloyal.'
      d. Tā   bù   kuānróng
         (s)he NEG tolerant
         'He is not tolerant.'
         'He is intolerant.'
      e. Tā   de fāngfǎ   bú   qiádáng
         (s)he DE method NEG appropriate
         'His method is not appropriate.' 'His method is inappropriate.'

In (199) and (198) *bù* is stacked, supporting that *bù* belongs to at least two different groups of negative markers: the group of T^{NEG}- and Foc^{NEG}-markers. However, as illustrated by (199) the low scope *bù* can also give rise to contrary readings.

(198) tā bù shì bú zhongcheng
       she NEG is NEG honest
       She is not dishonest.

(199) Tā jí   bú   shì kuanrong, de yě   bú   shì bù   kuānróng de.
       She and NEG is   tolerant, DE also NEG is   NEG tolerant
       'She is neither tolerant nor intolerant.'

Chinese has another frequently used marker, *méi*. This marker always co-occurs with *yǒu* 'have'. It is the typical negative marker for all tenses that express a completed or accomplished action (Dan 2006, Po-Ching & Rimmington 2006 [1997]), (200a)–(200b), and it is used to negate adjectives that consist of *yǒu* and a noun, as in (201a).

(200) a. Tā méi(yǒu) qù ōzhōu.
        He neg(-have) go Europe
        'He did not go to Europe.'
     b. Shéi méi(yǒu) tīng zuótian de guûangbō?
        who not(-have) listen yesterday DE broadcast
        'Who didn't listen to yesterday's broadcast?'   (Po-Ching & Rimmington 2006 [1997]:52)

(201) a. Zhéi běn   xiǎoshuō měi yǒu yísi
        this CLASS novel   NEG have meaning
        'This novel is not interesting'   (Po-Ching & Rimmington 2006 [1997]:52)
     b. Tā méi yǒu yísi
        he not have light
        'He is unconscious.'

I want to argue that *méi* when it negates an adjective in combination with the verb *yǒu* – is a suppletive form for the combination of *bù* and aspectual meanings associated with *yǒu* (Li & Thompson 1981).[71] For a sentence like (202) for instance the idea is that the negator *méi* is a suppletive T^{NEG}-marker in an embedded clause with the existential verb *yǒu*. Within one clause, the same reasoning as before seems valid: *bù* is the standard T^{NEG}-marker, whilst *mei* (*yǒu*), also a T^{NEG}-marker, is used in a more specific context and can therefore be considered to be in complementary distribution with it. As mentioned in footnote 23 and section 4.1, I will not discuss TAM-related markers further in this book. They constitute a research project on their own.

---

71 Croft (1991) pointed to the existence of a negative existential cycle: in stage A languages use the verbal negator in combination with the existential verb, in stage B they use a special 'suppletive' negative existential predicate which differs from the verbal negator and then in stage C the negative existential predicate is used as a regular verbal negator. Croft argued for Chinese that it moved from stage A to C without going through a fusional B-stage. Since Chinese keeps *bù* as the main standard negator and uses *méi yǒu* as a negator in perfective contexts (and in existential and possessive clauses), it seems that one cannot really equate *méi yǒu* with the standard negator. The discussions on *méi yǒu* and the differences with *bù* constitute a major bone of contention among linguists. It is beyond the scope of this book to go deeper into it.

(202)　Tā bú shì méi yǒu bú kuaile
　　　she NEG is NEG have NEG happy
　　　'She isn't not unhappy.'

Focussing on a more formal literary variety of Chinese, we can say that *fēi* can be identified as Q- and Class^{NEG}-marker and *bù* as a T^{NEG}- and Foc^{NEG}-marker. We assume for now that the contrary readings that can arise with *bù* are a consequence of pragmatic strengthening, which itself can arise due to the syntax of negative markers (as we will further discuss in chapter 5). Even though we will discuss informally how we could deal with the existence of different syncretism patterns within one language in section 4.3, for now we keep the option open that a more informal variety of Chinese could be argued to have another pattern.

4.2.3.2 Modern Standard Arabic

In Modern Standard Arabic (henceforth MSA)[72] *ghayr* behaves like a Q- and Class^{NEG}-marker. The marker *laa* on the other hand is syncretic for T en Foc-negation.[73]

Table 4.17: Modern Standard Arabic.

	T^{NEG}-marker	Foc^{NEG}-marker	Class^{NEG}-marker	Q^{NEG}-marker
Pattern 3	laa	laa	ghayr	ghayr

The Q- and Class^{NEG}-marker in MSA is *ghayr*. *Ghayr* can give rise to contrariety and functions as a characterising negative marker on the one hand, as in (203a)–(203c). On the other hand it can also express contradictory negation, functioning as a classifying negative marker, as illustrated by the examples in (204a)–(204b).

---

[72] Arabic is a Semitic language and the term Arabic most commonly refers to Modern Standard Arabic (MSA) or Classical Arabic (literary Arabic) (CA). Sometimes Arabic also refers to the vernaculars spoken in all the different regions of the Arab world. MSA and CA are not so different from each other. MSA is the spoken and written language of television, radio, press, books, whereas CA was the written language until the 18th century. The main differences between the two varieties of Arabic are stylistic and in terms of vocabulary. Lots of new vocabulary have entered the language to meet the needs of modern life. With respect to negation there is hardly any difference between MSA and CA. Besides MSA, all speakers of Arabic master at least one regional vernacular which is their mother tongue and which often differs a lot from MSA and CA (Ryding 2005).
[73] Many thanks to Hicham El Sghiar for help with the data.

(203) a. ghayru muqaddasin.
         NEG   holy
         'unholy.' (Ryding 2005:275)
      b. ghayru munaasibin.
         NEG   suitable
         'inappropriate.'
      c. ghayru mubaashirin
         NEG   direct
         'indirect' (Ryding 2005:649)

(204) a. ghayr mutadayin.
         NEG   religious
         'He is irreligious/non-religious.'
      b. ghayru islaamiyyin
         NEG   Islamic
         'non-Islamic' (examples adapted from Ryding 2005:649)

Ghayr scopes only over the predicate term, not over the (un)tensed predicate. Ghayr is structurally close to the adjective it modifies: it is the first term in a special construction, called the adjectival construct (Al Sharifi & Sadler 2009, Alsharif & Sadler 2009), construct phrase or iDaafa (Ryding 2005:223).[74]

The T^{NEG}-marker is *laa* in MSA. However, this is not an unproblematic claim, since *laa*, as a T^{NEG}-marker, typically does not occur in verbless sentences as those we investigate. In those cases *laysa* 'to not be' (see also Horn 2001b:449, Lucas 2009:20) is used, a negative verb.[75] Ouhalla (1993) suggests it consists of *laa*, a verbal copula *s* and agreement, an analysis that is followed by Benmamoun (2000:103). It only negates the present tense.[76] The verb *lays-a*, therefore, is specialised and limited to negating the present tense of *be*. I consider it a suppletive form for the combination of the T^{NEG}-marker *laa* and the present tense of the verb 'be', which is why I kept *laa* as the T^{NEG}-marker in the table. I will not discuss

---

[74] The construction with *ghayr* is relatively special since construct phrases normally consist of two nominals, whereas adjectival constructs normally have the adjective preceding the noun. In the construct with *ghayr* the first part is a nominal, which is the negative marker *ghayr*, whereas the second part is an adjective or adjectival participle.

[75] More straightforwardly than Mandarin Chinese, cf. section 4.2.3.1, MSA seems to be in Stage B of the Croft's Cycle.

[76] Like with other verbs, the negation of the perfect or past tense happens with *lam*. For the future tense *lan* is used (Ryding 2005:647, Lucas 2009:20). I consider *lam* and *lan* tense conditioned allomorphs of *laa*. They belong to the group of T^{NEG}-markers and are in complementary distribution with *laa*.

suppletive negative verbs in this book, because they do not express pure negation (cf. section 4.1).

(205) a. sum^catuka lays-at jayyidatan.
reputation.your NEG.be-AGR good.
Your reputation is not good. (Ryding 2005:643)

As a T^{NEG}-marker *laa* scopes over the tensed predicate, as in (206a). In this case it is a regular contradictory negative marker, giving rise to speaker denial.

(206) a. laa 'afhamu maadhaa taquulu.
NEG I.understand what you.saying
'I do not understand what you are saying.'
b. laa 'u-daxxinu.
NEG I.smoke
'I do not smoke.' (Ryding 2005:644)

laa can also be used as a predicate negative marker, not scoping over the tensed verb (Ryding 2005, Benmamoun 2000:96), as illustrated in (207a)–(207b).[77]

(207) a. laa lwilaayaatu lmuttaHidatu wa- laa littiHaadu lsuufiyaatiyyu
NEG the.states the.united and- NEG the.union the.Soviet
'neither the United States nor the Soviet Union' (Ryding 2005:646)

---

[77] In (ia)–(ic), *laa* is not used in combination with a finite verb, but it is used in a compound construction. It thus seems that *laa* is sometimes capable of expressing Class and/or Q-negation. The existence of *laa* in these compounds can point to older or newer layers of the language. It could also mean that Arabic has two available patterns for Class and Q-negation, depending on the predicate involved, a pattern that we also saw for Korean and Chinese. More research into Arabic would be necessary to understand this. For the purpose of this research I take it that *ghayr* expresses Q^{NEG}- and Class^{NEG}, though nothing crucially hinges on this as we will see in the discussion of the results in 4.3.

(i) a. laa-faqaariyy
NEG-vertebrate.adj
'invertebrate'
b. laa -nihaa'iyy
NEG- end-adj
'never-ending'
c. Harakatun laa-tahda'u qurba lmasjidi
motion NEG-stopped near the.mosque
'non-stop motion/movement near the mosque' (examples adapted from Ryding 2005:645)

b. laa ʕahad
   no one
   'No one'   (Aoun et al. 2010:36)

Another negator, *maa*, is also argued to be used as a focal negator (Benmamoun 2000:108), which is why I would argue it could be considered another Foc^{NEG}-marker. However, I have not taken it up in the table.

Summarizing, *ghayr* expresses Q-negation and Class-negation and *laa* expresses Foc- and T-negation. In the present tense of a copular clause the T^{NEG}-marker and the copular verb 'be' are replaced by the suppletive form *laysa*.

4.2.3.3 Persian

Persian has a syncretic form *qeyr-* to express Q- and Class-negation and *na* to express T- and Foc-negation, see table 4.18.[78]

Table 4.18: Persian.

	T^{NEG}-marker	Foc^{NEG}-marker	Class^{NEG}-marker	Q^{NEG}-marker
Pattern 3	na-	na-	qeyr-	qeyr-

Persian uses *qeyr-* as a Q^{NEG}- and Class^{NEG}-marker, (208a)–(208h). *Qeyr-* is derived from the Arabic noun *ghayr* which means 'other than','non', 'un-'. It either expresses contrary negation and has a characterising function, as in (208a)–(208e), or it express contradictory negation with a classifying meaning, (208f)–(208h).[79]

---

[78] I am very much indebted to Mansour Shabani and Karimouy Mitra Heravi for a lot of help with the data.

[79] There is another negative marker *nā*, with a long ā, spelled differently in Persian, which can be prefixed onto adjectival predicates and which gives rise to contrary readings, sometimes even lexicalized meanings, as in (ia)–(id).

(i) a. nā-binā
       NEG-seeing
       'blind'
    b. nā-omia
       NEG-hope
       'despondent'   (Reuben 1951:46)
    c. U   adame nā-rāhati   ast.
       he man   NEG-relaxed is
       'He is a sad man.'

(208) a. U qeyr-e herfehi   ast.
       He NEG-EZ professional is
       'He is unprofessional.'
       'He is nonprofessional.'
    b. U qeyr-e tabi'i   ast.
       He NEG-EZ natural is
       'He is unnatural'.
    c. metod-e   u   qeyr-e tejari   ast.
       Method-EZ his NEG-EZ commercial is
       'His method is non-commercial.'
    d. U qeyr-e qābel-e ehterām ast.
       He NEG-EZ able-EZ respect is
       'He is disrespectful.'
    e. U adame qeyr-e-ensăni ast.
       he man   NEG-EZ-human is
       'He is an inhuman/unhuman man.'
    f. U adame qeyr-e-mazhabi ast.
       he man   NEG-EZ-religious is
       'He is a non-religous person'
    g. Raftār-e   u qeyr-e amrikai   ast.
       Behavior-EZ his NEG-EZ American is
       'His behavior is un-/non-American'
    h. qeyr-e daneshgahi
       NEG- Ez   university.ADJ
       'non-academic'

---

    d. metod-e   u   nā-monāseb   ast.
       Method-EZ his NEG-appropriate is
       'His method is inappropriate'

Moreover, the Foc^{NEG}-marker na can be stacked on this other nā in (ii).

(ii) U adame na nā-rāhat,   balke rāhati ast.
      he man NEG NEG-happy, but   happy is.
      'He is not sad, but happy.'

These data suggest that Persian has an additional strategy for the Q^{NEG}- and Class^{NEG}-markers, which co-exists alongside the strategy with *qheyr*, comparable to how English also has several markers for Q-negation. However, this does not really change the picture for the pattern in the case of Persian. More data research is necessary to see how productive this strategy is compared to the *qeyr-*-strategy. Moreover, more stacking-data are needed to decide on the precise relation between *nā* and *qheyr*. For the purpose of this dissertation I do not consider this long *nā* in the overview of the syncretism patterns. I leave this issue for further research.

Qeyr- does not scope over the tensed predicate. It is in a complex predicate construction with the adjective. The close relationship between the negative marker and the adjective is expressed by the Ezāfe (Ez in the glosses).[80]

The Foc^{NEG}- and T^{NEG}-marker in Persian is *na*. When *na* takes scope over the finite verb, by affixing onto it, it is a T^{NEG}-marker (209).[81]

(209) Diruz   na-raft-am   madrese
       Yesterday NEG-went-1SG school
       'I didn't go to school yesterday.'   (Kwak 2010:623)

(210) a. U   ādam-e rāhati   ni-st
           (s)he man-EZ relaxed   NEG-is
           'He is not a relaxed person.'
       b. u   ba-vafa   ni-st
           (s)he with-loyalty   NEG-is
           'He is not loyal'

Na can also be used as a Foc^{NEG}-marker, a 'constituent negation' according to Kwak (2010). In (211a)–(211d) *na* functions as a contrastive negation, giving rise to contradictory negation. In (211e)–(211f) *na* is used as an adverbial modifier.

---

80 The Ezāfe following *qeyr-* is typical of Iranian languages. It connects a noun, adjective or preposition with its modifier. The function of the Ezāfe is not yet well-understood and many different approaches have been taken to explain how the Ezāfe regulates the relation between a noun, adjective or preposition and its complement. Proposals vary from considering it a contracted clause (Tabaian 1974), a non-verbal EzafeP (Moinzadeh 2005), a case marking head (Larson & Yamakido 2008), a PF-phenomenon (Samiian 1983, Ghomeshi 1996), etc. It is beyond the scope of this dissertation to go into this.

81 When *na-* prefixes onto the 3rd person singular of the verb *budan* 'to be', namely *ast*, as in (210a)–(210b), then the combination of the negative marker *na* and *ast* becomes *nist*. *Ni-* is thus an allomorph of *na* (Lambton 2003:12). Two other allomorphs are (Kwak 2010): *ne*, which occurs when negation precedes the progressive marker *mi-* (Taleghani 2006, 2008), as in (ia) and *ma*, which can occur with imperatives,(ib), though it is hardly ever used. I consider all these negative markers in complementary distribution with the T^{NEG}-marker and TAM-conditioned sentential negative markers.

(i)   a. Mariam ne-mi-tavānest-ø   taklif ro anjām   be-dah-ad.
          Mariam NEG-DUR-could-3SG task rā completion SUBJ-give-3SG.
          'Mariam could not complete the task.'   (Kwak 2010:622)
      b. Dige   ma-pors-ø.
          Any-more   NEG-ask-2sg.
          'Don't ask any more.'   (Kwak 2010:623)

(211)   a. Ali ketābo varaq zad-ø, na-xarid-ø.
           Ali book   page hit-3SG NEG-bought-3SG.
           'Ali turned the pages of the book, but did not buy it.'
        b. Na man chini   sohbat mi-kon-am, na ānhā
           NEG I   Chinese speak dur-do-1SG NEG they
           'Neither I nor they speak Chinese.'
        c. Man ketāb mi-xun-am,   na majale
           I   book dur-read-1SG, NEG magazine
           'I'm reading a book, not a magazine.'
        d. U na be Bruxel balke be Tehran raft-ø.
           he NEG to Brussels but   to Tehran went-3SG
           'He went not to Brussels, but to Teheran.'
        e. Ruzi do sā'at ketāb mi-xun-am,   na har ruz.
           a.day two hour book DUR-read-1SG NEG every day.
           'I read a book two hours a day, not every day.'   (Kwak 2010:624)
        f. na chandān pishtar
           NEG long   ago
           'not long ago'

The Foc^{NEG}-marker *na* can stack on *qeyr-*, as shown in (212). Stacking *qeyr-* on *na-* is not possible.

(212)   U adame na qeyr- e- mazhabi,   balke mazhabi ast.
        he man   NEG NEG- Ez- religious, but   religious is
        'He is not an irreligious person, but a religious person.'

Summarizing, *na* is the T^{NEG}- and Foc^{NEG}-marker in Persian and *qeyr-* functions as a Q- and Class^{NEG}-marker.

4.2.3.4 Malayalam

In Malayalam, *alla* is used as a T^{NEG}- and Foc^{NEG}-marker in adjectival predicational clauses and *a-* functions as a Class^{NEG}- and Q^{NEG}-marker, 4.19.[82] In what follows I discuss the different negation strategies in more detail.

In order to explain why I consider *alla*, and not the standard negator *illa*, the T^{NEG}- and Foc^{NEG}-marker, some explanation on copular clauses in Malayalam is necessary. In copular sentences two forms of 'to be' can be used, *aaṇe* and

---

[82] Malayam is a language spoken in South-India, more specifically in Kerala. It belongs to the group of the Dravidian languages, more in particular South-Dravidian (Krishnamurti 2003). I want to thank Maryann Madahavadthu for help with the data.

Table 4.19: Malayalam.

	T^NEG-marker	Foc^NEG-marker	Class^NEG-marker	Q^NEG-marker
Pattern 3	(-)alla(-)	-alla	a-	a-

uṇṭə. The different contexts in which both forms occur are not always easy to dinstinguish. However, *uṇṭə* is definitely used in existential contexts and universal contexts and *aaṇe* in defining, identifying and role-expressing copular clause. In some contexts there is overlap and both verbs can be used. These contexts are locational contexts and contexts in which the subject is in the dative form and said to undergo a certain experience. The meaning differences between the use of *aaṇe* and *uṇṭə* in these contexts is subtle. However, Mohanan & Mohanan (1999) argue that in these contexts only sentences with *aaṇe* give rise to a contextual presupposition.

(213) a. veedana kaalil aaṇe
pain leg.LOC be.PRS
'The pain is in the leg.'
b. kaalil veedana uṇṭə
leg.LOC pain be.PRS
'There is pain in the leg.'

(214) a. avannə pani aaṇe
he.DAT fever be.PRS
'He is feverish.'
b. avannə pani uṇṭə
he.DAT fever be.PRS
'He has a fever.' (Asher & Kumar 1997:151)

The two forms of 'to be', *aaṇe* and *uṇṭə*, have two forms of negation: *alla* and *illa* respectively.

(215) a. avannə pani alla
he.DAT fever be.NEG
'He isn't feverish.' (It is not fever that he is suffering from.)
b. avannə pani illa
he.DAT fever be.NEG
He doesn't have a fever.' (Asher & Kumar 1997:151–152)

The semantic difference between *alla* and *illa* was described by Kunjan Pillai (1965) as 'is not that' for the former and 'does/do not exist' for the latter. *alla* is concerned with the denial of the attachment of a given quality to an entity and *illa* with the denial of the existence of an entity, either in general or in a specific location (Asher & Kumar 1997:340).

Both *illa*, (216) and *alla*, (217) can be conjugated, i. e. they can get tense marking suffixed to their base and are hence often considered predicates incorporating the meaning of 'be'.

(216) a. aarum illa-aṉṉiṭṭə ṉaan buddhimuṭṭi
anyone be.NEG-PRF.PTCP I experience.difficulty.PST
'Nobody being there, I had great difficulty.'
b. avan illa-aṉṭə oru rasavum illa [or: illaate]
he be.NEG-PTCP a interest.even be.NEG
'Without him it's not at all interesting.'

(217) innale kaṉṭa paṭam nallatə alla-ayirunnu
yesterday see-RP picture good NEG-PST
'The picture (we) saw yesterday was not a good one.'

For regular verbal sentential negation *illa* is added to the verb, (218).

(218) avan innale vann-illa
he yesterday come-PST-NEG
'He didn't come yesterday.'

Amritavalli & Jayaseelan (2005) analyze Kannada and Malayalam *illa* as being either a negative finite existential verb, labelled *illa₁*, or a pure negative, *illa₂*. The reason for this is that *(-)illa* sometimes functions as a negative existential verb, being the counterpart of *uNTə*, (219), and sometimes as pure negation, (218). The proces, visible in Malayalam, is the process described by Croft (1991): negative existential verbs develop into standard negators, cf. section 4.2.3.1 and 4.2.3.2 and in particular footnotes 71–75.

(219) a. Avan iviDe uṉṭə.
he here be
'He is here.'
b. Avan iviDe illa.
he here NEG
'He is not here.' (Amritavalli & Jayaseelan 2005:202)

As such, Amritavalli & Jayaseelan (2005) provide an analysis which considers *illa* as a homophonous representation of two underlying structures: negation as such and also a negative copula. This idea is also present in Krishnamurti (2003:355–356)'s overview of the Dravidian languages.

However, given that we are considering predicational copular clauses (and not existential copular clauses), the study of *illa* cannot be the main focus of this section. In predicational clauses the relevant negator is the suffix *-alla* or the independent particle *alla*. We propose that the suffix *-alla* has the function of a Foc^{NEG}-marker, whereas the particle *alla* functions as a T^{NEG}-marker. Usually, the particle *alla* will be considered a negative copula.

(220)   avannə pani   alla
        he   feverish be.NEG
        'He isn't feverish'.(Asher & Kumar 1997:151)

When it functions as a Foc^{NEG}-marker, *-alla* gives rise to constituent negation, attaching to all constituents, including non-verbal ones as well, as in (221) and triggering nominalization on the verb.

(221)   a. avan-alla innale   vannatə
            he-NEG   yesterday come.NMLZ
            'It was not he that came yesterday.'
        b. avan innaley-alla   vannatə
            he   yesterday-NEG   come.NMLZ
            'It was not yesterday that he came.'   (Asher & Kumar 1997:154)

As a T^{NEG}-marker *(-)alla* is usually considered the negative counterpart of *aaṇe*, which is in most grammars or typological descriptions also described as a copula (Asher & Kumar 1997, Krishnamurti 2003, Nair 2012, Lindblom 2014). One could argue that in the structures in (221), which are usually regarded as cleft constructions, *alla* still functions as a negative copula with the Foc^{NEG}-marker spelling out the properties of a copula in addition to the properties of a negative focus marker. However, this analysis of *alla* as a negative copula is not required. Mathew (2013:258) analyzes the positive counterpart of *alla*, i. e. *aaṇe*, as a Focus Marker, following ideas by Mohanan (1982) and argues for a mono-clausal analysis in line with this assumption. I would like to tentatively follow that approach.

Keeping the analysis for the Foc^{NEG}-marker in mind, the question remains whether the particle *alla*, the T^{NEG}-marker, consists of verbal structure in Malayalam or is just a negative focal dependant of *aaṇe*. Given the predominant view in the literature to treat it as a negative copula, I will stick to that idea for now. However, if it is a copula, its form is nevertheless syncretic with the constituent negator *alla*.

Malayalam also has a negative marker that takes very low scope. *a-*, going back to the Proto-Dravidian negative marker *ā (Krishnamurti 2003:353), is such a negative marker and *alla* can be stacked on such predicates, both as a T^{NEG}- and Foc^{NEG}-marker.[83]

(222) a. Avan santhoshavaán alla.
 He happy be.NEG.
 'He isn't happy.'
 b. Avan a-santhushttan anu.
 He NEG-happy is
 'He is unhappy.'
 c. Avan a-santhushattan alla
 He NEG-happy be.NEG
 'He isn't unhappy.'

(223) Avante a-dharmikam-allá-tha perumattam.
 His NEG-moral-NEG behaviour
 'His non-immoral behaviour.'

The perfect acceptability of the sentences in (224) suggests that this marker gives rise to contrary negation, which would make it a candidate to be a Q^{NEG}-marker.

(224) Avan sathushttan alla, pakshe avan a-santhusttan-um alla.
 He happy be.NEG, but he NEG-happy-and be.NEG
 'He isn't happy, but he isn't unhappy either.'

(225) Avan a-santhushattan alla.
 He NEG-happy be.NEG.
 'He isn't unhappy.'

The following examples show that *a-* can also function as a Class^{NEG}-marker, (226).

(226) Avan a-chraistavan alla.
 He NEG-christian be.NEG
 'He isn't non-Christian.'

Summarizing, for predicational copular clauses *alla* is the T^{NEG} and Foc^{NEG}-marker, whilst *a-* can be considered the Q^{NEG}- and Class^{NEG}-marker.

---

83 Many thanks to Maryann Madhuvatu for help with the data and providing me with stacking data. Her transliterations and those from the grammars differ.

4.2.4 Pattern 4

4.2.4.1 Khwe

Khwe has *vé* as a T^{NEG}-marker, *-nya* as a Foc^{NEG}-marker and *o-* as a Class^{NEG} and Q-^{NEG}-marker. The summary of the pattern is in table 4.20.[84]

Table 4.20: Khwe.

	T^{NEG}-marker	Foc^{NEG}-marker	Class^{NEG}-marker	Q^{NEG}-marker
Pattern 4	vé	–nya	o-	o-

It has been argued that Khwe does not have a proper class of adjectives, but only deverbalized or denominalized adjectives (by means of the suffix *-ci*). A deverbalized adjective will use the tenseless or 'pure' form of the verb (Kilian-Hatz 2008:196–197) and precede a noun, thus giving rise to an attributive adjective. Many of the properties expressed by adjectives with copular verbs in English and the other languages we looked at are expressed by means of stative verbs in Khwe. (227a) shows the verb used to express 'be difficult' and (227b) shows that same verb in a tenseless form preceding the noun.

(227) a. N|é kx'uí-h kyéri-xàm-kyéri-na-hã.
   DEM word-3SG.F difficult-INTENS-difficult-II-PST1
   'This word is very difficult'
   b. kyéri-xàm-kyéri kx'úí-hè hè é
   difficult-INTENS-difficult word-3SG.F there it is
   'That's a very difficult word.'

However, one might also think about the behaviour of these stative predicates as predicates that are syncretic between being adjectives and verbs, depending on how they are used in the structure, i. e. whether they get tense suffixes attached to them or not. This is not far-fetched since also in languages that have adjectives, there are adjectives that can zero-convert to verbs, like for instance *cool/to cool*.

The privative prefix *ó-* combines with what the grammar of Khwe refers to as deverbalized adjectives and it is the only negative marker on deverbal adjectives

---

[84] Khwe is a Kalahari Khoe-language, which is a subgroup of the Central Khoisan language family (Kilian-Hatz 2008) spoken in some parts of Botswana, Angola, Namibia and South Africa. The total number of Khwe speakers is estimated at 8.000. Abbreviations: C = common gender, AG = nomen agentis, O = object, GRD = gerund.

that Khwe has. Its meaning is comparable to -*less* and *without*. I therefore want to argue that it is a Q^NEG-marker.

(228) ó-xéri-o
       PRV-end-LOC
       'be endless, never end'

I consider *ó* also a Class^NEG-marker, because it is also a common negator on gerunds, ending in -*xa*. Gerund-formation is illustrated in (229): 'the suffix -*xa* derives gerunds from nouns and process verbs, thus denoting an inherent quality' (Kilian-Hatz 2008:262).

(229) Tcárà-hɛ̀   n‖góá-xa
       field-3SG.F stone-GRD
       'The field has stones/is stony.'

(230) ó-‖àvò-ná-xá
       NEG-shoe-x-GRD
       'without shoes/barefoot'

Also in in (231), the classifying function of a Class^NEG-marker is clearly present by means of *ó*-: the negative marker clearly points to the absence of a certain property.

(231) Xà-má   ũ-á-hã́   ó-qéú-ci   ã́xó   á.
       DEM-3SG.M buy-II-PST1 NEG-be.red-DENOM jacket O
       'He bought a jacket that is not red.'

Non-verbal clauses, like the copular clauses we are interested in for the present study, can be negated by a clause-final *vé*, which is without any doubt a T^NEG-marker.

(232) Héútù xá-ḿ   dì à   vé.
       car   DEM-3SG.M POSS COP NEG
       'It is not his car.' (lit. The car is not his)

Regular declarative verbal clauses also take *vé* as the standard negator in Khwe. The fact that future and habitual markers erode, i.e. lose an -*e*, when -*vé* is present, suggests that *vé* is indeed a T^NEG-marker in Khwe, at least within regular verbal clauses.[85]

---

[85] Another negation strategy is the use of *hámbe*, (i). *Hámbe* is the contraction of 'there is' and *vé*, and the negative copula *yò*, which is used in empathic contexts. *Hámbe* can be considered a

(233) a. Xà-ná   cácà   à kx'áà-à-liò vé.
       DEM-3PL.C alcohol O drink-I-HAB neg
       'They are not used to drinking alcohol.'
     b. Tcá   à té |'úru-a-gò vé.
       2SG.M O 1.PL.C forget-FUT neg
       'We will never forget you.'   (Kilian-Hatz 2008:256)

vé can also attach to a constituent, as in (234). This usage of *vé* is reminiscent of a constituent negator, i. e. a Foc^{NEG}-marker.

(234) Tí mű̃ũ-a-hã̃ vé-mà.
      1SG see-II-PSTI NEG-3SG.M
      'I have never/not seen him.'   (Kilian-Hatz 2008:174)

However, Khwe seems to have another suffix *ŋya*, which can only negate the verbal event and which cannot take clausal scope. It can precede or follow other derivative suffixes that are attached to the verbal stem and it can be used as a negative marker on deverbalized adjectives. In certain contexts, it seems that *ŋya* and the privative *ó* are stylistic variants, (236).

(235) Tí ki yaá-ŋya-à-òè xó-hè nǎű̃ rè?
      1SG LOC come-NEG-1-HAB thing-3SG.F which Q
      'Why do you never come to me?'   (Kilian-Hatz 2008:257)

(236) a. ‖úu-nya   ‖géɛ-khóé-hɛ
         give.birth-NEG female-AG-3SG.F
      b. ó-‖úu   ‖gèɛ-khóé-hɛ́
         NEG-give.birth ‖female-AG-3SG.F
         'infertile/barren woman'

Based on the fact that this negative marker attaches to adjectives derived from action verbs, i. e. containing more event structure than adjectives derived from stative verbs, I would like to argue that the Foc^{NEG}-marker in Khwe is *ŋya*.

---

suppletive negative existential form. However, given that the study of existential verbs is not the main aim of this study, we abstract away from it and refer the reader to Veselinova (2013).

(i)   Khwé-nà   hámbe-o.
      Khwe-3PL.C be.absent-LOC
      'There are no Khews.'

Even though more research on Khwe is necessary to be confident about the picture that is being sketched here, it seems that Khwe has a T^{NEG}-marker, that is *vé*, a Foc^{NEG}-marker *ŋya* and a Class^{NEG}- and Q^{NEG}-marker *ó*.

4.2.5 Pattern 5

4.2.5.1 Moroccan Arabic

The variety of Northern Moroccan Arabic (MA) I describe here has a syncretic marker for Foc-, Class and Q-negation: *muši*. In addition MA uses an embracing negative marker, discontinuous or bipartite negation to express sentential negation on the finite verb: *ma…ši*. The pattern is summarized in table 4.21.[86]

Table 4.21: Moroccan Arabic.

	T^{NEG}-marker	Foc^{NEG}-marker	Class^{NEG}-marker	Q^{NEG}-marker
Pattern 5	ma (… ši)	muši	muši	muši

Q-, Class and Foc-negation is expressed by one continuous negative marker: *muši*. The marker can give rise to contrary negation and functions like a characterising negative marker, as in (237a)–(237d).

(237) a. Howa muši diani.
    he   NEG religious
    'He is irreligious.'
  b. Howa muši fħerħ an.
    He   NEG happy
    'He is unhappy.'
  c. Tasarufaat djalu   muši mezjanin.
    act-PL   of.him NEG good.
    'His behavior is not good.'
  d. Eliqtiraaħ djalu   muši munaasib.
    proposal of.him NEG suitable.
    'His proposal is unsuitable.'

The marker also functions as a classifying negative marker, as in (238).

---

[86] Many thanks to Hicham El Sghiar for help with the data. My informant is from Chefchaouen, Northern Morocco. My informant transcribed the continuous negator as *muši*, but this negator is sometimes also transcribed as *maši*.

(238) Elhadaf dyel munaddama kullu muši tijari
goal of.the organisation completely NEG commercial
The goal of the organisation is completely non-commercial.

Moreover, it can be used in contrastive contexts, like (239), which is a typical property of Foc^{NEG}-markers.

(239) Howa muši furħan, raħ mʕassub.
he NEG happy, is sad.
'He is NOT happy, he is sad.'

In all these examples illustrated here the negative marker does not take scope over the tensed predicate. Its scope is restricted to the untensed predicate and its predicate terms.[87]

The T^{NEG}-marker on the other hand is expressed by means of a bipartite construction *ma* ... *ši* in the variety of Northern MA under discussion, as in (240a)–(240c), typically giving rise to disagreement or denial (Lafkioui 2013), which we identified as a typical function of a T^{NEG}-marker.

(240) a. Howa ma-raħ-ši diani.
He NEG-be.3SG-NEG religious
'He isn't religious.'
b. Howa ma-raħ-ši ferħan.
he NEG-be.3SG.-NEG happy.
'He is not happy.'
c. Ma-ʕandou-ši l akhlaaq.
NEG have-NEG the moral
'His behavior isn't moral.'

(241) Omar ma-ši mrid
Omar NEG-NEG sick
'Omar is not sick' (Benmamoun 2000:7)

ma can also co-occur with other negative indefinites, but *ši* can only be used in the scope of *ma* in Northern MA. *ma* could be analysed as the only real negator with all indefinites in its scope as NPIs or one could say that the necessary co-existence of the two elements in the bipartite structure points to the inherent deficiency of *ma* and *ši*, which is why they need each other. No matter which approach one takes, it

---

87 The negative marker arose historically from the contraction of the third person masculine singular *hu* with the negative markers *mā-hu-ši* (Holes [1995] 2004, Benmamoun 2000, Lucas 2009).

is clear that the bipartite negation in MA is fundamentally different from the one in BUF (French), where the second part of the negation is the real negation *pas* and *ne* is a deficient expletive bit (cf. chapter 7 for the analysis).[88] Since in most varieties of Arabic *ši* became a phonologically reduced enclitic when it entered stage II of Jespersen's Cycle (Lucas 2009), i. e. the stage in the development of negative markers where the regular (old) negator needs to be accompanied by a new emphatic negator (see chapter 7), and given that *ši* still occurs in its full form in MA, as opposed to the other Arabic vernaculars where it often occurs in a phonologically reduced form š (Heath 2002), we can assume that *ši* in combination with *ma* is still a real NPI and not yet inherently negative.[89] The only inherently negative form under this reasoning is thus *ma*.

Summarizing, *muši* is syncretic for the Q^{NEG}-, $Class^{NEG}$- and Foc-^{NEG}-marker, whereas *ma* combined with an NPI like *ši* is used as the T^{NEG}-marker.

4.2.6 Pattern 6

4.2.6.1 Hungarian

In Hungarian *nem* functions as the T^{NEG}, Foc^{NEG} and $Class^{NEG}$-marker. The Q^{NEG}-marker is the suffix *tElEn*. The pattern is summarized in table 4.22.[90]

Table 4.22: Hungarian.

	T^{NEG}-marker	Foc^{NEG}-marker	$Class^{NEG}$-marker	Q^{NEG}-marker
Pattern 6	nem	nem	nem	-tElEn

The Q^{NEG}-marker in Hungarian is the suffix *-tElEn* which literally means 'lacking'.[91] The suffix combines with nouns and can in this respect be compared to *-less* (Zimmer 1964:77), but is also combined with deverbal adjectives. It can give rise to contrary negation and functions as a characterising negative marker, illus-

---

88 The marker *ma* goes back to the MSA and CA marker *mā*, which is extremely rare in written language. In other varieties of MA and other varieties of the Arabic vernacular in general this *ma* is the regular negative marker. In MA *ma* is not lengthened.
89 š is derived from the NPI *šayʕ* 'thing' in CA.
90 Hungarian is a Finno-Ugric language spoken in Central Europe. I am very grateful to Adrien Jánosi for help with the data.
91 The reason for the E in the representation of the suffix is that the suffix undergoes vowel harmony in accord with the stem: when the stem has a front vowel, the suffix will adapt and the same with back vowels. (Rounds 2001).

trated by the examples in (242).

(242) a. A módszere szakszerű-tlen.
the method.POSS.3SG professional-NEG
'His method is unprofessional.'
b. Ő boldog-talan.
(s)he happy-NEG
'(S)he is unhappy.'
c. Ő őszinté-tlen
(s)he honest-NEG
'(S)he is dishonest.'

Evidence for the claim that *-tElEn* is a Q^{NEG}-marker also comes from the fact that it can give rise to lexicalized meanings, as in (243).

(243) A viselkedése ember-telen
the behaviour.POSS.3SG human-NEG
'His behavior is inhuman/cruel.'

In section 3.3 we discussed the connection between lexicalized meanings and structural closeness between an affix and the predicate. The scope of the suffix is restricted to the predicate term.[92]

---

92 This suffix can also be used on nouns, (ia)–(ic), and verbs, (iic).

(i) a. A gyerek törvény-telen.
the child law-NEG
'The child is unlawful.'
b. Ő erkölcs-telen
(s)he moral-NEG
'(S)he is amoral/asocial.'
c. Ő eszmél-etlen.
(s)he conscious-NEG
'S(h)e is unconscious.'

(ii) a. ismer-etlen
know-NEG
'unknown'
b. kér-etlen
ask.for-NEG
'unrequested'
c. vár-atlan
expect-NEG
'unexpected'

Sometimes, the contrary reading expressed by *-tElEn* can be expressed by loanprefixes: Latin *iN-* or Greek *a-*, but this only happens with foreign words (244a) and their usage is marginal.

(244) a. a-szexuális
NEG-sexual
'without a (sign of) wish for sex'
b. in-toleráns
NEG-tolerant
'intolerant'

Sometimes *-tElEn* and a loanprefix can both occur with the same stem, as in (245a)–(245b). In this case the negative loanprefix goes on the adjective and *-tElEn* combines with the noun, without any change in meaning.

(245) a. ir-racionális
NEG-rational
'irrational'
b. ráció-tlan
ratio-NEG
'irrational'

The Class, Foc- and T^{NEG}-marker is *nem*. As a Class^{NEG}-marker, *nem* functions as a classifying adjective, (246).

(246) Nem kereskedelmi termékek
NEG commercial product.PL
'non-commercial products'

As a Class^{NEG}-marker *nem* takes low scope. Its low scope can be illustrated by the examples in (247). In the presence of a copular verb like *seem nem* occurs in a structurally different position depending on whether it instantiates Class- or T-negation. When *nem* occurs below the adverb *teljsen* 'completely', then it functions as a Class^{NEG}-marker. However, when *nem* scopes over the copular *tünt* and *teljesen*, it gives rise to sentence negation, (247b). The stacking example in (247c) shows *nem* in its different positions, giving rise to T- and Class-negation.

(247) a. A projekt teljesen nem-kereskedelminek tűnt.
The project completely NEG-commercial.DAT seemed.3SG
'The project seemed completely non-commercial.'
b. A projekt neg tűnt teljesen kereskedelminek.
The project NEG seemed.3SG completely commercial.DAT

'The project didn't seem completely commercial.'
c. A projekt neg tűnt teljesen nem-kereskedelminek.
The project NEG seemed.3SG completely NEG-commercial.DAT
'The project didn't seem completely non-commercial.'

As a Foc^{NEG}-marker *nem* can function in a contrastive context, (248a)–(248b), and as an adverbial modifier, as in (248c). When it functions in a contrastive context it is in the focus field of a sentence, which is in preverbal position in Hungarian.

(248) a. János nem BOLDAGTALAN, hanem BOLDOG.
John NEG unhappy but happy
'János is not unhappy, but happy.'
b. János nem A FELESÉGÉVEL táncolt.
Janos NEG the wife.poss.3sg.with danced
'It was not his wife that John danced with.' (Kiss 2004:130)
c. Nem mindenki A FELESÉGÉVEL táncolt.
NEG everybody the wife.poss.3sg.with danced.
'Not everybody danced WITH HIS WIFE.' (Kiss 2004:130)

The Foc^{NEG}-marker also sometimes expresses readings which are in other languages associated with Class-negation, as in the example in (249a), where *nem* functions as a classifying adjective, but occurs in the focus-field. (249b) shows the same sentence with regular sentence negation.

(249) a. Mi nem keresztények vagyunk.
we NEG Christian be.1PL
'We are non-Christian.'
'It is not Christian that we are.'
b. Mi nem vagyunk keresztények.
we NEG be.1PL Christian.PL
'We are not Christian.'

As a T^{NEG}-marker it takes sentential scope over the entire tensed predicate, (250).

(250) János nem táncolt a feleségével.
John NEG danced his wife.with.
'John didn't dance with his wife.'

A test which provides extra support for the low scope position of *nem* as a Class^{NEG}-marker compared to the scope positions of Foc- and T^{NEG}-markers is to see how *nem* as a Class^{NEG}-marker interacts with the NPIs *senki* 'anybody' and *semmi* 'nothing'. When *nem* is a Foc^NEG- and T^NEG-marker, it can license these NPIs in subject position, as shown in (251a)–(251b), and changes to *sem* under their influence.

(251) a. Senki sem [_VP hívta fel a feleségét]
nobody NEG called up his wife
'Nobody called up his wife.'
b. Senki sem [_FP A FELESÉGÉT hívta fel]
nobody NEG his wife.ACC called up
'Nobody called up HIS WIFE.'

However, when *nem* is a Class^NEG-marker, it cannot license *semki*, as in (252a), unless when there is an extra *nem* or *sem* inserted on the verb, as illustrated in (252b).[93]

(252) a. *Semmi tünt teljesen nem-kereskedelminek.
Anything seemed.3SG completely NEG-commercial.DAT
b. Semmi sem tünt teljesen nem-kereskedelminek.
Anything neg seemed.3SG completely NEG-commercial.DAT
'Nothing seemed completely non-commercial.'

These data support the fact that *nem* has different readings which coincide with different positions.[94]

---

[93] Foc- and T^NEG-marker *nem* typically change into *sem* under the influence of the indefinites *senki* and *semmi*.

[94] Hungarian, like MSA, has a suppletive negative form for the existential predicate *van* 'be', i. e. *nincs(en)*; the plural form is *nincsenek* corresponding to the affirmative *vannak*. So when the sentential negative marker *nem* combines with the 3SG of the existential 'be', a suppletive form is used, as illustrated by the examples in (ia)–(ic).

(i) a. Attila nincs jól.
Attila NEG.be.3SG well
Àtilla is not well.'
b. Attila nincs a házban.
Attila NEG.be.3SG in the.house
'Atilla is not in the house.'
c. Nincsenek régi könyvek a szekrényben.
NEG.be.3PL old books in the.closet
'There are no old books in the closet.' (Rounds 2001:270)

As for the other languages, I will not dwell on negative existentials in this book, but I refer the reader to Veselinova (2013, 2014) for more typological insights regarding negation and existentials.

Summarizing, Hungarian has the syncretic marker *nem* as a T^{NEG}-, Foc^{NEG}- and $Class^{NEG}$-marker, but has a different Q^{NEG}-marker, *-tElEn*.

4.2.6.2 Hebrew

Hebrew,[95] a Northwest Semitic language, shows the same syncretism pattern as Hungarian, illustrated in table 4.23: it has *lo* as a T^{NEG}-, Foc^{NEG}- and $Class^{NEG}$-marker and *bilti* as a Q^{NEG}-marker.

Table 4.23: Hebrew.

	T^{NEG}-marker	Foc^{NEG}-marker	$Class^{NEG}$-marker	Q^{NEG}-marker
Pattern 6	lo	lo	lo	bilti

Lo is used as the main negator expressing sentence negation in main and subordinate clauses, with verbal, (253), nominal and adjectival predicates. I hence consider it the T^{NEG}-marker. At first sight it seems also to be the negative marker used for all other discerned types of negation.

(253) a. hu lo yada
      he NEG knew
      'He did not know.'
   b. hu bevaday lo yada
      he certainly NEG knew
      'He certainly did not know.' (Hetzron 1997:327)

However, in between *lo* and the adjectival predicate a modifier like *very* can be inserted, (254b). This is meaningful, since this shows us that *lo* does not need to have a very close connection to the stem, a property we expect to be inherent to Q^{NEG}-markers.

(254) a. lo raxoq
      NEG far
      'not far'
   b. ha-lo me'od raxoq
      the-NEG very far
      'the not very far' (Agmon 2013:814)

---

95 Many thanks to Yael Gaulan for help with the data. All errors are mine.

Moreover, *lo* can also be used to negate adverbs, degree phrases and certain quantifiers, a property we assigned to Foc^{NEG}-markers, (255).

(255)   lo   harbe 'anašim yod'im
        NEG   many people   know
        'Not many people now.'   (Glinert 2013:813)

The fact that *lo* can be stacked, as in (256), supports the idea that it is syncretic between a T^{NEG}-marker and a Foc^{NEG}-marker.

(256)   Hu lo lo   same'ax.
        He NEG NEG   happy
        'He isn't unhappy.'

More support for the fact that it functions as a Foc^{NEG}-marker comes from (257), where *lo* is clearly used as a modifier of *only*. However, it also seems in this example that *lo* can be used as a Q^{NEG}-marker in giving rise to contrary readings. The question is now whether these readings arise as a consequence of pragmatic strengthening or because *lo* is also a Q^{NEG}-marker.

(257)   ze   lo   raq lo   'eti   'ela gam lo xuqi
        it's NEG only NEG ethical but also NEG legal
        'It's not only unethical but also illegal.'   (Glinert 2013:813)

I will argue that *lo* is not a Q^{NEG}-marker, because gradable adjectives can also be negated with the prefix *bilti-*, (258)–(259). With *bilti* no modifiers can be inserted between *bilti-* and the adjective, (258b). This is indicative of the fact that *bilti-* is close to the stem and hence a candidate to be considered a Q^{NEG}-marker.

(258)   a.   ha-me'od bilti ma'aśi
             the-very NEG practical
             'the very impractical'
        b.   *ha-bilti me'od ma'aśi.   (Agmon 2013:814)

(259)   a.   davar laxalutin bilti pašut
             thing totally   NEG simple
             'A thing which is totally not simple.'
        b.   hi yoter bilti nisbelet mi-meno
             she more NEG bearable than-DAT.3.SG.M
             'She is more unbearable than he is'
        c.   ha-šelet haxi bilti muvan   ba-arec
             The-sign most NEG understood in-the.country
             The most uncomprehendable sign in thecountry

The use of *bilti-* is restricted to gradable adjectives and participles in Modern Hebrew, whereas it was more widely used in Biblical Hebrew (Agmon 2013:815). There are a few frozen forms of verbs used as adjectives, (260).

(260)   bilti ye'amen
          NEG believe
          'unbelievable'

When *bilti-* negates participles it does not denote a temporal property, but it creates an atemporal meaning of classification or kind-tagging, as in (261).

(261)   bilti me'uyaš
          NEG manned
          'unmanned'

In general, Agmon (2013) argues that *bilti-* gives rise to contrary negation, whereas *lo-* gives rise to contradictory negation, hence the incompatibility of *bilti* with predicates that do not allow for a middle between two opposites:

(262)   a.   *bilti rišoni
               NEG prime
               Intended: 'unprime'
        b.   *bilti zaxar
               NEG male
               Intended: 'unmale'
        c.   *bilti xai
               NEG alive
               Intended: 'unalive'

Based on this discussion, I want to argue that *bilti-* is the Q^{NEG}-marker in Hebrew. There are a few other markers, which I consider unproductive Q^{NEG}-markers: *i-* and *a-*. *i-*, (263), was relatively productive in the early revival period of Hebrew, since it was used to translate the prefixes *un-* and *dis-* from European languages. *i-* is also used with nouns to express that a certain property or quality is lacking, (263a). *Xoser* is also used to express privation, (263b). The *i-* used with adjectives has been mostly replaced by *bilti-* and *lo*.

(263)   a.   'i-ha-te'um
               NEG-the-coordination
               'lack of coordination'
        b.   haya   xoser-te'um
               there-was lack-of.coordination

'There was lack of coordination.' (Glinert 2013:813)

(264) a. i-regulari
NEG-regular
'irregular'
b. i-rasyonali
NEG-rational
'irrational' (Agmon 2013:815)

A- is also sometimes used, but it is extremely unproductive and adopted from European languages, (265).

(265) a. a-mini
NEG-sexual
'asexual'
b. a-musari
NEG-moral
'amoral'

Since *bilti-* is so clearly a contrariety inducing marker, I consider *lo* the Class^{NEG}-marker, in spite of the fact that Glinert (2013:813) states that *bilti-* can be translated as 'non-, un-, in-'. However, he gives no examples of *bilti-* used with the meaning of *non-* and it contradicts Agmon's (2013) work on negative adjectives in Hebrew. Also given that the following phrase, (266), can only be translated by stacking *lo-* upon *bilti-* and given the classifying nature of the *lo*-negation in (268), we can deduce that the Class^{NEG}-marker in Hebrew is *lo-*.

(266) Ha-hitnahagut ha-lo bilti musarit shelo.
the-behaviour the-NEG NEG moral of-his
His non-immoral behaviour.

(267) Ha-hesber shelo mamash lo intuitivi.
the-explanation of.his really NEG intuitive
'His explanation is extremely non-intuitive.'

(268) Hu lo lo nocri.
He NEG NEG christian
'He isn't non-Christian.' (= He has another religion)

Summarizing, the T^{NEG}, Foc^{NEG} and Class^{NEG}-marker is *lo* and the Q^{NEG}-marker is *bilti*.

4.2.6.3 Dutch

While a lot of research has been done on negation in Dutch and Flemish, mainly discussing the role of negative quantifiers, double negation and negative concord patterns (Haegeman 1995, Zeijlstra 2004a, Haegeman & Lohndal 2010), very little research has been devoted to the different types of negation that can combine within one clause with adjectival predicates, as discussed in this book. Dutch shows the same pattern as the one exemplified in detail by Hungarian and Hebrew. Dutch has *niet* as a T^{NEG}-, Foc^{NEG}- and $Class^{NEG}$-marker and *on-* as a Q^{NEG}-marker in copular clauses. The pattern is summarized in table 4.24.

Table 4.24: Pattern 6: Other languages.

	T^{NEG}-marker	Foc^{NEG}-marker	$Class^{NEG}$-marker	Q^{NEG}-marker
Dutch	niet	niet	niet(-)	on-

An example of the Q^{NEG}-marker is in (269).[96]

(269) Hij is on-gelukkig.
 he is NEG-happy
 'He is unhappy.'

(270) Het is on-mogelijk iedereen tevreden te stellen.
 It is NEG-possible everyone pleased to make
 'It's impossible to make everyone happy.' (EANS 2002)

When *niet-* is used as a $Class^{NEG}$-marker, it is written with a hyphen, unlike the *niet* used as a Foc^{NEG}- or T^{NEG}-marker. An example of *niet-* as a $Class^{NEG}$-marker is in (271).

(271) Nieuwe goden zijn niet-christelijk.
 new gods are NEG-christian.
 "New gods are non-Christian". (from CHN 2013)

---

[96] Like many other languages discussed in this book, Dutch also has a couple of unproductive negative markers like *a-* from Greek, as in *atheistisch* 'atheist' or *asociaal* 'asocial', or *dis-* as in *gedisconnecteerd* 'disconnected'. Moreover, it also has the suffixal *-loos* that corresponds to English *-less* and that is not taken up here because Dutch has a dedicated Q^{NEG}-marker *on-*. All non-attested examples in this chapter are provided with my own judgments. I am a native speaker of Dutch (Flemish).

Booij & Audring (2018:215–216) compare Dutch *on-* with *niet-* and argue that when *on-* combines with relational adjectives like *Nederlands* 'Dutch' it coerces the adjective into a qualifying adjective, as opposed to *niet-*, (272), which does not have this coercing property. This observation squares well with the subcategorization of *on-* as a Q^{NEG}-marker and *niet-* as a Class^{NEG}-marker and with the data we discussed for English (Zimmer 1964).

(272)   a.   on-Nederlands
               NEG-Dutch
               'un-Dutch'
       b.   niet-Nederlands
               NEG-Dutch
               'non-Dutch'

Instead of *niet-*, *non-* can also be used as a Class^{NEG}-marker, (413). However, *non-* is mainly used with loanwords from English or with bases derived from Latin via French as in (273). In (273) *non* can be replaced by *niet-*.

(273)   85 procent van onze communicatie is non verbaal.
         85 percent of our communication is NEG verbal
         '85 percent of our communication is nonverbaal.'   (Van der Sijs 2010)

When *niet* is used as a Foc^{NEG}-marker it modifies adverbs, as in (274a), or it appears in front of the constituent it wants to focus on, as in (274b), giving rise to a contrastive negation. In the latter case the negative marker does not appear in its canonical position, i. e. preceding the adjectival predicate in copular clauses, (274c), which is the position *niet* takes as a T^{NEG}-marker in copular clauses.

(274)   a.   Niet lang geleden bezocht hij zijn moeder.
               NOT long ago   visited he his mother
               'Not long ago he visited his mother.'
       b.   Hij was niet gisteren   ziek, maar vorige week.
               He was NEG yesterday ill,   but   last   week.
               'He was not yesterday ill (but last week).'
       c.   Hij was niet ziek.
               he was NEG ill
               'He was not ill yesterday.'

With respect to stacking it is possible to stack a T^{NEG}-marker on a Q- or Class^{NEG}-marker, as in (275a)–(275b), a Foc^{NEG}-marker can be stacked on a Q^{NEG}-marker, as in (275c) and (275d) shows that even three negative markers can be grammatically stacked.

(275) a. Hij was niet on-gelukkig.
           he was NEG NEG-happy
           'He was not unhappy.'
       b. Deze scholen zijn helemaal   niet uitsluitend niet-christelijk.
           These schools are completely NEG only   NEG-christian
           'These schools are not at all only non-christian.'
       c. Zijn bestaansminimum   was NIET zomaar on-voldoende, maar
           His subsistence minimum was NEG only   NEG-sufficient, but
           echt   compleet   ontoereikend.
           it was completely deficient.
           'His subsistence minimum was not insufficient, but shamelessly deficient!'
       d. Hij was niet echt   NIET ongelukkig.
           he was NEG really NEG NEG-happy
           'He wasn't really not unhappy.'

Summarizing, the T^{NEG}-, Foc^{NEG}- and $Class^{NEG}$-marker in Dutch is *niet* and *on-* is the Q^{NEG}-marker.

4.2.7 Pattern 7

The patterns discussed in this section are fully syncretic patterns. I exemplify this pattern in detail with Indo-European Czech and the Carib language Hixkaryana. I conclude by a brief discussion of languages that also seem to have this pattern.

4.2.7.1 Czech

Czech shows a fully syncretic pattern. The same negative marker *ne* is used for T, Foc-, Class and Q-negation.[97]

Table 4.25: Czech.

	T^{NEG}-marker	Foc^{NEG}-marker	$Class^{NEG}$-marker	Q^{NEG}-marker
Pattern 6	ne-	ne	ne-	ne-

---

[97] Czech is a West-Slavic language spoken in Central-Europe. Many thanks to Jakub Dotlačil and Radek Šimík for help with the Czech data.

As a Q^{NEG}-marker *ne-* attaches onto an adjectival predicate. It gives rise to contrariety readings, as in (276a) and (276b), and sometimes even to lexicalized readings, as in (277a)–(277b), a sign of structural closeness.[98]

(276) a. Je ne-loajální.
 is NEG-loyal
 'He is disloyal.'
 b. Je ne-tolerantní.
 is NEG-tolerant
 'He is intolerant.'

(277) a. Je ne-přátelský
 is NEG-friendly
 'He is hostile'/ 'He is adverse'
 b. Je ne-mocný.
 he NEG-powerful.
 'He is ill.' (Kovarikova et al. 2012:824)

ne- can also function as a $Class^{NEG}$-marker and give rise to contradictory classifying readings, as in (278a)–(278d). Sometimes both Q- and Class-readings are possible, (278d).[99]

(278) a. Jeho metoda je ne-profesionální.
 his method is NEG-professional
 'His method is nonprofessional.'

---

[98] Some foreign prefixes, like Greek *a-* and Latin-based *iN-* can idiosyncratically be used in combination with certain stems of foreign origin, and in such cases they are interchangeable with *ne-*, i. e. there is no noticeable meaning difference between (ia) and (ib). However, these adjectives are rarely used in Czech.

(i) a. On je ne-morální.
 he is NEG-moral
 'He is amoral/immoral/non-moral.'
 b. On je a-morální.
 he is NEG-moral.
 'He is amoral.'
 c. *On je im-morální.
 he is NEG-moral.

[99] Admittedly, it is hard to know whether the $Class^{NEG}$-marker exists in Czech, since if it exists, it is syncretic and one of the main ways to test the presence of a $Class^{NEG}$-marker is to see whether it can select for a negative predicate that already consists of a Q^{NEG}-marker. However, when Q^{NEG}-marker- and $Class^{NEG}$-markers are syncretic, they never seem to stack.

b. Jeho metoda je ne-komerční.
   his method is NEG-commercial
   'His method is noncommercial.'
c. Jeho metoda je ne-adekvátní.
   his method is NEG-adequate
   'His method is inadequate.'
d. Je ne-americký.
   is NEG-American
   'He is un-American.'
   'He is non-American.'

Ne can be used as a Foc^{NEG}-marker as well. This is clear from an example like (279), in which *ne* functions as a contrastive negative marker. In (279) *ne* stacks on another *ne* which behaves like a Q^{NEG}-marker, illustrating that Foc-negation takes scope in a higher position than Q-negation. Like other Foc^{NEG}-markers, *ne* can also be used as an adverbial modifier, as in (280).

(279) On je ne ne-šťastný, on je šťastný.
      he is NEG NEG-happy, he is happy.
      'He is not unhappy, but happy.'

(280) a. Oni jsou tři ne zrovna ne-šťastní muži.
         they are three NEG exactly NEG-happy men.
         'They are three not really unhappy men.'
      b. Ne dnes, zítra.
         NEG today, tomorrow
         'Not today, but tomorrow.'   (Naughton 2005:212)

When *ne-* prefixes onto the copular verb *být* 'to be' (Naughton 2005:134–135), it gives rise to sentential negation and functions as a T^{NEG}-marker, (281).[100]

(281) Ja ne-jsem šťastný.
      I NEG-am happy.
      'I am not happy.'

The T^{NEG}-marker *ne-* can be combined with *ne* as a Foc^{NEG}-marker and with *ne-* as a Q^{NEG}-marker, (282), illustrating the different scope positions for the syncretic marker.

---

100 When negation combines with the third person singular of *být*, i.e. *je*, the result is a suppletive or irregular negative form *není* (Naughton 2005:134–135, Janda & Townsend 2000:37). This type of negative allomorphy triggered by person features is outside the scope of this book. I intend to take this up in future work.

(282) On ne-ní ne ne-št'astný.
 he NEG-is NEG NEG-happy.
 'He isn't not unhappy'

Summarizing, Czech is syncretic with respect to the different classes of negative markers distinguished above. The negative marker *ne-* is used throughout, apart from some loanwords which can be prefixed with Latin and Greek *iN-* or *a-*.

4.2.7.2 Hixkaryana

Hixkaryana, a Carib language spoken by a group of people on the banks of the river Nhamundá in Brazil, has one syncretic negative marker *-hɨ* functioning as the T^{NEG}, Foc^{NEG} and $Class^{NEG}$ and Q^{NEG}-marker in the language, summarized in table 4.26. However, this is not what it looks like when one checks a grammar (Derbyshire 1979) of the language. In what follows I explain why I analyse the negation pattern like this.

Table 4.26: Hixkaryana.

	T^{NEG}-marker	Foc^{NEG}-marker	$Class^{NEG}$-marker	Q^{NEG}-marker
Pattern 6	-hɨ	-hɨ	-hɨ	-hɨ

In Hixkaryana sentence negation is expressed by means of a derivational process. This process turns a verb into a negative adverbial. This negative adverbial functions then as the complement of the copula, which is the usual complement of copular verbs in Hixkaryana. There are hardly 'any real adjectives' in Hixkaryana (Derbyshire 1979:33), which means that states or properties are expressed by what is referred to as derived adverbials.

Standard negation in Hixkaryana is expressed by means of the derivational suffix *-hɨra*, which depending on the phonological context alters to *-hra* or *-pɨra*. It is added to the verb stem (Derbyshire 1979:48), as in (283).[101]

(283) a. ki-amryeki-no
 I-hunt-IMM.PST

---

[101] There is a small subclass of verb and noun stems which combines with *-mra*:

(i) ahoxe-mra
 strength.of-NEG
 'not strong, weak' (Derbyshire 1979:177)

'I went hunting'
    b.   amryeki-hɨra w-ah-ko
          hunt-NEG   I-be-IMM.PST
          'I did not go hunting.'

For constituent negation, *-hɨra* is attached to adverbials and postpositional relators without changing anything else in the sentence. As is obvious from the examples (284) and (285), most negative antonyms are formed by adding the negative marker to the positive simple adverb. The use of the negative marker to give rise to contrary readings suggests that these markers are Q^{NEG}-markers.

(284)   a.   Krawame-hra ihoko   wehxakoni.
                hard-NEG   occupied.with.it I.was
                'I worked on it without difficulty.'
       b.   Waywi yereyeye   warata hona, karye-hra.
             arrow he.put.it.down shelf   onto, high-NEG
             'He put down the arrow on the shelf, low down.'

(285)   a.   kawo
                tall
                'tall'
       b.   kawo-hra
             tall-NEG
             'short'
       c.   tiyoke
             sharp
       d.   iyo-hra
             sharp-NEG
             'dull'

The following example with *hra* clearly expresses a low contrastive negation, a property typical of a Foc-negator:

(286)   Kasawa hona ito-hra   wahko. Mutuma hona haxa   itono.
        Kasawa to   going-NEG I-was. Mutuma to   CONTR I-went
        'I didn't go to Kasawa, but to Mutuma.'   (Derbyshire 1979:49)

The same negator is also used to express other typical instances of constituent negation:

(287)   a.   towenywa-hra
              one-NEG
              'not one'

b. rowti   me-hra   na-ha mosoni
   my.brother DENOM-NEG he.is this.one
   'This is not my brother.'

Nominal and verbal constituents can also be negativized by means of the suffix *-hɨnɨ (-hnɨ, -pɨnɨ)*.[102] Negative nominals can have two different meanings depending on whether the underlying noun is a possessed or nonpossessed item. With possessed nominal items the meaning of the negative is: one who is without that item'. This meaning resembles the properties ascribed to negatives markers like English *-less*, as illustrated in (288);

(288) ɨhe-hnɨ   mokro
       one.wife-NEG that.one
       'He is one who does not have a wife.'   (Derbyshire 1979:50)

With non-possessed items the meaning is the 'negation of the item' and resembles mostly negative markers like *non(-)*, as in (289):

(289) toto-hnɨ
       human-NEG
       'one who is not a human being' (i. e. non-human)

It also seems that *-hɨnɨ* can function as a typical constituent negator, i. e. as a Foc^{NEG}-marker, by attaching to nominals as in (290) or to verbs, as in (291).

(290) Waraka ntono? Noro-hnɨ. Kaywerye   haxa ntono.
       waraka he.went he-NEG it.was.Kaywerye who went.
       'Did Waraka go? No, not he. It was Kaywerye who went.'
       (Derbyshire 1979:50)

(291) emokoto-hnɨ   moro,   titko   ymo
       one.falling-NEG that-one, Brazil.nut.tree AUG
       'That one, the big Brazil nut tree, is one that will not fall.'
       (Derbyshire 1979:50)

It thus seems that, depending on the categorial nature of the predicate, Hixkaryana has 2 different negative strategies that can both be used as Foc, Class and Q-negators. However, only *-hira* also seems to function as a real T^{NEG}-marker. *-hɨnɨ* only occurs in equative (reduced) sentences and not as the adverbial complement of tensed copular clauses. A closer look at the two negative strategies shows that

---

[102] A small subclass of nominal stems takes *-mnɨ*.

they have one morpheme in common, i. e. *-hɨ-* (which can undergo phonological changes and reduction). I want to argue that Hixkaryana has one syncretic negator, i. e. *-hɨ-* for all lexical categories and that depending on which category the negator attaches to extra derivational morphemes like *-ra* (to form adverbials) or *nɨ* (to form nominals) are added. More research on Hixkaryana is needed to make this analysis more precise.

4.2.7.3 Other languages

Other languages that show the same fully syncretic pattern is the East-Slavic language Russian (Zimmer 1964:61–66, Wade 2011 [1992, 2000]), illustrated in (292),[103] and the South-Slavic language Macedonian, which is illustrated by some stacking examples in (293)–(295).[104] Both Slavic languages show a pattern that is similar to Czech, see table 4.27.

(292) a. Ego povedenie ne ochen ne-khristianskoe
His behavior NEG very NEG-Christian
'His behaviour is not very un-Christian.'

b. ?On ne ne khristianin
He NEG NEG Christian
He isn't non-Christian.'

c. Ego obyasnenija absolutno ne- intuitivnyje
His explanations absolutely NEG- intuitive
'His explanation is extremely non- intuitive.'

d. ne-davno
not-long.ago
'not long ago'

e. He ne javlajetsa ne schastlivym.
He NEG be NEG happy
'He isn't not happy'

(293) Toj ne e srekjen, no ne e ni nesrekjen.
he NEG is happy, but NEG is either NEG.happy
He isn't happy, but he isn't unhappy either.' [Macedonian]

(294) a. Toj ne e nehristijanin.
He NEG is NEG.christian
He isn't non-Christian.'

---

103 Thanks to Vadim Kimmelman for help with the Russian data respectively.
104 Thanks to Aleksandar Aleksovski for help with the data.

b. Negoviot odnos ne e mnogu nehristijanski.
   behaviour his NEG is very NEG.christian
   His behaviour is not very un-Christian.

(295) a. Context: A says: He is not unhappy. B contradicts this and says:
      b. Toj ne e nenesrekjen.
         he NEG is NEG.NEG.happy.
         'He isn't not unhappy. (He is sad)

The Uto-Aztecan language Tümpisa Shoshone (Paminta) (Dayley 1989b,a) and the Austronesian language Malagasy (Rasoloson 2001, Rajaonarimanana 2001) are also fully syncretic, see table 4.27.

Table 4.27: Pattern 7: Other languages.

	T^{NEG}-marker	Foc^{NEG}-marker	$Class^{NEG}$-marker	Q^{NEG}-marker
Russian	ne	ne	ne	ne-
Macedonian	ne	ne	ne	ne-
Malagasy	tsy	tsy	tsy-	tsy-
Tümpisa Shoshone	ke(e)	ke(e)	ke(e)	ke(e)

4.3 Summary and discussion

The table in (296) presents an overview of the languages discussed and the syncretism patterns in these languages. When we order the negative markers per language according to their scope properties, i. e. going from those which take widest scope to those which take narrowest scope (or the other way around), only contiguous syncretisms can be detected. All syncretisms detected are in adjacent cells in the paradigm. As we discussed in chapter 2 for case the absence of non-contiguous syncretisms is meaningful and points to hidden layers of syntactic structure. In the next chapter I explore how this can be translated into syntactic structure.

(296)

	T^NEG	Foc^NEG	Class^NEG	Q^NEG
Greek	dhen	oxi	mi	a-
English	n't	not	non	un-
French (formal)	ne ...pas	pas	non	iN-
Korean	(-ci) an(i) (ha-) (-ci) mos (ha-)	an(i) mos	pi- mol-	pul- mol-
French (informal)	pas	pas	non	iN-
Swedish	inte	inte	icke-	o-
Turkish	degil	degil	gayri/olmayan	-siz
Japanese	nai	nai	hi-	hu(/bu)/mu
Azerbaijani	deyil	deyil	(qeyri)/olmayan	qeyri
Khwe	vé	ŋya	ó-	ó
Chinese	bù	bù	fēi	fēi
MS Arabic	laa	laa	ghayr-	ghayr-
Persian	na	na	qheyr-	qheyr-
Mayalayam	alla	alla	a-	a-
Moroccan Arabic	ma (ši)	muši	muši	muši
Hungarian	nem	nem	nem	-tElEn
Hebrew	lo	lo	lo	bilti-
Dutch	niet	niet	niet-	on-
Russian	ne	ne	ne	ne-
Macedonian	ne	ne	ne	ne-
Czech	ne-	ne	ne-	ne-
Malagasy	tsy	tsy	tsy	tsy
Hixkaryana	-hi-	-hi-	-hi-	-hi-
Tümpisa Shoshone	ke(e)	ke(e)	ke(e)	ke(e)

For now I want to discuss a bit more what this paradigm tells us. Since we distinguished four different categories of negative markers, strictly speaking 15 different patterns could logically arise, visualized in (297).[105]

---

[105] I want to thank Michal Starke for sending me his summary (and therefore his view on) of my work. His summary was very helpful and I used it for the discussion of the logically possible orders in (297) and (298).

(297)

1	A	A	A	A
2	A	A	A	B
3	A	A	B	A
4	A	A	B	B
5	A	A	B	C
6	A	B	B	A
7	A	B	B	B
8	A	B	B	C
9	A	B	A	A
10	A	B	A	B
11	A	B	A	C
12	A	B	C	A
13	A	B	C	B
14	A	B	C	C
15	A	B	C	D

Of these 15 logically possible orders, 7 are *ABA patterns and we expect them not to arise: these are marked with shading in (298).

(298)

1	A	A	A	A
2	A	A	A	B
3	A	A	B	A
4	A	A	B	B
5	A	A	B	C
6	A	B	B	A
7	A	B	B	B
8	A	B	B	C
9	A	B	A	A
10	A	B	A	B
11	A	B	A	C
12	A	B	C	A
13	A	B	C	B
14	A	B	C	C
15	A	B	C	D

This leaves us with 8 patterns that are expected to occur. The table in (299) shows that 7 of the 8 logically possible orders are attested in the sample that we discussed. One pattern seems to be missing.

(299)

1	A	A	A	A	Czech, Hixkaryana etc.
2	A	A	A	B	Hungarian, Hebrew, Dutch
3	A	A	B	A	
4	A	A	B	B	Chinese, MS Arabic, Malayalam, Persian
5	A	A	B	C	French (CF), Turkish, Japanese, Swedish, Azerbaijani
6	A	B	B	A	
7	A	B	B	B	Moroccan Arabic
8	A	B	B	C	not attested?
9	A	B	A	A	
10	A	B	A	B	
11	A	B	A	C	
12	A	B	C	A	
13	A	B	C	B	
14	A	B	C	C	Khwe
15	A	B	C	D	Greek, English, French (BUF), Korean

The first question that comes to mind when we see all the patterns and the one missing pattern is whether this is a meaningful missing pattern and whether this tells us something about the structure of the clause. The missing pattern is one where the syncretism crosses the lexical-functional divide or the divide between what is normally dealt with in syntax versus morphology. It could be that this is not a coincidence, were it not that a careful reconsideration of some of the data actually points us to the existence of the pattern in French, as I have already mentioned in the discussion of *le bon usage* French in section 4.2.1.2.

As we noticed at a few points in the discussion of the languages in the sample, often a language has several negative markers for one type of marker. Sometimes it is easy to decide which marker is productive and which one is not (as for English *iN-/dis-*). However, this is not always the case. For instance in our discussion of BUF (French), we also discussed the use of *non* as a Foc^{NEG}-marker, next to its position as a $Class^{NEG}$-marker. We saw how contrastive *non* can be stacked on the $Class^{NEG}$-marker, (140b), repeated here as (300b).

(300) a. Le but de cette organisation est non non-lucratif, mais
the goal of this organisation is NEG NEG-lucrative, but
commercial.
commercial.
The goal of this organisation is not non-profit, but commercial.
b. Les déchets sont non non-dangereux, mais vraiment mortels si
the trashes are NEG NEG-dangerous, but really mortal if
on les touche.
one them touches.

'This trash is not non-dangerous, but really life-threatening if you touch it.'

We decided to leave *non* out of the picture for the syncretism pattern of *le bon usage* French. Extra support for the fact that both *pas* and *non* can target the same position for negation comes from the data in (301)–(302). These data show that when *pas* and *non-* co-occur, double negation arises since *non-* can get a very low reading as a Class-marker and *pas* the reading of a Foc^{NEG}-marker, (301). However, when *non* stacks on *pas*, *pas*—not being a Class^{NEG}- or Q^{NEG}-marker—can only have the function of a Foc^{NEG}-marker and *non* can now only take its widest possible scope, i. e. the scope of a Foc^{NEG}-marker. Since both negative markers now try to get their negative features licensed by the same NegP in clausal syntax, a concord reading arises. This idea will become more clear once we have discussed the internal and external syntax of negative marker, but the implicit proposal here is that one way for concord to arise may be when two constituents with the same internal structure target the same scopal position for negation. We will see for bipartite negation in *le bon usage* French in chapter 7 that concord, if bipartite negation is considered some sort of concord, may also arise due to other reasons, like deficient negative markers, as is the case for *ne* in *ne ... pas*.[106]

(301) a. Il s'arrête, pas non in-quiet.
he himself-stopped, NEG NEG NEG-calm
'He stopped, not not worried.'

b. Il a éte pas non in -quiet, mais totalement en panique.
he has been NEG NEG NEG -calm, but completely in panic
'He hasn't been not restless, but completely in panic.'

(302) Il s'arrête, non pas in-quiet, mais curieux.
he REFL.stopped, NEG NEG NEG-calm, but curious
'He stopped, not worried, but curious.'
(Grevisse & Goosse [1936] 1993:1446)

So if we include *non* and consider it an important negative marker within some variety of French, then the syncretism pattern that arises, is the missing pattern. This picture of French is visualized in table 4.28. So it seems that if we zoom in on a particular negative marker of a language, which is not the dominant marker, the unattested pattern turns out to be attested.

---

[106] Another way for concord to arise is when n-words and NPIs are syncretic and co-occur, as discussed for French in De Clercq (2019a).

Table 4.28: French

	T^{NEG}-marker	Foc^{NEG}-marker	Class^{NEG}-marker	Q^{NEG}-marker
Pattern 8	(ne) pas	non	non(-)	iN-, (dé(s)-)
	pas	pas	non(-)	iN-, (dé(s)-)

Since the pattern is attested within a particular variety of French we can – relatively safely – hypothesize that there will be other languages that also show this pattern.

Something that came up during the discussion of the different languages is that within one language there may be different patterns or different competing negative markers for the same type. We saw that this was the case in English with respect to the register-related sentential *not* vs. *n't*, but also at the level of the prefixes, where we saw that there are productive and unproductive negative markers. The situation for English will be discussed in more technical detail in section 6.2. Also for Chinese we discussed that register-related differences may have an influence on the type of negative markers used. With respect to Korean we saw that there are different negative markers used depending on the origin of the predicate. The French type of pattern-alternation is therefore clearly not unique and not surprising. However, all of these patterns will ultimately require a different analysis. Nanosyntax, the model used in this book, is ideally equipped to capture both language internal variation, as well as variation amongst languages. The differences between different varieties of one language will boil down to differences in the internal structure of negative markers, i.e. structural differences in the lexicon of negative markers (cf. Starke 2014b) or the predicates they combine with. The Korean syncretism-alternation for instance would not be treated as a consequence of a different internal structure of the negative marker, but of differences in the structure of Sino-Korean vs native Korean predicates. Predicates from native Korean origin could be argued to spell out more structure, which prevents them from combining with the lowest negative markers, in line with recent research by Caha et al. (2019) and Vanden Wyngaerd et al. (2020). If this assumption is on the right track, then this would mean that the pattern for Korean can safely be considered the main pattern and that deviations from that pattern follow as a consequence of the internal structure of the predicates the negative markers combine with. A similar reasoning can be entertained for the difference between predicates belonging to literary and non-literary registers in Chinese.

Another issue with respect to (296) is whether it is meaningful that some patterns seem more widely attested than others. Again it is hard to be sure about this given that – even though the sample under discussion is typologically varied – it is still a relatively small sample. It is likely that the picture shifts if we consider more languages. At present it seems that the orders 1, 2, 4, 5 and 15 are best represented. 7, 8 and 14 have less representatives in the sample. More research is necessary to see whether this is meaningful. Most crucially, *ABA-patterns are not attested, suggesting that the natural scope of negation is morphologically supported and hence that morphology is meaningful and indicative of underlying structure. I will explore this idea further in the next chapter.

5 The internal syntax of a negative marker

In this chapter I interpret the syncretisms we detected for the sample of languages discussed in chapter 4 in terms of the nanosyntactic program introduced in chapter 2. In what follows I explain how the syncretisms and the nanosyntactic methodology provide insight into the internal structure of a negative morpheme. This leads to a radical decomposition of the negative morpheme into a layered structure. Negative markers turn out to be featurally and structurally complex with [Neg] being only one of the features constituting a negative marker.[107]

The proposal developed in this chapter and in the rest of this book is in some ways reminiscent of work proposed by Poletto (2008, 2017). She proposed a structurally complex Split NegP on the basis of Italian dialects. In spite of some similarities, there are also many differences, most importantly related to the type of negative markers studied. Whilst the current proposal looks at syncretism patterns across the functional-lexical divide or across the syntax-morphology divide, Poletto's work is concerned with sentential negative markers only. I discuss her work—and the differences and similarities between our proposals in chapter 8.

In the next section I explain step by step what the different arguments and assumptions are to decompose negative markers.

5.1 The negation sequence

In this section I discuss how the syncretism patterns discussed in chapter 4 are meaningful and how they show that morphology is not arbitrary. The sequence used in discussing the negative markers in the previous chapter, i.e. the sequence in (303), respects the natural semantic scope of negation, i.e. from wide to narrow or narrow to wide, and the study of syncretism patterns across a variety of languages showed that this order is also supported by the morphology, i.e. by the syncretisms. This section discusses this issue further.

The core assumption within nanosyntax is that syncretism patterns point to structural relatedness and closeness, i.e. syncretic markers are closer to each other than non-syncretic markers. If we order the detected syncretism patterns of the 23 languages studied in chapter 4 in such a way that the syncretisms target contiguous cells in a table, then it turns out that the sequence that arises on the basis of the morphology of scopally different negative markers reflects the semantic scope of negation, cf. (303).

---

[107] The idea of negation as featurally and/or structurally complex is also present in Haegeman & Lohndal (2010:199).

(303) $T^{NEG} - Foc^{NEG} - Class^{NEG} - Q^{NEG}$

The morphology supports the idea that Q^{NEG} is closer to $Class^{NEG}$ than to Foc^{NEG} and T^{NEG} is closer to Foc^{NEG} than to $Class^{NEG}$. A closer look at the table in (296) indeed shows that there are languages which have syncretic Q^{NEG}- and $Class^{NEG}$-markers (e.g. Chinese, Persian, MSA) and syncretic Foc^{NEG}- and T^{NEG}-markers (e.g. Chinese, Persian, MSA, English, French, Czech, Hungarian), but we do not find any language which has a syncretic Q^{NEG}- and Foc^{NEG}-marker unless the $Class^{NEG}$-marker is also syncretic (as in Moroccan Arabic). This shows that Q^{NEG}- and $Class^{NEG}$-markers are somehow closer or more similar than Q^{NEG}- and Foc^{NEG}-markers. Moreover, no language in the sample has a Q^{NEG}-marker that is syncretic with the T^{NEG}-marker, unless the Foc^{NEG}- and $Class^{NEG}$-marker are also syncretic (as for instance in Czech). This shows that the Q^{NEG}-marker and the T^{NEG}-marker are further apart or more different with respect to each other than the $Class^{NEG}$-marker and the Foc^{NEG}-marker.

The typological generalisation that emerges is as stated in (304):

(304)   If a language has marker X to give rise to *Q-negation* and that language has marker X to give rise to *T-negation* then *Class-negation* and *Foc-negation* will also be expressed by means of marker X.

Based on this generalisation and in line with the nanosyntactic tenet with respect to syncretisms (Caha 2009, Starke 2009, Baunaz et al. 2018), I argue that syncretisms point to relatedness and structural closeness. From the 15 possible sequences for the four types of negative markers, cf. chapter 4 table (297), the negation sequence that the syncretism patterns point to also respects the scope/stacking properties of the four different types of negative markers. As such, the syncretism patterns and the natural scope of negation point in the same direction, establishing a unique order for these four types of negative markers: $T^{NEG} - Foc^{NEG} - Class^{NEG} - Q^{NEG}$.

I refer to this order as the negation sequence or the Universal Negation Contiguity Hypothesis, (305).[108]

---

[108] The Hypothesis is formulated along the lines of Caha's 2009 Universal Case Contiguity Hypothesis, (i):

(i) a. Universal (Case) Contiguity:
     b. Non-accidental case syncretism targets contiguous regions in a sequence invariant across languages.
     c. The Case sequence: NOM–ACC–GEN–DAT–INS–COM (Caha 2009:49)

(305) The Universal Negation Contiguity Hypothesis
a. Negation syncretism targets contiguous regions of negative markers invariant across languages.
b. The negation sequence: T^{NEG} – Foc^{NEG} – $Class^{NEG}$ – Q^{NEG}

Summarizing, if one adopts the idea that syncretisms point to contiguity and relatedness – the syncretism patterns established in chapter 4 allow one to order the negative markers leading to the same sequence also obtained on the basis of scope.

5.2 Decomposition

Given that the scope positions in the clausal spine for the four different types of negative markers are not contiguous, the contiguity laid bare by the syncretisms must be structurally present at another point in syntax. The tree in (306) illustrates the different scopal positions for the different types of markers and is the same tree we used in (64) in chapter 3.

(306)
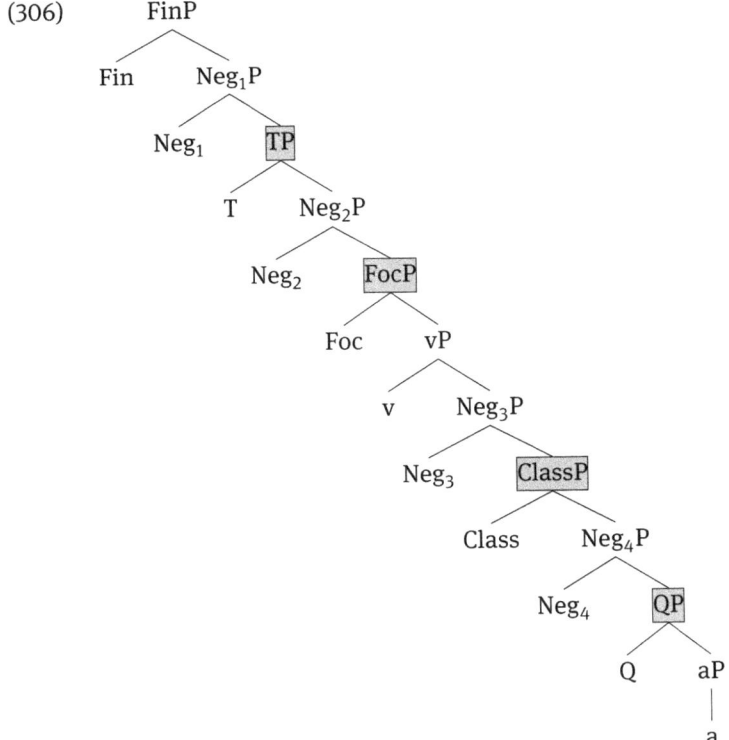

The syncretisms point to the organization and contiguity of features inside a negative marker, i. e. they tell us something about the internal make-up of negative markers, just like the case syncretisms discussed by Caha (2009) point to how features inside case are contiguous, but not to how case behaves in clausal syntax where it is clearly usually non-contiguous. In what follows this idea will be worked out in a more technical way trying to explain in a step-by-step fashion how we get from the syncretisms to decomposition.

In order to decompose the negative morpheme I start from a sub-classification system, also used by Caha (2009) to decompose case, and which is based on Johnston (1996). I introduced this system in chapter 2 in order to show how case is decomposed. The system allows for a translation of the sequence based on the syncretisms of negative markers, to a sub-classification, which eventually results in a hierarchical structure.

The four negative markers can be grouped into one set, which we label W, which is the set of negative markers ordered into a sequence on the basis of the syncretisms. In order to derive a sub-classification on the basis of this sequence, we need to branch off the different markers systematically, starting either from the left or from the right, i. e. either with the Q^{NEG}-marker or with the T^{NEG}-marker, since we do not know based on the syncretisms which marker is most complex. When the first type of the sequence is branched off from the set W, a new set X arises, and so on. As such, two sub-classifications arise, depending on whether we start splitting off T, (307), from the set of all negative markers or Q, (308).

(307)   {T, Foc, Class, Q} = W

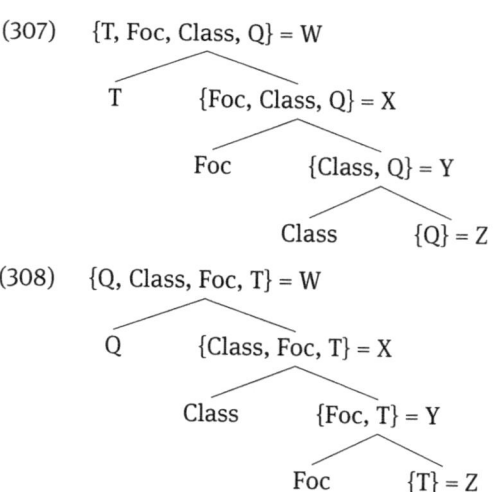

(308)   {Q, Class, Foc, T} = W

This subclassification gives us insight in the number of features that each negative marker consists of: a negative marker consists of as many features as the set it belongs to. In the next step, which is called a 'cumulative classification' (based on Caha (2009:21)), each type of the negative markers under scrutiny here is classified in terms of the number of sets it belongs to. Again we can do this classification in two different ways, since we do not know whether the sequence starts with Q or with T. For the decomposition in (307) the cumulative classification is in (309). For (308) it is in (310).

(309) a. W = T-marker
       b. W, X = Foc-marker
       c. W, X, Y = Class-marker
       d. W, X, Y, Z = Q-marker

(310) a. W = Q-marker
       b. W, X = Class-marker
       c. W, X, Y = Foc-marker
       d. W, X, Y, Z = T-marker

If the negative marker belongs to different sets, this can be understood as that the negative marker consists of different distinctive features. A negative marker that does not belong to a particular set, lacks the distinctive feature associated with that set. In (311) and (312) the letters representing the sets have been replaced by N1, N2, N3, ... Again I present the decomposition for both possible directions of the negative sequence.

(311) a. N1 = T-marker
       b. N1 + N2 = Foc-marker
       c. N1 + N2 + N3 = Class-marker
       d. N1 + N2 + N3 + N4 = Q-marker

(312) a. N1 = Q-marker
       b. N1 + N2 = Class-marker
       c. N1 + N2 + N3 = Foc-marker
       d. N1 + N2 + N3 + N4 = T-marker

Instead of N1, N2, N3, N4 we will now use the distinctive labels per type of marker, i. e. T, Foc, Class and Q.[109]

(313) a. T = T-marker
       b. T + Foc = Foc-marker
       c. T + Foc + Class = Class-marker

---

[109] De Clercq (2013) used N1, N2, N3 etc throughout.

    d. T + Foc + Class + Q = Q-marker
(314) a. Q = Q-marker
    b. Q + Class = CLASS-marker
    c. Q + Class + Foc = FOC-marker
    d. Q + Class + Foc + T = T-marker

However, even though a sub-classification like this one yields subatomic features whilst keeping the contiguity of the negation sequence (and thus avoiding non-contiguous syncretisms), it cannot capture all possible syncretism patterns. The sub-classification in (313) for instance cannot capture a syncretism of Q, Class, Foc to the exclusion of T (a pattern present in Moroccan Arabic), since the feature T, present in a Q^{NEG}-marker, $Class^{NEG}$-marker and Foc^{NEG}-marker is also present in the T^{NEG}-marker. The sub-classification in (314) on the other hand cannot capture a syncretism of T, Foc and Class to the exclusion of Q (as present in Hungarian), because the feature Q present in the T^{NEG}-marker, Foc^{NEG}-marker and $Class^{NEG}$-marker is also present in the Q^{NEG}-marker.

If we supplement this system with the Elsewhere Principle (Minimize Junk), as described in (30) in chapter 2 and repeated here in (315), then a syncretism between T, Foc and Class to the exclusion of Q (as for the decomposition in (22)) is possible.

(315) *Elsewhere Condition* or *Minimize Junk*
    In case two rules, R1 and R2, can apply in an environment E, R1 takes precedence over R2 if it applies in a proper subset of environments compared to R2 (Caha 2009:18).

Imagine for instance the hypothetical negative markers in (316a) and (316b).

(316) a. {T, Foc, Class, Q} ⇒ /Phon A/
    b. {Q} ⇒ /Phon B/

At this point the system can spell out Phon B for the Q^{NEG}-marker alone, because it takes precedence over the spell out Phon A, since it applies in a proper subset of the situations Phon A applies in. Phon B will thus be the spell out of the Q-^{NEG}-marker, whilst Phon A will be the spellout of the T^{NEG}-, Foc^{NEG}- and $Class^{NEG}$-marker.

By means of cumulative sub-classification and the Elsewhere Principle, the Universal Negation Contiguity Hypothesis can be captured. Syncretisms between negative markers are thus a surface reflection of the presence of contiguous subatomic features inside negative markers, i. e. the Universal Contiguity Hypothesis is a consequence of how syntax is organised at the nanolevel.

In line with nanosyntactic assumptions and the cartographic 'one feature one head' tenet (see chapter 2), each of these features in the decomposition in (313)–(314) is a syntactic head. When we now organise these heads in terms of binary branching trees, then we get a hierarchically organised tree in which the negative morpheme is split up in different negation layers, each instantiating a syntactic feature. The structure for the decomposition in (313) is in (317): the T^{NEG}-marker consists of only one feature in this decomposition and therefore comes lowest in this structure. The structure for the decomposition in (314) is in (318): in this decomposition the Q^{NEG}-marker consists of only one distinctive feature and thus comes lowest in this structure.

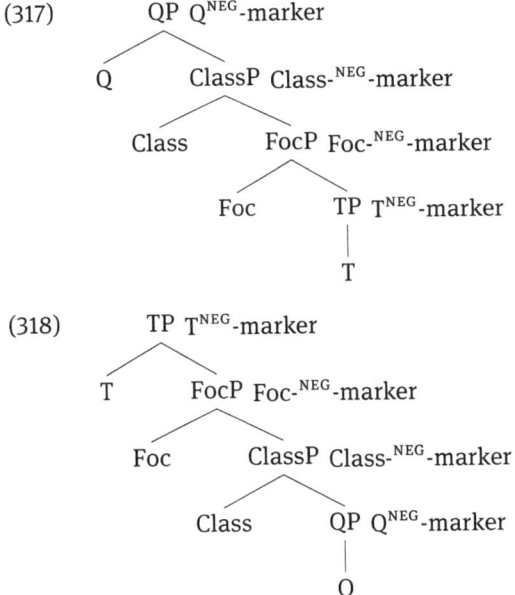

I adopt the structure in (318) as the correct structure. In the next section I provide arguments for this choice. However, one more element needs to be added for the structure to give rise to semantic negation: a [Neg]-feature. I propose to have this negative feature at the bottom of the sequence, supporting the intuition that a negative marker starts out with semantic negation.[110] The nanospine we con-

---

110 There are no radical arguments in favour of having it at the bottom and not for instance at the top of the spine. Ideally, one would want all the non-negative features together to compositionally give rise to negation and to be able to get rid of the negative feature as such. Unfortunately, I have to postpone this to future research.

tinue working with is in (319). Note also that the bottom of this spine contains two heads: the reason for this is that in many languages negative markers are prefixes. However, in languages with suffixal negative markers the bottom of the negative spine would be unary. I come back to this in section 5.4.

(319)
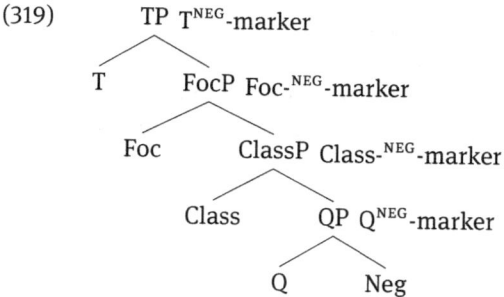

In the next section I provide two arguments for why I decided on the hierarchical structure in (319).

5.3 Containment

In this section I offer support for the decomposition in (314) and the negative spine in (318), updated with a negative feature in (319). The main hypothesis underlying the spine is that T^{NEG}-markers do not only consist of the feature T, but they also consist of the features Q, Class, Foc and of course Neg.[111] The Foc^{NEG}-marker consist of the features Foc, Class, Q and Neg whilst the $Class^{NEG}$-marker consists of Class, Q and Neg. Important to mention here is that a T^{NEG}-marker cannot be equated with the feature T. It is the spellout of the cumulation of Neg, Q, Class, Foc and T.

The first argument for the structure that I adopt is a diachronic argument. The English markers *un-*, *a-* and *-iN* are derived from Proto-Indo-European (PIE) **n-*, which is a variant of **ne-* (Harper 2013). *Non-* on the other hand consists of that same **ne* and the Latin word *oinum*, meaning 'one' (Horn 2001b:453). *Non-* is hence morphologically and featurally bigger than *un-*, *iN-*, *a-*. Also *not* (Harper 2013) is morphologically bigger than *un-*, *iN-*, *a-*. It is the unstressed variant of

---

[111] As we go along, it will become clear that in some languages, like for instance *le bon usage* French, cf. chapter 7, the lexical tree for a T^{NEG}-marker is only a subpart of the negative spine. In this case the T^{NEG}-marker is featurally impoverished and shows clitic-like behavior. I postpone this discussion to chapter 7.

naught, which consists of PIE **ne* and Old English (OE) *wiht* which means 'person, creature, thing' (Horn 2001b:455, Harper 2013). These diachronic data suggest that Q^{NEG}-markers are contained in T-, Foc- and $Class^{NEG}$-markers. Unfortunately, these diachronic data do not say anything about the relationship between *non-* and *not*, i. e. it is not clear whether a $Class^{NEG}$-marker is contained in a Foc- and/or T^{NEG}-marker.

A second argument for the spine in (318) comes from grammaticalisation. This process provides support for the negative spine I propose. Sentential negative markers, which I call T^{NEG}-markers, often find their origin in minimizers, like French *pas* or regular indefinites, like Old English *wiht* (as described above). An example of a negative marker which is derived from a minimizer comes from French. Originally *pas* is derived from the noun, *un pas* 'a step' and is thus a minimizer, i. e. it denotes a small quantity. Minimizers ideally occur in the scope of negation as a way to emphasize the preverbal negative marker. The minimizer *pas* evolved from being used as an emphatic adverb in the scope of the negative marker *ne* until it became used as a negative marker itself. In *le bon usage* French, neither *ne* nor *pas* can give rise to sentential negation on their own. *pas* must thus have evolved in this stage into a real negative marker with emphatic force, a Foc^{NEG}-marker, that still needed the help of *ne* (Grevisse & Goosse [1936] 1993). In Colloquial French on the other hand *pas* can be used on its own as a sentential negative marker (Pollock 1989, Rowlett 1998a) and it has thus acquired the status of a T^{NEG}-marker. From a diachronic point of view thus quantificational features and focus features are an inherent part of the grammaticalisation of what I call T^{NEG}-markers. From the perspective of grammaticalisation the spine with T^{NEG}-markers at the top and Q^{NEG}-markers at the bottom reflects the evolution which indefinites or nouns undergo to give rise to sentential negation. This grammaticalisation process is also reflected in Poletto (2008)'s work, which I discuss in greater detail in chapter 8. Poletto puts markers like Italian *non* at the top of her Split NegP (in ScalarP) and markers which originally meant *nothing* at the bottom of her Split NegP (in QP). The proposal in this chapter to have Q^{NEG}-markers contained in T^{NEG}-markers has thus been independently confirmed by research, which is methodologically different and which focused on sentential negative markers with verbal predicates. One could of course wonder why a Foc-feature would be part of the regular expression of sentential negation, i. e. of a T^{NEG}-marker. I want to argue that even in T^{NEG}-markers, Foc is still a relevant feature, since if a negative marker loses its emphatic power and becomes too bleached, the entire cycle will necessarily start all over again and the marker will start combining with new emphatic adverbs and loose its negative force. Actually, the presence of Foc is crucial for negation to give rise to sentential negation.

Without the presence of Foc, a negative marker will lose power and be renewed. We will discuss this formally in chapter 7.

Based on the support presented in this section, I assume that the structure in (319)—which I proposed is underlyingly present in a negative marker—captures the order of the feature composition of negation well: Foc, Class, and Q^{NEG}-markers are contained in T^{NEG}-markers (and not the other way around). In the next section I explain how negative markers can be spelled out in nanosyntax.

5.4 Spellout

In this section I show how the spellout of negative markers for formal English works. However, spelling out these negative markers does not make them part of clausal syntax straight away. In chapter 6 I will elaborate on how negative markers get inserted into clausal syntax, but here I discuss how the spellout of a negative marker works in isolation.

The post-syntactic lexicon of English consists of at least the following Lexical Items (LI) for negation, illustrated in (321)–(323). Each lexical item consists of phonological material (indicated between slant brackets) and syntactic structure, in line with Starke (2014a:245)'s premise on the organisation of the lexicon:

(320) The lexicon contains nothing but well-formed syntactic expressions.

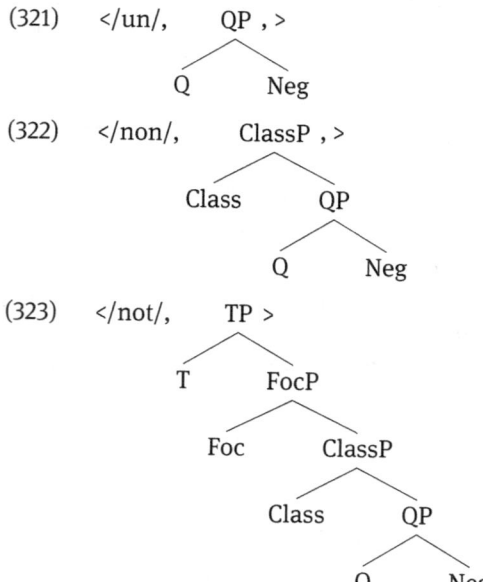

Note in the LIs in (321)–(323) that the bottom of the negative nanospines in English has a binary grouping. The reason for this is that most negative markers in English are PRE-elements. Recapitulating briefly what we explained in section 2.3, Starke (2018) proposes to make a distinction between prefixes and suffixes in terms of a difference in the bottom of their lexical trees. Prefixal elements, i. e. any word or prefix preceding a predicate (henceforth PRE-elements), have a binary grouping at the bottom, as illustrated in (324). As a result of this, they are inserted as complex specifiers in the main spine. Suffixal elements (henceforth POST) have a singleton at the bottom of their lexical spines and are the consequence of movement that does not leave traces, (325).

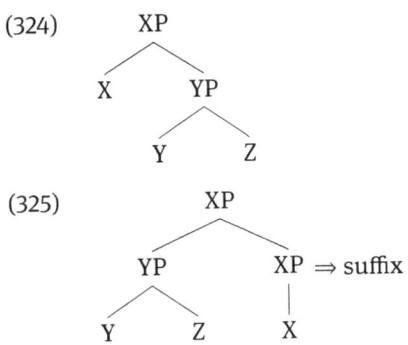

English is far from the only language with negative markers that precede the predicate and hence should be analyzed as having binary bottoms. It has been argued by Dryer (1988) that 70% of the 345 languages in his sample, i. e. 227 languages, have a negative marker that precedes the predicate. Of course, Dryer only studied sentential negative markers, so if you take all types of negative markers into account, this number will most probably decrease. Nevertheless, 70% is quite significant and has confirmed Jespersen's NegFirst principle, which he defines in the following way: "to place the negative first, or at any rate as soon as possible, very often immediately before the particular word to be negated (generally the verb)". (Jespersen 1924:4, labelled NegFirst by Horn (2001b:292–293)). The fact that Starke proposes to capture this distinction between PRE and POST elements structurally can thus be used to capture what has been known as the NegFirst principle. In what follows I show how the different English PRE negative markers get spelled out individually.

After Neg and Q are merged as a binary grouping, the lexicon is checked at the level of QP, (326). There are at least three LIs that are possible candidates to be inserted according to the Superset Principle, i. e. (321), (322) and (323). Due to the Elsewhere Principle, (321) will be inserted. This negative spine can be inserted in the specifier of a NegP for the derivation of a word like *unhappy*. I elaborate further on how nanospine and clausal spine match in chapter 6.2.

(326)   QP ⇒ un-
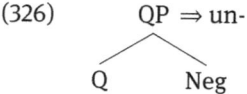
         Q   Neg

The derivation of the negative spine could be stopped here. However, it could also continue merging when a negative adjective like *non-American* needs to be derived. Then another feature, i. e. Class, will be merged, as in (327). The lexicon is checked again at the level of ClassP. Due to the Superset Principle, (322) and (323) are candidates for insertion. However, due to the Elsewhere Principle (322) will be inserted, because (322) is a perfect match. The spellout of ClassP overrides the spellout of QP.

(327)   ClassP ⇒ non
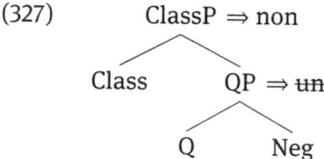
       Class   QP ⇒ ~~un~~
                Q   Neg

Again the derivation could stop here, but syntax could also continue merging a low scope contrastive negation like *not happy (but sad)*. In that case Foc is merged, as in (328). The lexicon is checked again, but no perfect match is available in the lexicon. There is (323), which contains the spine that is merged in syntax. Due to the Superset Principle, (323) can be inserted for the syntactic structure in (328). The reason that the lexicon does not have a perfect match for the spine in (328) is a consequence of syncretism: *not* functions as a Foc- and T^{NEG}-marker in formal written English. The spellout of the FocP-node overrides the spellout of the ClassP-node.

(328)   FocP ⇒ not
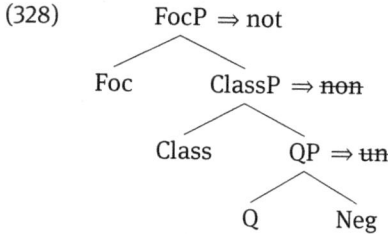
       Foc   ClassP ⇒ ~~non~~
              Class   QP ⇒ ~~un~~
                        Q   Neg

The derivation could stop here, but for a copular clause like *She is not happy*, a negative marker with sentential scope needs to be inserted in syntax. So syntax merges an extra feature, T, as in (329). The lexicon is checked and (323) matches the structure in syntax. The spellout of TP overrides the spellout of FocP. However, due to the fact that *not* is syncretic for Foc- and T-negation this does not result in a different exponent. Again it is crucial to realize that the derivations here are nano-derivations, i. e. at the level of the word. In chapter 6 I will explain how the interaction between main spine and nanospine works and how these negative markers get inserted in clausal syntax.

(329)

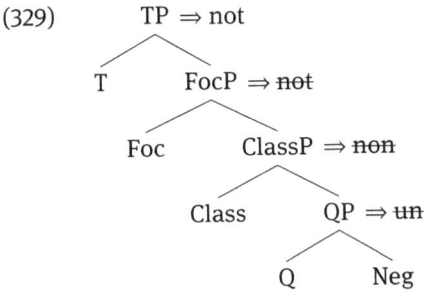

Moreover, I will also discuss in chapter 6 section 6.4.2 how the spellout of *n't*, the register related variant of sentential *not*, can be derived and how the competition between productive and unproductive affixes like *un-* vs. *iN-* and *dis-* can be regulated and spelled out in nanosyntax, (96).

5.5 Conclusion

In this chapter I showed how contiguous syncretism patterns between negative markers in scopally different positions point to structure within what is normally considered one unit, i. e. the negative marker. I decomposed this negative marker into four subatomic features, which I labelled in accordance with the scope positions of the negative markers in clausal syntax T, Foc, Class and Q. In addition to these four features I proposed that there is a Neg-feature that provides semantic negation. I organized these features into a hierarchical structure, which has T at the top and Neg at the bottom and provided arguments for this hierarchy. I will refer to this hierarchy as the negative nanospine. This chapter also showed how negative markers can be spelled out in isolation. We did not explain yet how these markers get inserted into a full clausal structure. This will be done in the next chapter.

Part III: **Negative markers and their clausal syntax in English and French**

6 The external syntax of negative markers in English

The main aim of this chapter is to explain how the negative nanospine of the four scopally different negative markers in English gets inserted in clausal syntax. At a more abstract level, this chapter shows how the same technology can spell out and capture negative markers that have up until now been treated in different modules of the grammar, i. e. morphology and syntax.

I argue in this chapter that most negative markers in English are inserted as complex specifiers, much like adverbs are inserted in the specifiers of dedicated heads in Cinque's (1999) work or subjects are inserted in the specifier of vP across most generative models. I argue that this is a consequence of the fact that markers in English usually precede the predicate they modify, and are hence structurally different from suffixal elements, cf. the discussion in section 2.3 based on Starke (2018) and his proposal for the structurally different nature of PRE and POST elements. I will also explain how suffixal negative markers like *-less* and register related variants like *-n't* can be treated, and how unproductive Q^{NEG}-markers get their spellout in competition with the productive negative marker *un-*.

Finally, the current chapter provides full clausal derivations in nanosyntax. As far as I know, this has not yet been done before and even though I am aware of many shortcomings in presentation and in the execution, I hope to spark off discussion on how this could be done by presenting them here.

6.1 Introduction

The tree structure in (330) again provides an overview of the different positions for negation in the clausal spine, i. e. it provides the FSEQ for negation at the clausal level. Note that the same features that we argued play a role at the level of the negative nanospine are replicated at the clausal level, be it interspersed with other features. The contiguity that we argued for plays a role at the nanolevel and the syncretisms of the different negative markers are a reflection of this contiguity. However, at the clausal level this contiguity is not visible. To the contrary, in between the different positions for NegPs there are intervening levels of structure and these intervening levels of structure are even necessary at the level of the clause, i. e. there should not be contiguity, because Neg is not selected by Neg in the main spine, just like T is not selected by T or C by C, an idea worked out and discussed in detail as the *Neg-Neg constraint in De Clercq & Vanden Wyngaerd (2017b, 2019a), Collins (2018), as we already discussed in chapter 3.

(330)

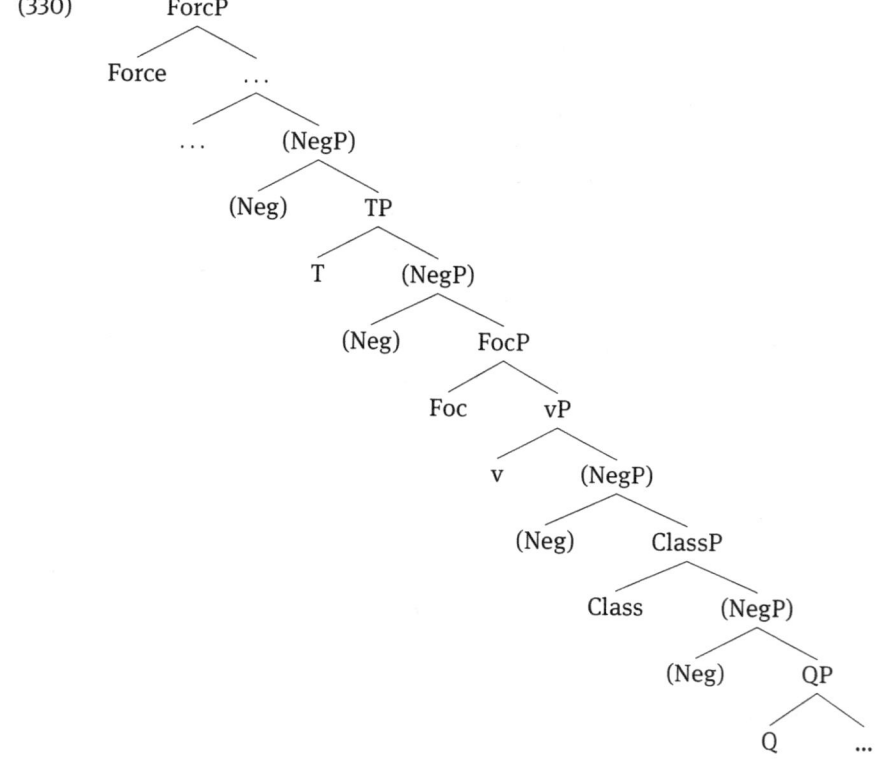

As is clear from the structure in (330), which we will refine as we go along, I propose that a NegP can optionally project on top of every of the four negation-related features. The suggestion that NegP is optional in the fseq is not new (Starke 2004) and has been argued for on the basis of the fact that negation is marked compared to affirmation, i. e. affirmation is rarely morphologically realized, but negation almost always (Greenberg 1966), negation leads to more processing difficulties in language acquisition than affirmative sentences (Horn 2001b), negative sentences have been argued to be less frequent than affirmative sentences (De Swart 2010) etc. As such, negative markers can appear in at least all the four positions indicated in the tree in (330) with (Neg), but not every type of negative marker can appear in any of these positions. Important to mention in relation to these optional positions is that there are naturally more positions for negation than those illustrated in the simplified tree structure in (330). As we discussed in section 3, Foc^NEG-markers may project as NegP over each possible FocP in the clause, which we saw could be many different positions, as discussed in Simpson & Wu (2002). The picture in (330) thus only provides the scope position for Foc^NEG-markers on top of the main adjectival predicate in a copular clause, but the idea is that this same marker can also appear on NPs, AdvPs and PPs in the clausal spine, in subject, or adverbial position, i.e. on each constituent that in itself gives rise to a predicate. These instances of Foc^NEG-markers give rise to what is usually referred to as constituent negation or adverbial modification of negation and they are not represented in the structure in (330).

In the specifier of each of the optional NegPs in (330) a complex negative nanospine can be inserted. The idea of inserting a complex specifier or complex left branch is well-known from the generative tradition, since this is also how subjects are inserted in complex specifiers and how adverbials are inserted in dedicated functional heads (Cinque 1999). However, the mechanism for how the insertion of a complex specifier happens in the main clausal spine is hardly ever discussed in any detail – at least to the best of my knowledge. It is somehow assumed that this specifier is assembled in another workspace and then somehow plugged into the derivation. How this exactly happens and how these different derivations interact is not usually explained. In the next section we will provide an algorithm for how this happens. This algorithm was already introduced in section 2.3 and applied to case morphemes there, but we will show in the next section how it can be used for the insertion of complex specifiers in general and for negative markers in particular.

Descriptively, we could say that the size of the negative nanospine will be indicative of where it will get inserted. A negative marker which consists of a T-feature will project in the specifier of a NegP at the level of TP, a negative marker which consists of a Foc-feature will project in a NegP at the level of FocP, etc. A similar hypothesis is present in Endo & Haegeman (2014). They propose that the internal syntax of the adverbial clause is indicative of its insertion position in clausal syntax (see also Williams 2003, Williams 2009:6–7, De Clercq & Vanden Wyngaerd 2017b). Put formally, the internal structure of the negative nanospine will be a requirement of the clausal FSEQ. The higher in the FSEQ a Neg-feature is merged, the more structure the nano-spine will need to consist of in order to match the features of the FSEQ at the point of insertion. As an illustration of what it looks like, the sentence in (331), which consists of a sentential negative marker, is depicted with a syntactic tree in (332). (332) consists of a negative nanospine that is inserted at the level of the optional NegP above TP. The negative nanospine consists of the features that match the structure of the FSEQ up until that point.

(331) John is not happy.

(332)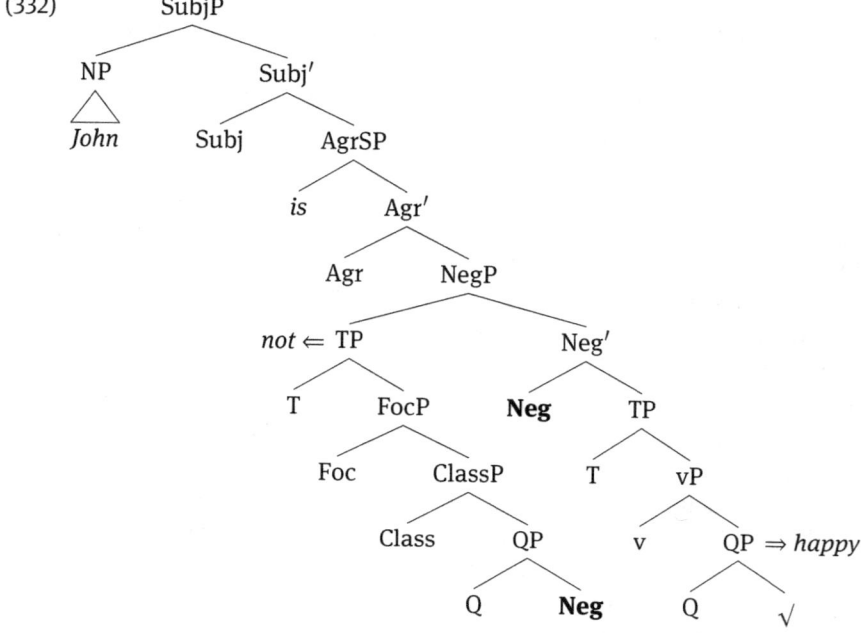

Observe that the sentential NegP in the clausal spine in (332) seems to get its semantic negativity from two negative heads (both boldfaced in the tree). For that reason, Starke (2004) argues that empty heads like, for instance the empty Neg-head in the clausal spine in (332), are superfluous, if the contentful element is provided by the specifier. Starke proposes that specifiers project and provide the feature required by the FSEQ. In the present case, it is the Neg-head in the specifier that is responsible for the projection of NegP and not the head in the main spine. We could thus simplify the tree in (332) to the one in (333), with the semantically vacuous Subj, Agr, and Neg heads removed from the main spine, since these heads are provided by the internal structure of the complex specifier.

(333)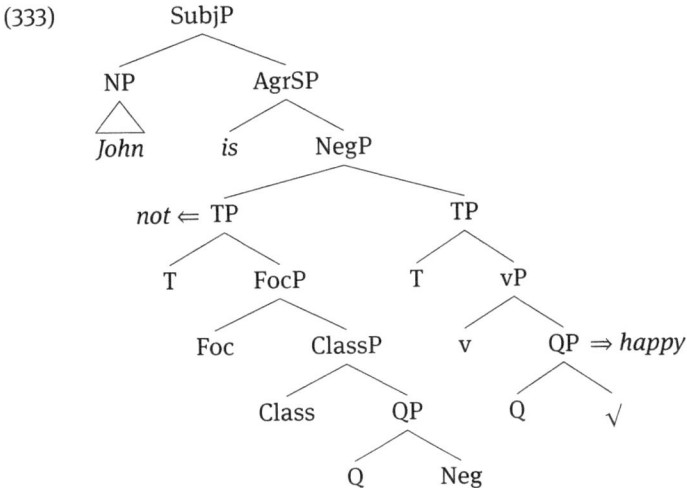

One could wonder why it is NegP that projects in the case of these complex negative specifiers and not the other features in the negative nanospine. We want to argue that all other features in the complex negative nanospine have already been projected and spelled out in the clausal spine by the time this specific complex negative marker is merged in clausal syntax. This will become more clear when we do a step-by-step derivation in section 6.2. Before we proceed to a step-by-step discussion of the spellout algorithm applied to negative markers, we need to discuss some further issues related to the tree structure in (333). Within a nanosyntactic system that makes use of phrasal syntax and that uses fine-grained featurally distinctions, the landing position for the subject will not be SpecTP or SpeccIP, because 1) there will not be one TP, since tense will be decomposed into different types of tense and 2) TP spells out tense morphology on the verb (and is also a part of the spellout of a negative marker as we will discuss) and 3) subjects will also be decomposed, in line with ideas by McCloskey (1997), Kiss (1996), Cardinaletti (1997, 2004), Rizzi (1981, 2004), Danckaert & Haegeman (2017) and hence give rise to dedicated positions of their own. Even though a lot of work still needs to be done in nanosyntax, and these topics constitute research projects on their own, it makes sense to argue that the subject will be attracted to dedicated subject positions in the syntactic tree, as illustrated informally in (333). In (333) the position proposed is SubjP (Cardinaletti 1997, Rizzi 1981, Cardinaletti 2004, Rizzi 2004, Danckaert & Haegeman 2017), a position for subjects of predication, but I follow the literature in assuming that there are more positions between the C-domain and TP dedicated to subjects.

Crucial to mention here is that this is a book on negative markers and not one on the full structure of the clause within Nanosyntax. When I provide derivations in section 6.2 they are meant to give the reader an idea of how nanosyntax COULD go about integrating what happens at the level of the word with clausal syntax. Naturally, the labels that I use to deal with verbs, tense, subjects and other grammatical categories are not fine-grained enough to do justice to Nanosyntax and sometimes even cartography. I stick to well-known and sometimes general labels if they are not crucial for the point I want to make in order to be able to focus on what this book is about: negative markers and their internal and external syntax.

Having laid out the basic ideas and some caveats, we are now ready to discuss the insertion mechanism for PRE-negative markers, the spellout algorithm and the nature of complex negative specifiers in greater detail for different types of negative markers.

6.2 Insertion of negative PRE-markers

If negative markers had unary bottoms, unlike the lexical structures we proposed for most negative markers in section 5.4, then they would be inserted as suffixes. Let me explain this. Imagine that the lexical item for the T^{NEG}-marker in English is as in (334). Once a predicate with copular verb is merged in syntax and spelled out, and after tense morphology is added, a Neg-feature will be added. After merge of this Neg-feature (336), the predicate XP would have to move out of the way to be able to spell out the negative marker (cf. the spellout algorithm in (335)). This would allow us to insert the negative marker and we could in consecutive steps build up the T^{NEG}-marker by means of phrasal spell out. However, the word order would – at the end of the derivation – be *Predicate not*, as in (337), and we would need to resort to non-spellout driven movements to solve the word-order problem. But what would be the trigger of this non-spellout driven movement?

(334)   < /not/,   TP >

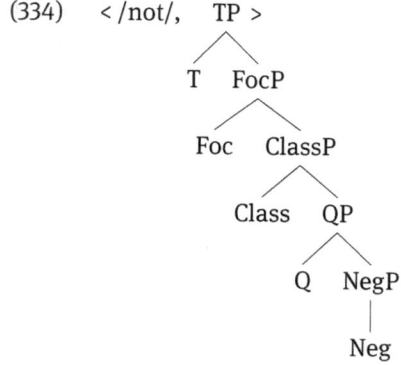

(335) a. Insert feature and spell out (= do not move)
b. If fail, try a cyclic (spec-to-spec) movement of the node inserted at the previous cycle
c. If fail, try a snowball movement of the complement of the newly inserted feature and spell out.
d. If merge-f has failed to spell out (even after backtracking), try to spawn a new derivation providing feature X and merge that with the current derivation, projecting feature X to the top node.

(336) NegP
     /\
  Neg XP

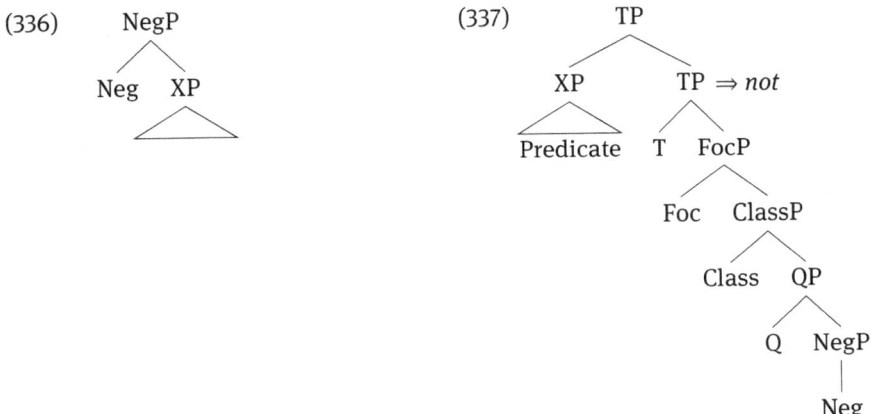

(337) TP tree with XP (Predicate), T, FocP (Foc, ClassP (Class, QP (Q, NegP (Neg)))), TP ⇒ not

In order to avoid vacuous and unwanted non-spellout driven movements, another solution needs to be tried. What we proposed is that (most) English negative markers have binary bottoms, as in (338)–(340), in line with Starke (2018)'s proposal that PRE- and POST-elements are structurally different creatures, whose difference can be captured in syntax (discussed in section 2.3 for case).

(338) </un/, QP >
          /\
        Q Neg

(339) </non/, ClassP >

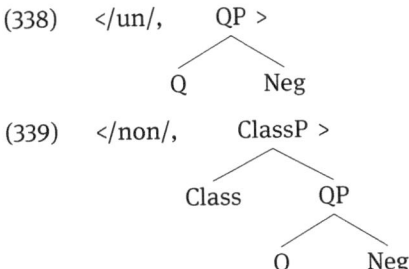

(340)   ⇐/not/,   TP >

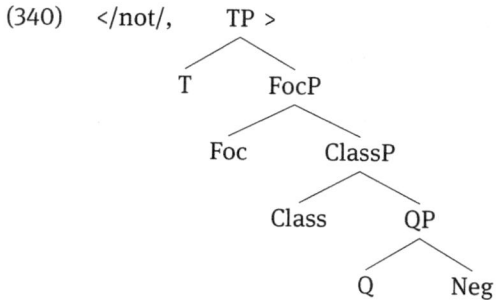

If we look again at the structure we dealt with in (336), then it is clear that in this case, even after the predicate has moved out, which is the first step in the spell out algorithm, neither of these negative markers can be inserted, because the structure for the negative marker in (337) does not match with any of the lexical items in (338)–(340) due to the binary bottoms of the lexical items. After all movement steps of the spellout algorithm (Starke 2018:245) have been tried, the final step in the algorithm will be tried, which is spawning a new derivation. In what follows I will explain how this works for several derivations. Even though some of it may come across at first as unintuitive or cumbersome, I want to emphasize that the procedure follows a strict and predictable algorithm, which seems to be preferred over stipulating that a complex specifier (for instance a subject) is inserted without saying anything about how and where this subject is assembled and how it can interact with the main clause.

If we consider the derivation of an adjective like *professional*, as in (344), then we need to start from the derivation of a noun, since this adjective is denominal, (341). The insertion of the nominal in (341) happens on the basis of Free Choice, i. e. the structure in (341) corresponds to a multitude of possible lexical trees and hence the Choice as to which nominal gets inserted is free. However, once the choice is made, deviation from that choice is not possible anymore. We call this the Faithfulness Condition (Caha et al. 2019).[112]

(341)   *profession* ⇐ nP

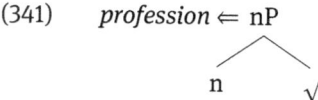

---

[112] It is possible to deviate from the choice made before, when there is a pointer at a later point in the derivation, which allows the structure to be overwritten. An example for such a derivation would be *good*, which would be the result of Free Choice at the level of aP, and then the insertion of *better* which is allowed to overwrite the root due to the fact that the suppletive stem of *bett-* contains a pointer to *good*. I refer the reader to Caha et al. (2019) for more discussion of this issue.

In order to form the adjective, the adjectivizing suffix -*al*, is added. We assume that this suffix consists of an adjectivizing head, a Q-feature which contributes gradability (Corver 1997b, De Clercq & Vanden Wyngaerd 2017b) and a Class-feature, which restricts the meaning of a gradable adjective to a neutral classifying property. The lexical tree for -*al* is in (342).[113]

(342) </al/   ClassP>

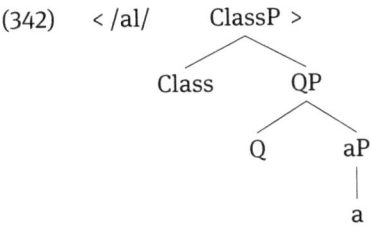

Thanks to the Superset Principle, the suffix -*al* can be inserted in (343) and is a perfect match with the syntax in (344). The structure in (343) gives rise to a gradable characterising adjective *professional*, whilst the structure in (344) gives rise to a classifying adjective.

(343)

(344)

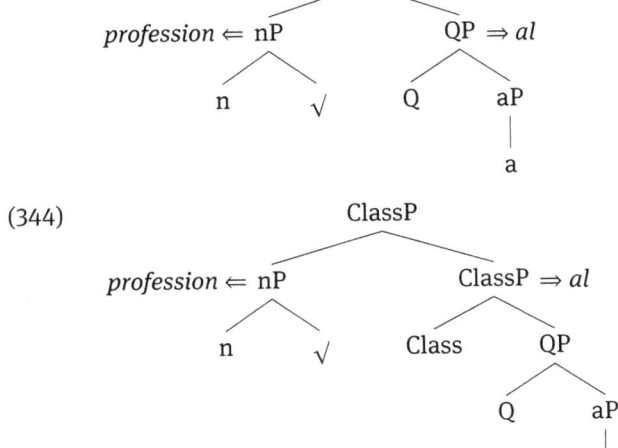

---

[113] The internal structure of *al-* is presumably more complex and may need a feature corresponding to the type of noun it combines with to discern it featurally from an adjectivizing suffix like -*ful* that combines with abstract mass nouns. See section 6.4.1.

Support for the different structures and the feature structure of *-al* comes from examples like (345)–(346), where the gradable and non-gradable meaning of *professional* is disambiguated by means of the negative markers. In (345) adding the negative marker disambiguates the adjective and allows only a classifying reading of the property denoted by *professional*, whereas the negative marker in (346) allows a gradable, characterising reading of the property denoted by the adjective *professional*.

(345) a. Context: Amie is an actress. However, she never obtained a degree for acting. Her friend says:
b. She is nonprofessional.
c. #She is unprofessional.

(346) a. Context: Amie is an actress. However, she is never on time at rehearsals, tries to get roles by gossiping about others, etc:
b. #Her behaviour is nonprofessional.
c. Her behaviour is unprofessional.

The data in (345)–(346) do not tell us anything about the order of Class and Q in the spine. Nevertheless, there is support that the order in (344) is the right order, i. e. non-gradable predicates are derived from gradable predicates and not the other way around. The hierarchy for negation (based on the syncretism patterns) is the first piece of evidence for that, but there is also evidence from within the domain of adjectives for the containment relationship Class > Q. Whereas non-gradable adjectives (like *pregnant*) can be easily coerced into gradable adjectives (e. g. *very pregnant*), the opposite is not true, i. e. adjectives like *happy* do not easily become non-gradable adjectives. If Q is a necessary ingredient of the functional structure of adjectives and ClassP is an optional feature, capable of turning scalar predicates into non-gradable classifying predicates, then it follows that the lexical structure of a non-gradable predicate like *pregnant*, (347), can, thanks to the Superset Principle, also spell out the syntax of a gradable adjective. However, the lexical tree of a predicate like *happy*, (348), will not contain [Class], and hence will not be able to spell out a non-gradable predicate.

(347) </pregnant/, ClassP >

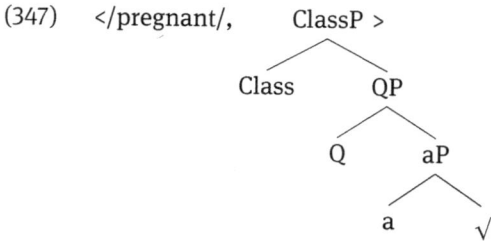

(348) </happy/, QP >

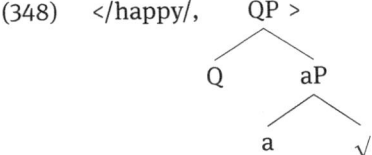

As we saw in (345)–(346), negative markers can appear in combination with adjectives like *professional* and even help in disambiguating the different layers of meaning: the negative marker *un-* then combines with a QP giving rise to a qualitative property, whereas the negative marker *non-* combines with a ClassP, giving rise to a non-qualitative but classifying property.

If we now move to the technicalities of spellout and we want to spell out the negative marker for a sentence as in (346), then at the point Neg is merged in clausal syntax, it seems there is no lexical item of the items in (338)–(340) that can spell out the structure in (349), not even after we apply the regular movement rules of the nanosyntactic spellout algorithm, (335). This is shown for roll-up movement in (350). The reason for this is clear: the bottom of all lexical items for negative markers is binary and consists at least of Q and Neg, but these features are not present after movement in (350).[114]

(349)

(350)

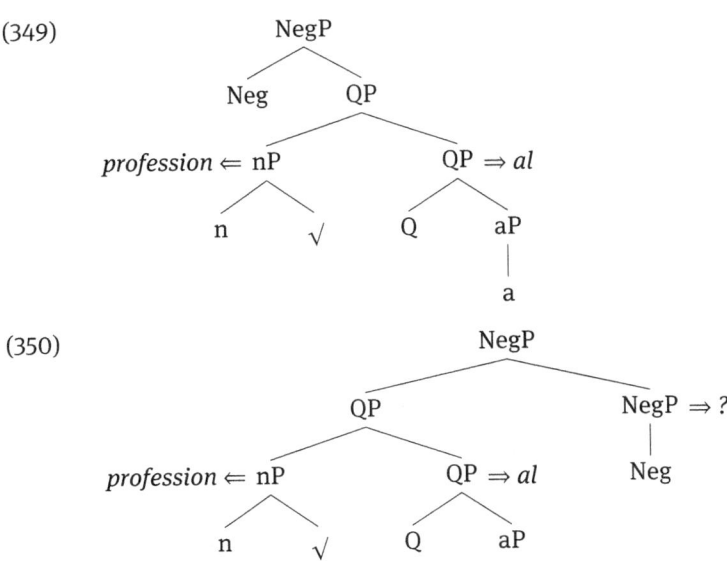

As a Last Resort strategy, a new derivation can be spawned, as proposed by Starke (2018) and explained for case in section 2.3. This is the point where the notion of

---

[114] *-less* and *n't* are exceptions to this, but they consist of other features that prevent spellout, as will be discussed in 6.4.

the complex specifier kicks in. Complex specifiers are completely normal parts of syntax but, as far as I know, there has been no systematic proposal for how complex specifiers should/can be integrated in clausal syntax. In what follows we present a first attempt at a more systematic way to deal with this, since merging complex specifiers has now become part of a spellout algorithm, i. e. it arises due to the structure of the lexicon and the need to spellout syntactic structure. When a new derivation is merged, it grows together with the main spine. Since merging a new derivation is more costly than movement, the new derivation will grow as long as possible, before it is closed off and merges with the main derivation, which then upon its turn continues merging structure. For the case at hand, the first feature that is merged is Neg, which is the one the FSEQ needed and could not get spelled out. It is this NEG feature that will project, because it will be the only feature in the negative nanospine that will not have been projected yet in the clausal spine. The other feature merged is Q. The reason that this feature is merged has to do with the structure of the FSEQ for negative markers, which has Q at its bottom and T at the top. At the level of QP the lexicon is checked and this phrase gets a spellout, (338), resulting in *un*, as shown in (351) and explained in chapter 5.

(351)

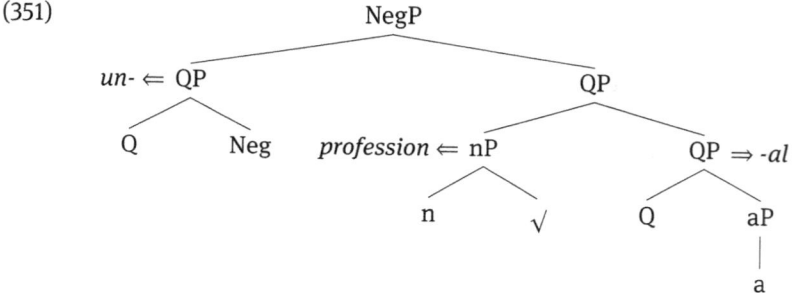

If we want to merge the structure for the non-gradable adjective in (345), then we merge a bigger adjectival structure, which includes ClassP. In accordance with the different scope positions for negation, the Neg-feature will be merged on top of ClassP, resulting in the same spellout problem as before, so a new derivation will be spawned. However, the structure of the negative marker is not yet what we need at the level of QP: the main clause consists of a ClassP-adjective, so it is in need of a Class[NEG]-marker, because the complex specifier needs to match the requirements of the main spine at that point. This newly spawned derivation will grow until it meets the requirements of the FSEQ at that particular point, i. e. it will grow until it reaches ClassP. At the level of ClassP the LI in (339) will be inserted and the new derivation will close off and merge with the main spine, thus creating the complex specifier. The structure that we end up having is the one in (352), with the NegP in the main clause as a projection of the negative head in the complex specifier and the features in the complex specifier matching the derivation at the level of the clause.

(352)
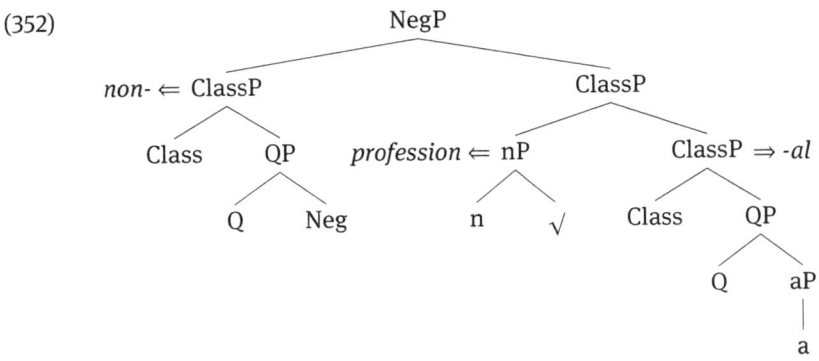

The same happens whenever Neg is merged in any of the scopal positions in the clausal spine in English: every time a new derivation will be spawned, it will grow in concord with the main clause, until it has reached the requirements of the clausal FSEQ. After that, the main clause will resume growing.

If we now go back to the derivation of the sentence in (331), i. e. *John is not happy*, then exactly the same happens at the point when Neg is merged in clausal syntax. Since the lexicon of English does not contain a lexical item that will enable spellout straightaway or after trying the regular steps in the nanosyntactic spellout algorithm, a new derivation will be spawned, in the way illustrated for the previous derivation. The first merge step will result in the spellout of *un*, (353).

(353)
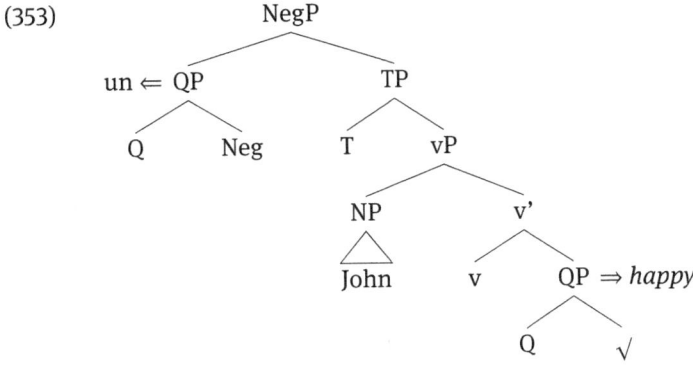

The new derivation will have to grow and spell out the different layers of the negative nanospine (as explained in chapter 5) until it meets the requirements of the clausal FSEQ, i. e. it will grow until TP, as illustrated in (354):

(354)
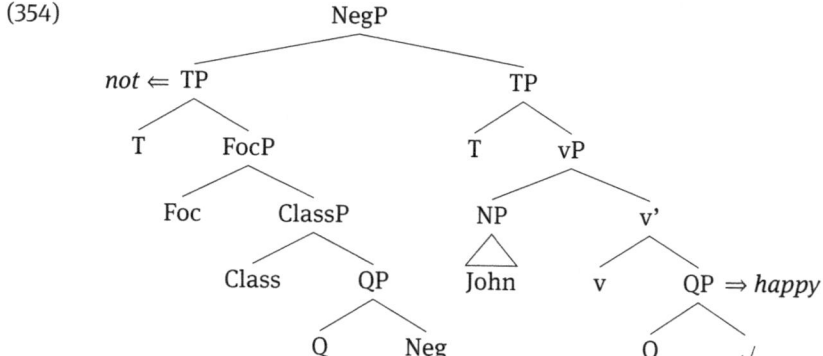

After that, the derivation will continue growing at the clausal level, i. e. AgrS will be added and the subject will move to a dedicated subject position, as we will discuss in section 6.4.2.

One may wonder at this point what happens when a negative marker, both prefixal and non-prefixal, is accented as in the sentences in (355):

(355)   a.   I'm happy to see that you've finally learned to act in an UNcareless way.
        b.   I'm NOT happy.

The effect of a negation carrying the main sentence accent seems to have the effect of giving rise to echo negation (Seuren 1976) or metalinguistic negation (Horn 1985, 2001b). The sentences in (355) seem to be associated to a speaker presupposition (Stalnaker 1978), i. e. the presupposition that the person in question's behaviour is usually careless, (355a), or that the speaker was supposed/expected to be happy by the interlocutor, (355b). The accented negative marker denies that existing presupposition (Vanden Wyngaerd 1999), i. e. functions as a plug rather than a hole (as negation usually does, cf. Karttunen 1973), thanks to polarity emphasis (Breitbarth et al. 2013b) or polar focus (Watters 1979). I want to argue that it is possible for all negative markers to attract the main accent and hence receive in situ polar focus. In a syntactic account to focus this would involve the option to merge a polar focus head on top of every projected NegP. However, one could also simply argue that the focus-marked element, i. e. the negative marker, gets a focus feature associated with it (Wilder 2013). Due to this focus feature the negative marker and the predicate it negates can outscope the entire proposition by moving covertly, as in the proposals by Erlewine & Kotek (2018), to a left peripheral focus position (Rizzi 1997), from where it can negate both the presupposition associated with the proposition and the proposition itself. A detailed investigation of these negative markers carrying sentence accent needs to be postponed to future work.

Before we move on to discuss the derivation of *n't* and how to derive POST-markers like English *-less*, some explanation on how to derive unproductive affixal negation is required.

6.3 Unproductive affixal negation

As things stand now and given the proposal for the lexical items in English in section 5.4, merge of the binary grouping Q and Neg will result in the spellout of *un-* in English. However, as we know, this is not always the correct spellout. Sometimes adjectival predicates combine with an unproductive Q^{NEG}-marker, i. e. *iN-* and *dis-* (cf. section 3.3.4). It is unclear at this point how the competition between the productive and the unproductive prefixes is regulated. I argue in this section that the spellout of these unproductive markers can be made possible by pointers, a tool used in nanosyntax to spell out idioms (Starke 2011a, 2014a), irregular or suppletive forms (Starke 2011a, De Clercq & Vanden Wyngaerd 2017a) or syncretisms in multidimensional paradigms (Caha & Pantcheva 2012, Vanden Wyngaerd 2018). The system is applied here to English unproductive prefixes, but is also valid for unproductive negative markers in other languages (like French, Czech, Hebrew, Hungarian, ...).

In what follows I first introduce how idioms or irregular forms can be spelled out in nanosyntax and then I apply this to the negative markers *iN-* and *dis-* in English.

6.3.1 Pointers

In nanosyntax irregular verb forms can be spelled out by making use of pointers (Starke 2011a, 2014a).[115] A pointer is a reference in the lexical tree of a lexical item (i.e. LI) to another LI. Pointers are used to account for suppletion, such as they are found in irregular past tenses (e. g. *bring-brought*).[116] The intuition behind point-

---

[115] For another introduction into spelling out idioms see Baunaz & Lander (2018b).
[116] The example is merely intended to illustrate how pointers work. It is not my intention to present the complete functional structure needed to derive past tense in English.

ers is that it allows to store links between lexical items in the lexicon. The verb *bring* could be listed in the lexicon in the way illustrated by (356a); its suppletive past tense *brought* would have the entry in (356b), with a past tense feature and a pointer to *bring*, the LI in (356a).

(356)   a.   < /bring/, [$_{VP}$ V], BRING >
        b.   < /brought/, [$_{T_{PST}P}$ T$_{PST}$ *bring*], BRING >

The pointer should be interpreted in such a way that *brought* may be inserted at T$_{PST}$P when in the previous cycle *bring* has been inserted. When the syntax merges VP, the LI in (356a) can be inserted, as shown in (357). Subsequently, past tense is merged, as in (358):

At this point, the lexicon is consulted and *brought* is inserted, overwriting the earlier spellout *bring*. Note that this derivation requires no movement, and therefore takes precedence over a movement derivation (according to the spellout algorithm), which would be needed to derive regular forms with the *-ed* suffix. This nonmovement derivation is restricted in its application thanks to the pointer in the entry of *brought*, which ensures that the nonmovement derivation is only available if in the previous cycle *bring* was inserted. This will avoid the situation that *brought* would get inserted for all verbs. With a regular verb like *walk-ed*, the root *walk* will spell out VP, with the suffix realising T$_{PST}$P after leftward movement of VP.

In the next section I show how this system of pointers can help in linking a specific unproductive negative marker to a specific word.

6.3.2 Spellout of unproductive Q^{NEG}-markers

I propose that the spellout of *iN-* (as in *impatient*) or *dis-* (as in *dishonest*) in English is the consequence of a lexical item which points to the structure for a regular Q^{NEG}-marker on the one hand and to a listed adjective on the other hand. The implication here is that these unproductive forms are stored as idioms or irregular forms.

First I present the derivation and LIs for *impatient* and then for *dishonest*.[117] To derive the spellout of *impatient*, the following LIs are used: an LI for regular Q-negation, repeated here as (359), an LI for the adjective *patient* as in (361), an LI which consists of two pointers, one to prefix *iN-* and one to the adjective *patient*, which will derive *impatient*. There is no conceptual nor phonological information associated to (362), since this information is in this particular case obtained from the parts pointed to.

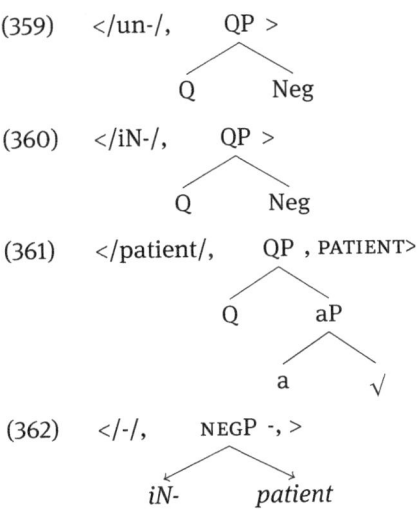

(359) </un-/,   QP >
                 Q   Neg

(360) </iN-/,   QP >
                 Q   Neg

(361) </patient/,   QP , PATIENT>
                     Q   aP
                         a   √

(362) </-/,   NEGP -, >
              iN-   patient

In what follows I will explain step by step how we derive *impatient*. However, I first need to say something about the two lexical items for negation in (359) and (360). As the reader may have noticed immediately, both lexical items have the same structure, which means that they will compete with each other for every single regular Q^{NEG}-marker. This is an unwanted result, since we do not want *iN-* to be inserted whenever *un-* is needed. We also disprefer storing *impatient* as one lexical item, as in (363), that overwrites the regular *un-* and *patient*, since this would obliterate the fact that *impatient* is clearly perceived as consisting of two

---

117 Newell (2008) argues that *iN-* conveys adjectival categorization, as opposed to *un-*. One of the stronger pieces of evidence supporting this claim is the fact that when *iN-* is combined with an acategorial root, it becomes adjectival, as in *inane*. Gibert Sotelo (2017) picks up on this and combines it with De Clercq's (2013) analysis of *iN-*, arguing that *iN-* has three features: [Q], [Neg] and [a]. Even if this categorial feature were adopted, this would not fundamentally change the need for pointers under the present analysis, because the co-occurrence of *iN-* with particular adjectives is unsystematic.

parts, a negative part *iN-* that is the irregular counterpart of *un* and the positive adjective *patient*.

(363)   </impatient/, NegP >

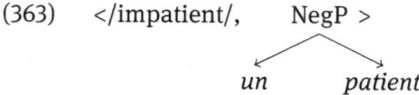

In order to block the insertion of *iN-* in the regular situations, I adopt an idea proposed by M. Starke (p. c.) and developed in De Clercq & Vanden Wyngaerd (2019b) concerning unproductive French lexical items. To be unproductive means to be not directly accessible for the syntactic computation, i. e. the lexical item in (360) is not accessible when the negative specifier is merged. It is only accessible when it is pointed to.

So when we start merging, the adjective is merged first and spelled out as *patient*. A [neg] feature will be merged, but since there are no lexical items with a unary [neg] bottom; this will not lead to a spellout, not even after movement of the adjective has taken place, as in (364).

(364)

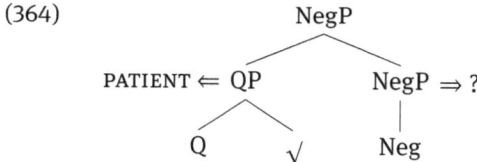

Consequently, the derivation will continue in a separate workspace, i. e. a complex specifier will be merged and spelled out as the Q^{NEG}-marker *un-*. The specifier is merged with the main derivation, and the lexicon is checked again at the phrasal node NegP. At this point, we need to say something about this part of the spellout procedure, since we have not yet mentioned checking the phrasal level at this point. However, this step happens every single time phrasal spellout has taken place and an extra spec-level has been created, either by movement or by merging a complex specifier. This extra layer of structure will also be checked against the lexicon. If no idiom, i. e. stored chunk with pointer, is available, the derivation simply continues merging. Absence of spellout at this level, does not lead to a crash, since the relevant feature has been spelled out (in this particular case Neg). So with respect to this particular NegP in (365), the lexicon contains a LI which has a pointer to *patient* and a pointer to *iN-*, the irregular negative prefix now becomes available and will replace the regular prefix *un-*.

(365)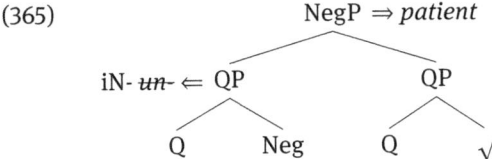

The same happens with an adjective like *dishonest*.¹¹⁸ The LIs are in (366)–(368). The LI for *dishonest* points to the irregular affix *dis-*, (367), and to the adjective *honest*.

(366)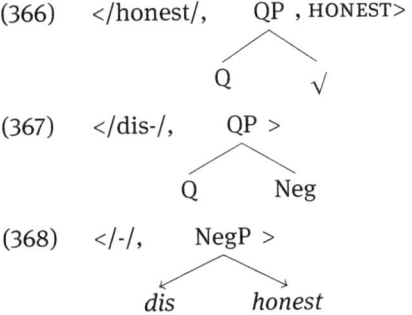

The derivation proceeds as outlined above for *impatient*, as shown in (369):

(369)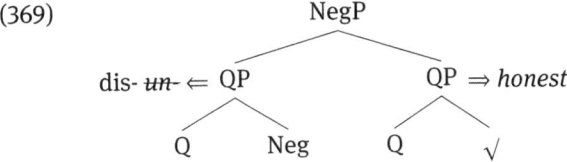

Under the present proposal the unproductive Q^{NEG}-markers are part of a series of listed unproductive negative adjectives that are stored and can only be accessed via pointers. As such, the irregular nature of the prefix is captured while keeping the intuition that they are similar to the Q^{NEG}-marker *un-*. The unproductively Q-negated adjectives are thus stored as lexical items without phonological and con-

---

118 Gibert Sotelo (2017) does not analyse Spanish *des-* as an intrinsically negative prefix, but argues that *des-* spells out a Source-path and that the negative meaning is a consequence of the interaction of this Source path in *des-* with the scalarity in the adjective.

ceptual information, but with two pointers, pointing to an unproductive negative prefix and to the positive adjective.[119]

6.4 Insertion of negative suffixal markers

Although most negative markers in English are PRE-elements or prefixal, two frequently used negative markers are suffixal. One is the denominal suffix *-less*, which has not been discussed much up until now, and the sentential negative marker *n't*, which is most commonly used in spoken English. In this section, I discuss the derivation of *-less* and *n't*.

6.4.1 *-less*

In section 3.3.4 above we discussed how the denominal negative marker *-less* cannot be combined with other Q^{NEG}-markers. We therefore concluded that these markers are in complementary distribution and share a substantial part of their featural make-up. However, this marker does not precede the predicate, but follows it and it turns nominals into adjectives, unlike the other Q^{NEG}-markers. In line with what we discussed in sections 5.4 and 6.2, the implication of the suffixal nature of the marker *-less* is that it has a unary bottom. We propose that the lexical item of *-less* is as in (370), spelling out the same features as for a regular Q^{NEG}-marker, in addition to a categorial *a*-feature.

(370) </less/,   NegP , >

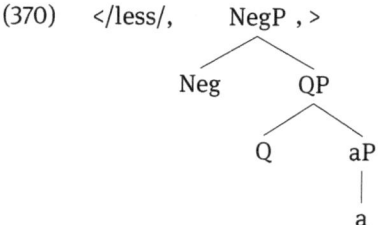

Note that unlike the other negative markers, this POST marker has Neg at the top. This explains why *-less* is not inserted every time a Neg is merged in the clausal spine. The reason why *-less* cannot be inserted in contexts when Neg is merged in

---

[119] The suppletive forms of the copular verb 'be' in MSA *laysa* or *není* in Czech and the existential verb *nincs* in Hungarian could also be derived by means of pointers. I will not elaborate further on these forms in this book.

the clausal spine is due to the Superset Principle. Consider the simplified syntactic derivation in (353) to illustrate this point. We see the derivation before the complex negative specifier is merged, i. e. as here in (371).

(371)
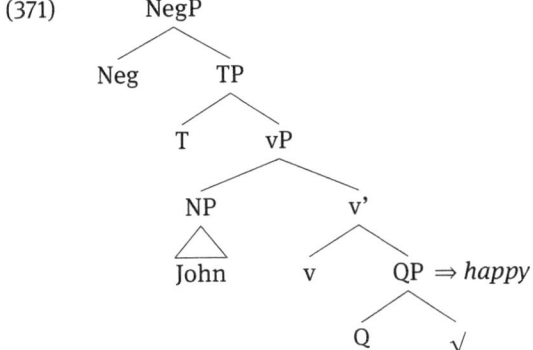

At this point, it is not an option to insert -*less*, not even after moving out the complement, as in (372), because of the Superset Principle.

(372)
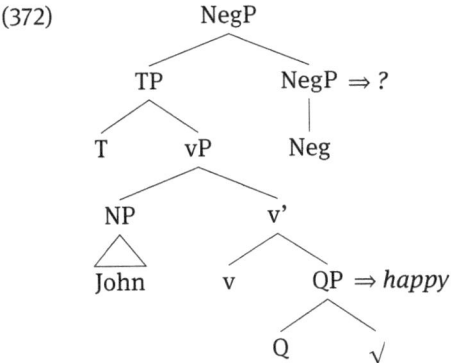

Even though -*less* has a unary bottom, the Neg-feature is at the top in the lexical tree in (370) and hence cannot match the syntactic structure, since the lexical tree does not contain the syntactic tree as a constituent. There is simply no way to insert -*less* in this syntactic configuration.

I will illustrate now how -*less* can be inserted for a word like *hopeless*. Assume the LI for *hope* in (373) and for -*less* as introduced in (370).[120]

---

[120] There is probably more functional material in the noun *hope*, but I abstract away from it for the sake of the present discussion.

(373) </hope/, nP , HOPE>

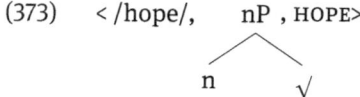

After syntax merged the structure that can be spelled out by *hope* (or any other mass noun), the little *a* feature, which turns nominals into adjectival structure, and the Q-feature, responsible for gradability, are merged. Thanks to the Superset Principle *-less* can spell out these features. However, *-less* will get competition from other suffixes at this point. One of these suffixes that will get into competition is the positive counterpart of *-less*, i. e. *-ful*. Due to the Elsewhere Principle it will be *-ful* that will win the competition, both at the level of aP and at the level of QP, and will be inserted after movement of nP to SpecaP and then consecutively to SpecQP.

(374)

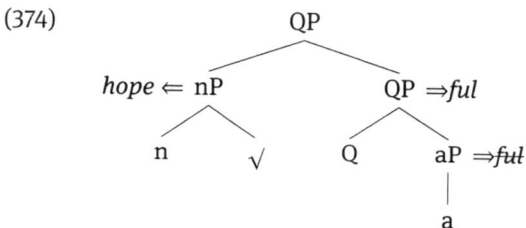

However, with the next merge step [neg] will be added to the derivation. Again without movement there is no spellout possible, but if the nP moves to SpecNegP, as in (375), *-less* can be inserted, since there is a perfect match now, also deriving the right word order.

(375)

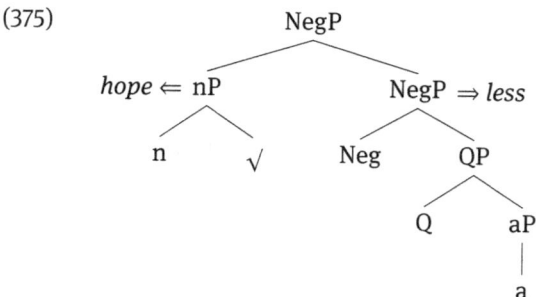

In the next section the derivation of the most common sentential negator *n't* will be discussed.

6.4.2 *n't*

In this section I want to discuss how the contracted sentential negator *n't* can be analyzed within the present nanosyntactic framework. Up until now I have mainly discussed the negator *not*, which is a PRE-marker like many other negators in English. However, given that *n't* is the only negator which unambiguously yields sentence negation and which looks like a suffix and hence a POST element, it is worthwhile devoting some discussion to this negator. As we will see, we will argue that *n't* is not a POST-marker, in spite of appearances.

The form *n't* has been argued to have come into use in the English spoken language around the year 1600 (Jespersen 1913). The rise of *n't* seems to have coincided with the loss of morphological agreement on the verb and an increase in the use of *do*-support (Jespersen 1917, Kroch 1989, Roberts 1993). Roberts (1993:305) argues that the rise of the use of the contracted *n't* goes hand in hand with the change from phrasal negation to head negation.[121] The underlying idea in this type of account is that *n't* is a reduced form of *not*, an idea present in many works on the syntax or grammar of English negation (Jespersen 1917, Roberts 1993, Zeijlstra 2004a:55). In essence this means that *n't* is considered a clitic in these approaches, an idea which has been strongly refuted by Zwicky & Pullum (1983), who consider the reduction a transitional phase to the current stage of *n't* as an inflectional affix. In what follows I will first present Zwicky & Pullum's (1983) arguments to consider *n't* an affix instead of a clitic, to then move on to the account that I will argue for in this book, i. e. that *n't* and the auxiliaries *n't* attaches to are stored in the lexicon as chunks, similar to how idioms are stored.

(376)   a.   You haven't been there.
         b.   You have not been there.

Under Zwicky & Pullum's (1983) account inflectional affixes (like plural *-s*, past tense *-ed*) differ from clitics (like *'s*, *'ve*) in being more selective with respect to a host, in showing arbitrary gaps or morphological and semantic idiosyncrasies in a paradigm, in forming one syntactic unit with their host, and in not being able to attach to other clitics. In what follows I illustrate some of their arguments. A first argument comes from subject-auxiliary inversion. This syntactic operation seems to be fed by the contraction of *n't*, as illustrated by the contrast in (377), where *n't* and the auxiliary seem to form one unit.

---

[121] That change more generally ties in with a preference for lowering of AGR to V instead of raising of V to AGR. Under such an approach, the newly formed negative head in NEG blocks movement of the verb to AGR, which is then left to be inserted by *do*.

(377) a. *Have not you been there?
       b. Haven't you been there?

Support for this comes from the contrast with *'ve* and *'s*, which do not trigger that effect, as shown in (378) (Zwicky & Pullum 1983:506). *n't* forms a unit with the auxiliary, whereas this is not the case for *'ve*, *'s*, supporting the idea that *n't* is an affix.

(378) a. You could've been there.
       b. *Could've you been there?

Another argument for the affixal nature of *n't* is in (379a) (Zwicky & Pullum 1983:506–7), which shows that *n't* cannot attach to other clitics, whereas clitics usually can stack, as shown in (379b). Hence, *n't* cannot be a clitic.

(379) a. *I'dn't been doing this unless I had to.
       b. I'd've done it if you asked me.

Another argument in favour of treating *n't* like an inflectional affix is the existence of morphological gaps, e. g. **mayn't* and **amn't*.[122] Moreover, there is an idiosyncratic form *ain't* which has no positive counterpart and which corresponds to negated *have, has, am, are* and *is*. Next to phonological idiosyncrasies, such as the deletion of /t/ in negative auxiliaries like *mustn't*, there are also semantic idiosyncrasies, as illustrated by the modals in (381). Whereas contracted and uncontracted negation trigger the same reading in (380), this is not the case with (381). While (381a) says that non-attendance can be forgiven, (381b) says that attendance cannot be forgiven.

(380) a. You must not go home.
       b. You mustn't go home.
(381) a. A good christian can NOT attend church and still be saved.
       b. A good christian CANnot/CAN'T attend church and still be saved.
           (Zwicky & Pullum 1983)

According to Zwicky & Pullum (1983), examples like those in (381) are problematic for accounts that derive *n't* from *not*, i. e. for the clitic-approach to *n't*, because these facts clearly illustrate that *n't* is different from *not*.

---

[122] See Bresnan (2001), Thoms (2017) for discussion of *amn't* in Scots. See also the results of the project Scots Syntax Atlas on https://scotssyntaxatlas.ac.uk/project-team/ See Yang (2017) for a mathematical approach to why this gap arises in language acquisition.

All the facts discussed above suggest that *n't* is not a clitic but an affix. However, since it takes an auxiliary and gives an auxiliary, it is clearly not a derivational affix. It is added to forms that are inflected for tense and therefore it makes sense to argue that it is an inflectional affix.

I want to adopt Zwicky & Pullum's (1983) arguments, in particular in so far as they are an argument against the idea that *n't* is simply the reduced version of *not*. Moreover, I adopt the idea in their proposal that auxiliaries with *n't* are assembled in morphology and not in syntax. The present account translates these ideas in nanosyntax by spelling out the auxiliary and the negative inflectional affix as one chunk, i. e. by means of phrasal spellout. In addition, I want to point to two further pieces of support for Zwicky & Pullum's (1983) claim.

First, as we saw in our discussion in chapter 4, from a typological perspective it is quite common for negation to be an inflectional affix and to form a negative verb in combination with an auxiliary or copular verb. Quite some languages in the sample have negative existential verbs or negative copular verbs, i. e. specific negative counterparts for the affirmative existential verb (e. g. Hungarian, MS Arabic, Chinese, Turkish, Malayalam etc.), as also mentioned in the typological sample in chapter 4. The English array of negative verbal forms, as illustrated in (382), looks like an instantiation of this phenomenon. The table is based on Yang (2017:219).[123]

(382)

could	couldn't		should	shouldn't
did	didn't		was	wasn't
does	doesn't		would	wouldn't
had	hadn't		am	*amn't
has	hasn't			ain't
have	haven't		are	aren't
	ain't			ain't
is	isn't		can	can't
is	ain't		dare	*daren't
might	mightn't		do	don't
must	mustn't		may	*mayn't
ought	oughtn't		shall	*shan't

It is not unlikely that one of these negative auxiliaries will at some point develop into a negator of its own, negating another auxiliary verb, much as discussed by Croft (1991). However, I will not dwell on the question whether English has entered Croft's cycle but will continue with the discussion at hand.

---

[123] It is beyond the scope of this book to go into the details of all these different lexical forms and in particular to provide a full analysis of the morphological gaps and the use of the tense/*phi*-feature conditioned suppletive form *ain't*.

A second piece of support for Zwicky & Pullum's (1983) analysis of *n't* as an (inflectional) affix comes from the nature of negative markers in English. The negative markers *non-*, *un-*, *dis-* and *iN-* are also affixes, be it derivational ones. Consequently, the majority of negative markers in English are affixal in nature. It is only the low scope Foc^NEG-marker that is not affixal. *n't* seems to have most in common with *iN-* and *dis-* in the sense that it cannot be productively used with all verbal forms, but only with a limited set of verbs. Like the other affixal markers, *n't* is part of a complex unit and cannot be spelled out independently. We will argue that *n't* is part of the spellout of lexically stored negative verbs, which spell out hierarchically ordered features including person features, NEG, T and ASP and Event-related features. English *n't* is in this way a real instantiation of the close link between tense/inflection and negation, as advocated for in section 3.3.1.

In what follows I will present the derivation of a sentence like *John isn't happy* and also how the derivation of this sentence differs from the derivation of a sentence like *John is not happy*. What this account of English negation shows is how the structure of the lexicon determines syntactic variation (Starke 2014b) i. e. the fact that there are two ways to express sentential negation in English, *isn't* and *is not*, is a consequence of the structure of the lexicon, i. e. the availability of stored chunks for negation and auxiliaries in addition to the availability of regular negative markers. The derivations presented here will be more detailed than those in previous chapters.

Syntax starts by merging a structure compatible with a gradable predicate, as in (383). At the level of QP, there will be many entries that consist of the right structure. In accordance with the principle of Free Choice, cf. section 6.2, the lexical item in (384) will be inserted.

(383)　　　　QP
　　　　　　／＼
　　　　　 Q　　√

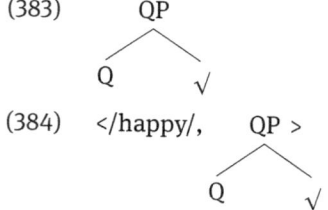

(384)　　</happy/,　　QP >
　　　　　　　　　　　／＼
　　　　　　　　　　 Q　　√

After the adjective *happy* is merged, the feature SMALL CLAUSE (Williams 1980), SC will be merged. I adopt this feature here to mediate the relationship between the non-verbal predicate and the subject. Merge of that feature will not lead to any spellout and so a complex specifier will be merged, giving rise to the subject and to a small clause structure in conformity with proposals in Stowell (1981), as in (385). Since it is not the aim of this book to get deeper into the how and why's of the merge of a subject in a predicate relationship, I move on here and I leave it for future research which features exactly are involved in merging a subject. After merge of the features related to the subject, the complex derivation will be closed off and merge in the main clause resumes.

(385)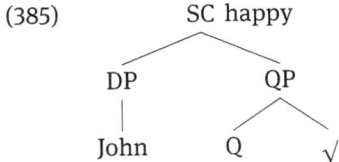

Since we want to build a copular clause, a linking/copular verb will be merged at the next level. I will use the more fine-grained labelling from Ramchand (2008), who distinguishes different event structural types depending on the lexical aspect of predicates and the role of the arguments in predicate structure. Dynamic verbs involve a Process Phrase, but stative predicates, including predicative copular constructions lack this projection, because they cannot have an undergoer argument but only rhematic and non-aspectual arguments. As such they only consist of an Event$_{Initiator}$ Phrase, which will be the next head that will be merged in syntax, (386). EVENT$_{Initiator}$ can be compared to PRED, which is also considered a crucial feature that turns non-verbal small clause complements into a predicate (Bowers 1993, Zwart 1997). EVENT$_{Init}$ was represented by the more common label vP in the earlier tree structures in this book.

(386)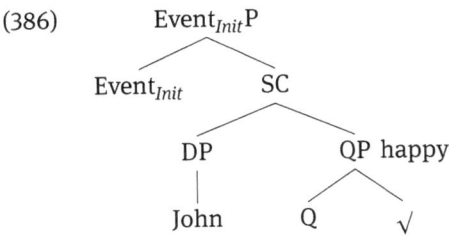

EVENT$_{Init}$ needs to provide us with the copula verb *be*. Before we continue with how insertion of *be* can take place, we need to say something about the internal structure of the copula *be*. I want to argue that the base of the copula *be* has the structure in (387), with the required EVENT$_{Init}$ head for stative predicates and an Aspectual feature for default simple Aspect. The internal structure of *be* will thus be able to capture not only the lexical role of *be*, but also its aspectual role (i. e. as auxiliary), and the fact that it interacts with illocutionary properties of the clause. For the inflected forms (*is, isn't, am*, etc) the idea is that these are all stored as chunks in the lexicon with a pointer to the verb *be* and with tense, person and number features added, as in (388)–(389). For the negative counterparts a NegP is added. Since it is not the intention to write a book on agreement morphology or aspectual morphology, I would like to emphasize that the internal structure of these verbal forms is possibly more complicated with respect to person/number and aspectual features and that the presentation in (388)–(391) is therefore possibly a simplification in this respect.

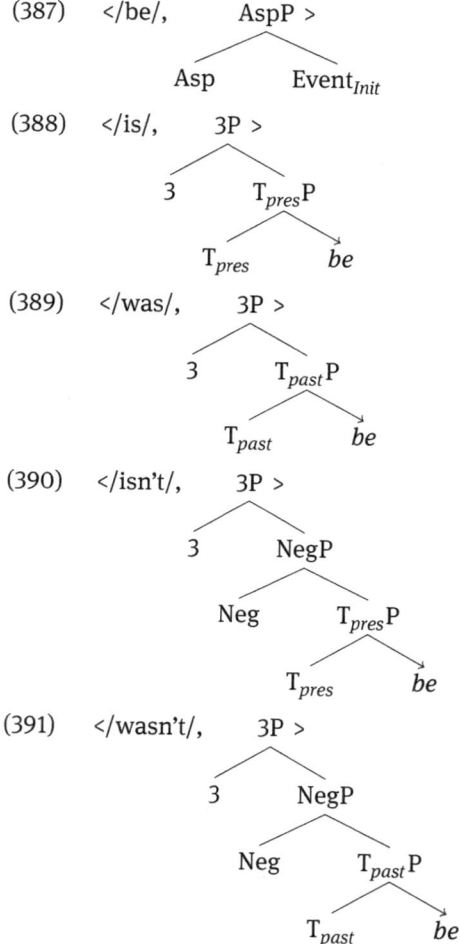

We left off with the merge of Event$_{Init}$, the head responsible for stative predicates. However, since copula *be* is not a suffix, it has a binary bottom, (387), and hence there will be no lexical item in English that has a lexical tree with a unary bottom with EVENT$_{Init}$ as its bottom feature. The first three steps in the spellout algorithm

6.4 Insertion of negative suffixal markers — 187

will be tried, as explained in sections 2.3 and 6.2 and repeated here in (392), but this will not lead to lexical insertion.

(392) a. Insert feature and spell out (= do not move)
       b. If fail, try a cyclic (spec-to-spec) movement of the node inserted at the previous cycle
       c. If fail, try a snowball movement of the complement of the newly inserted feature and spell out.
       d. If merge-f has failed to spell out (even after backtracking), try to spawn a new derivation providing feature X and merge that with the current derivation, projecting feature X to the top node.

As a final resort mechanism a complex specifier will be merged, as in the final step of the algorithm (d), to provide the fseq with the required Event_{Init}-feature. So at the point when a complex specifier is merged as a last resort, Event_{Init}, and the next feature required by the verbal fseq of copular verbs, Asp, will be merged, as in (393), leading to the spellout of *be* in the complex specifier.

(393)

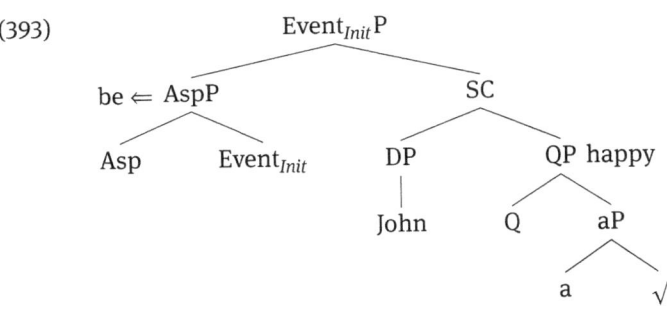

The new subderivation will continue as long as possible from this point in accordance with the verbal fseq for copular predicates. The critical reader will notice at this point that there is a small difference between how the complex specifiers for negation are merged and how complex specifiers for predicates/subjects are merged. Both complex specifiers merge a spine in accordance with the requirements of the fseq, i.e. the negative fseq, the verbal fseq, the fseq for subjects etc. However, whereas negative complex specifiers continue merging up until the point that the features in the complex negative specifier match the features in the clausal fseq, complex specifiers for predicates (and subjects) merge features according to the verbal fseq that have not yet been merged in the main spine. One of the ways to explain this is that there is a difference between how optional adverbial complex specifiers, like negation, are created and how complex specifiers that provide non-optional material, like predicates and subjects, are created. More research is necessary to determine whether the two proposed methods of complex specifier creation are indeed valid and whether the difference indeed coincides with functional differences of the constituents under discussion. For now, we will assume that there is such a difference and continue with the derivation for the copular verb 'be'.

The next feature in the verbal fseq is a tense-related feature. In this particular case, T_{pres} will be merged, (394), and (388) will be inserted. Insertion of *is* is not a violation of the Faithfulness Condition, discussed in 6.2, because the pointer to *be* in the lexical item of *is* allows the previously chosen lexical item to be overridden by this form. Next the optional feature [neg] can be merged. At this point there will be an immediate spell out available, because of the lexical item in (390). Merge continues, the person feature 3 is merged,(394), resulting again in the spellout of *isn't*, in conformity with the LI in (390).

(394)

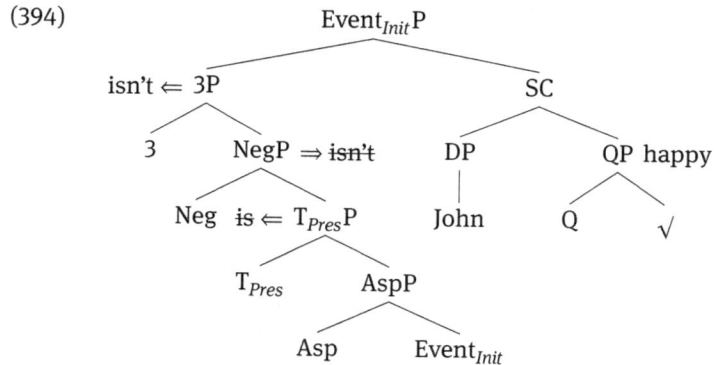

At this point the new derivation will come to its end, since all features relevant to the verbal fseq will have been tried to be spelled out. The complex specifier is closed off and the next feature of the fseq, i. e. AgrS will be merged in the main spine. Note that there is only one feature of this verbal fseq that is projected in the main spine, i. e. the base feature of the verb, $Event_{Init}$. More research is needed to know whether it is always the base feature that projects, or whether it could be the top feature as well. What also needs to be studied is whether there are advantages to merging the 'new' features merged in the complex specifier for the verbal predicate once more in the main spine, followed by subsequent movement of the complex spec to these features in the main spine, as such 'licensing' or 'validating' the features in the complex specifier. I do not wish to take a stance on this now and I leave this issue unresolved for now, since it does not bear on issues related to negation. Nevertheless, the final steps of the derivation, i. e. getting the subject and agreement with the subject in the right place, will illustrate how this type of movement of a complex specifier, i. e. syntactic movement, alternates with phrasal spellout.

AgrS will not find an immediate spellout, not even after spellout-driven movement. However, the complex constituent that was just closed off, consisted of agreement features and hence could be the right candidate to spell out AgrS. So what we are proposing now is that a constituent that has been merged before can be moved to satisfy the requirement of the fseq at a higher point. Introducing syntactic movement in a system that has for now been dominated by phrasal spellout requires that we update the algorithm that has been described before as a spellout algorithm, section 2.3, with a syntactic movement step. I want to propose that before merge and the first attempt to spellout phrasally, the derivation should be screened for whether syntactic movement can provide the required feature. As such, an attempt for syntactic movement preceeds merge and spellout-driven movement, allowing featurally rich constituents that have been merged at an early point in syntax to be internally merged at a higher point in syntax. I proposed these ideas for the first time in De Clercq (2019a) where I applied them to negative concord and n-words. The spellout algorithm, as we saw it, hence needs to be updated with a syntactic movement step, as in (395), which is ultimately also attempting to satisfy/spell out a feature, but then via internal merge.

(395) a. **Probe the derivation and attract a constituent with the next feature required by the fseq, i.e. F. If there is no such constituent available, move to b.**
  b. Merge F and spell out (= do not move)
  c. If fail, try a cyclic (spec-to-spec) movement of the node inserted at the previous cycle
  d. If fail, try a snowball movement of the complement of the newly inserted feature and spell out.
  e. If merge-f has failed to spell out (even after backtracking), try to spawn a new derivation providing feature X and merge that with the current derivation, projecting feature X to the top node.

As a consequence of this, the complex specifier *isn't* will be moved to the specifier of AgrSP, as in (396). The next feature to be merged is a feature hosting the subject. I adopt Subj here in an informal way, again keeping in mind that I am aware that there are more subject positions (cf. the introduction to this chapter). Again the derivation will be probed and the features on *John* will allow this constituent to be projected in SpecSubjP, according to step a in the algorithm in (395). The final movement steps are illustrated in (396).

(396)

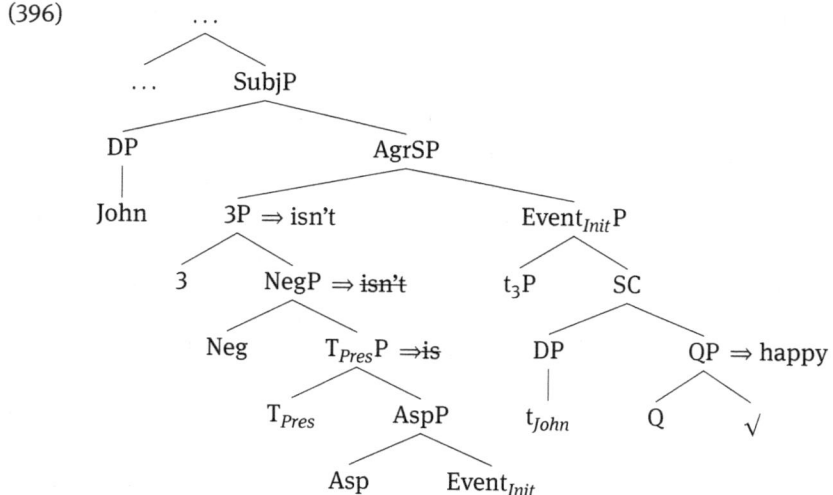

For the sentence *John is not happy* the complex specifier that projects Event$_{Init}$P will not consist of the optional NegP. I see two possible options for why this is the case. The first option is related to the fact that the lexicon of the formal variety of English does not consist of lexical items like (390), with a negated auxiliary chunk. As such, when [Neg] is merged in the complex specifier, the only option is to merge a complex negative specifier within the complex specifier, leading to a problem when [3p] will get merged: this feature will not get any spell out, leading to backtracking of the derivation, i. e. undoing the complex negative specifier, and merge of the next feature in line, [3], which will get a spell out at the point. The second option is that it could be argued that in the complex specifier that builds the copula one has the choice to merge the Neg below the agreement related feature [3] or to keep that for the main spine, given that NegP is an optional feature. I tentatively adopt the first hypothesis, but the result is the same under both hypotheses: *is* will be merged in the complex verbal specifier and at the level of the clausal spine, before AgrSP is merged, [Neg] will be merged in the main spine, leading to the insertion of the complex NegP, creating sentential *not*, as in (397). All other steps in the derivation are the same as explained before, but now there is no option to resort to the stored chunks spelling out *isn't*.[124]

---

[124] The underlying idea in this chapter is that *do*-support and its negative counterpart is a consequence of the fact that English has – also for these items – stored chunks in the lexicon, which kick in whenever negation intervenes in the spellout of the regular portmanteaus for tense and agreement in English. However, it is beyond the confines and the aim of this book to provide a full account of *do*-support and related issues like lowering or raising. I refer the reader to Pollock

(397)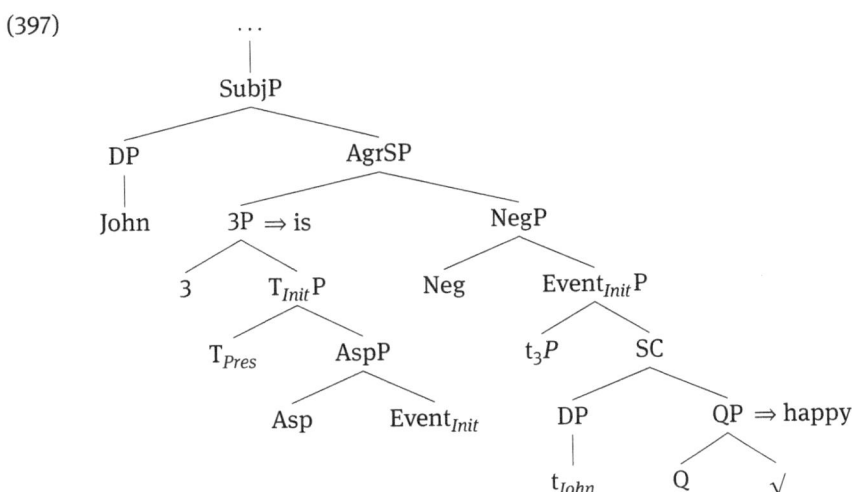

6.5 Conclusion

This chapter aimed at showing how complex negative markers of scopally different types, usually treated in different modules of the grammar, can be derived in syntax by means of the same spellout algorithm and the same technology. Moreover, the chapter explained why *un*, *non* and low scope *not* cannot be merged at the level of TP and why *n't* cannot be inserted at the level of QP. These facts are no longer a stipulation now, but they follow from the internal structure of negative markers that was laid bare by the study of syncretism patterns, cf. chapter 4. Moreover, the chapter also discussed how unproductive negative morphology can be captured by means of pointers and how the negative marker *n't* does not have an isolated spellout, but is part of a stored negative verb. In addition, it was explained how the difference between PRE and POST negative markers is a consequence of the structure of the lexicon. In the next chapter, the negative nanospine developed in this book will be used to explain bipartite negation and the diachronic development from stage IIb (BUF) to stage III (CF) in Jespersen's Cycle.

(1989), Vikner (1995), Bobaljik (2002), Alexiadou & Anagnostopoulou (1998) for discussion of the Verb Raising Parameter and to Chomsky (1957), Lasnik (1981), Kroch (1989), Roberts (1985), Halle & Marantz (1993), Bobaljik (1995), Embick & Noyer (2001), Han & Kroch (2000) and many others for accounts dealing with *do*-support.

7 Diachronic change in French

7.1 Introduction

In this chapter[125] I show how the system developed in this book offers all tools needed to tackle the change in the expression of sentential negation from le bon usage French, (398a) (henceforth BUF) (Grevisse & Goosse [1936] 1993, Rooryck 2017) to Colloquial French (henceforth CF), (398b).

(398)   a.   Je n' ai pas faim.
                 I NEG have neg hunger
                 'I'm not hungry.'
        b.   J' ai pas faim.
                 I have NEG hunger
                 'I'm not hungry.'

The analysis developed in this chapter can also be used to account for other types of bipartite negation, as for instance the pattern we see in Afrikaans. At the end of this chapter I will briefly explain how the system set up could be used to approach Afrikaans bipartite negation in copular clauses. However, the focus of this chapter will be French. I first explain why it is hard to capture bipartite negation in a formal system and what proposals have been made, then I explain how bipartite ne…pas can be derived for *le bon usage* French. Finally, I discuss how the change to stage III of Jespersen's Cycle, i. e. to CF, can be captured. I refer the reader to section 4.2.1.2 for a discussion of the different stages in Jespersen's Cycle and how it applies to the French negation system.

7.2 Bipartite negation

7.2.1 Asymmetry and formal analyses

What this section focuses on is the obligatory presence of *ne* and *pas* for the expression of sentential negation in BUF and how these facts follow naturally from the decomposition of negation. More in particular, the analysis presented here accounts for the paradox that *ne* and *pas* give rise to: each of them seems to convey negation, but they do not give rise to a double negation effect. Whereas the inherent negativity of *pas* is evident from the fact that *pas* is also a constituent

---

[125] Some parts of this chapter go back to De Clercq (2017). However the analysis has fundamentally changed. A related paper on French negative concord is De Clercq (2019a).

https://doi.org/10.1515/9781501513756-007

negator, the inherent negativity of *ne* is less immediately obvious. However, there must be something crucial about *ne* that forces it to be present in the realisation of sentential negation in bipartite patterns in BUF.

The paradox with respect to *ne* ...*pas* has been accounted for in the literature mostly by means of asymmetric approaches to the problem (cf. Breitbarth & Haegeman 2010:68 for the term): either by considering *pas* to be the only inherently negative element with *ne* acquiring negativity via Dynamic Agree (Rowlett 1998b:28; Rizzi & Roberts 1996:76) or Agree (Roberts & Roussou 2003:154–155, Roberts 2007:64–81) or by considering *pas* to be semantically negative with *ne* an NPI (Zeijlstra 2009). A problem with respect to the latter approach is that if *ne* were an NPI, then its obligatory presence in CF in data like (399) remains unexplained, (399).

(399)   Julie *(ne) boit   plus.
        Julie ne   drinks more
        'Julie no longer drinks.'

The reason why asymmetric approaches are favoured is because formal systems are, due to their categorial nature, better equipped to capture asymmetry than symmetry or near-symmetry. Under an asymmetric approach one of the two markers needs to be made non-negative, whilst the other one should be negative. But if this is the case it is hard to argue why the non-negative element is still necessary in a particular stage of Jespersen's Cycle and how the interdependence works at the point in history when both elements are equally necessary to render sentential negation (cf. Willis 2011:94), i. e. in stage IIb, the stage BUF is in (cf. section 4.2.1.2).

The trigger for change from stage I to stage II and from stage II to stage III is the topic of an ongoing debate in the literature. There are proponents of a pull-chain approach (Breitbarth 2009:85) and proponents of a push-chain approach (Breitbarth 2009:86). The current proposal can be categorised as a push-chain approach. Under a pull-chain approach, the original preverbal negator *ne* in French is considered the trigger for change. The idea is that at some point this marker was so strongly phonologically weakened that it became too weak to express negation on its own (Jespersen 1917). Arguments against this approach have come from Posner (1985:177), who argues that phonological weakening does not necessarily lead to the development of a new negator, as is the case with the negator in South Central Italian dialects. Under a push-chain approach, the origin of change lies in changes within the new negator, i. e. it is the use of a new emphatic marker that pushes the original negator away Meillet (1921), (Hansen 2013:51–53). This empathic element is first optionally used with the preverbal negator, until it becomes a compulsory element to express sentential negation in Stage II. When the new negator starts functioning as a regular negator, it pushes away the preverbal negator and the language enters stage III (Willis et al. 2013:1–50). According to Detges & Waltereit (2002) and Kiparsky & Condoravdi (2006) it is due to the overuse of the emphatic construction that the negative construction is bleached over time and ultimately replaces the original preverbal negation. For French this means that the strengthening of the preverbal *ne* is optional at first. However, at some point the generic noun *pas* is used as an emphasizer for negation (next to other emphasizers). When this noun grammaticalises as a new category and consistently starts co-occurring as a negative adverb with the preverbal negator, it pushes aside the preverbal negator *ne* (Willis et al. 2013:1–50).

Most problematic for the current asymmetric approaches is that they force *ne* to be present for the expression of sentential negation by stipulation. Under the present account, we try to do away with this stipulation and argue that in BUF both negative markers lack the necessary features to give rise to sentential negation, i. e. both are featurally defective. As such, they need each other to give rise to sentential negation. The difference between *ne* and *pas* in BUF boils down to a structural difference in this approach: *ne* consists of a Mood and Tense feature, whereas *pas* consists of Foc, Class, Q and Neg. Only the combination of T, Foc, Class, Q and Neg can yield what is conceived of as sentential negation and hence two lexical items need to be activated to express sentential negation in BUF. With respect to CF this analysis implies that at some point the lexical structure of *pas* grew and started spelling out five features, making *ne* redundant for the expression of sentential negation. Therefore, the present analysis is a push-chain approach. The structural growth of *pas* and the concomitant increasing deficiency of *ne* (Cardinaletti & Starke 1999, Breitbarth et al. 2013c) are thus crucial in the diachronic change that takes place between *le bon usage* French (Stage IIb of Jespersen's Cycle) and colloquial French (stage III). Under the current approach the idea that emphasis is crucial for *pas* to become a real (constituent and bipartite) negator, as advocated for in the other push-chain approaches discussed above, is kept, but the current proposal deviates from the previously mentioned approaches in that emphasis is not lost in *pas* in the change from stage IIb to stage III. It is rather the case that *pas* acquires more features, allowing it to be used in more environments and hence pushing aside the old negator. It is possible that the extended use of *pas* will lead to a loss of emphasis over time, with new markers developing emphatic negative properties, thus pushing aside *pas* followed by loss of emphasis. However, it is hard to predict that this will be the cycle of change for French *pas*. Under the current approach it is assumed that loss of emphasis took place in *ne* when it entered stage IIb.

As such, the nanosyntactic tenet that the internal structure of lexical items determines the syntactic variation (Starke 2014b) is exemplified in this chapter

7.2.2 BUF analysis

In this section I propose an analysis for bipartite negation in a sentence like (400).

(400)   Il   n'est pas heureux.
        he NEG is NEG   happy
        He is not happy.

I propose that the lexicon of BUF contains the following lexical items for negative markers:

(401)   a.   < /iN-/, [$_{QP}$ Q Neg] >
        b.   < /non/ [$_{ClassP}$ Class [$_{QP}$ Q Neg]] >
        c.   < /pas/ [$_{FocP}$ Foc [$_{ClassP}$ Class [$_{QP}$ Q Neg]]] >
        d.   < /ne/ [$_{MoodP}$ Mood T]] >[126]

With respect to LI (401d) I assume that it is due to the fact the lexical item of *ne* consists of more features than just a T-feature that *ne* can also be used as an expletive marker in *le bon usage* French. Rowlett (1998a) mentions the examples of expletive *ne* in (402).

(402)   a.   Elle a   peur que tu   ne sois   là.
             She has fear that you NE be.SUBJ there
             'She's worried you might be there.'
        b.   Je doute qu' il   ne soit   là.
             I doubt that he   NE be.SUBJ there
             'I doubt he's there.'   (Rowlett 1998b:28)

The association of *ne* with (subjunctive mood) as in (402a)–(402b) has fed into the feature structure of (401d). Polarity and subjunctive mood have often been argued to be linked, since both occur in nonveridical contexts, i. e. contexts where

---

[126] As mentioned in the introduction to this chapter the idea is that *ne* lost its emphatic features once it entered stage IIb. The negative spine for *ne* was still complete in stage IIa. However, due to the structural growth of *pas* (acquiring focus features in stage IIa), *ne* loses features, i. e. it loses all its negation related features below T including its negative anchor, turning it into a deficient negative marker.

the truth of a proposition p is open in the sense that p is not entailed or presupposed (Giannakidou (1998, 2016)). Moreover, the rich variety of TAM-conditioned negative allomorphs of the stantard negator mentioned in chapter 3 (section 3.3.1 footnote 23) strongly suggests that what I have referred to as the T-layer in sentential negative markers possibly needs to be decomposed further, including Mood- and possibly Aspect-related features. I keep this for future research, but I want to mention this again since this makes the sudden appearance of [Mood] in (401d) less surprising.[127]

To move away from the more complex issues related to the spellout of irregular verbs in French, I will use the copular verb *sembler* in the rest of this section for the analysis of the sentence in (403).

(403)   Elle ne semblait pas heureuse.

Syntax will start Merge with the adjective in the way that is familiar by now, leading to the spellout of *heureuse*, followed by merge of the subject in the complex specifier SC, standing for SMALLCLAUSE, right above it, leading to a small clause structure. I use SC here, but I leave in the middle what feature is responsible for the creation of small clauses and I refer the reader to Stowell (1983), Bowers (1993) for discussion of small clause structures. Next the feature relevant for the copular verb will be merged. As we did for the analysis of the English sentences in chapter 6, I follow Ramchand (2008) and argue that stative predicates like copular verbs consist of a feature EVENT_{Init}. In addition, a default Aspectual feature will be merged, which allows them to be linking verbs at the propositional level. It will not be possible to spell out EVENT_{Init} with or without movement and hence the last step in the algorithm, (395), will be tried. A complex specifier will be merged with the EVENT_{Init} feature and ASP feature at the bottom, which will provide the label in the fseq.

---

[127] I assume it is possible that *ne* consists of even more features, including for instance other features above TP, since its association with comparative than-constructions, as in (i).

(i)   Marie est plus grande que n' est son frère.
      M.   is more tall   than NE is her brother
      'M. is taller than her brother is.'

However, this assumption does not change anything about the current analysis, hence I will not dwell on it.

(404)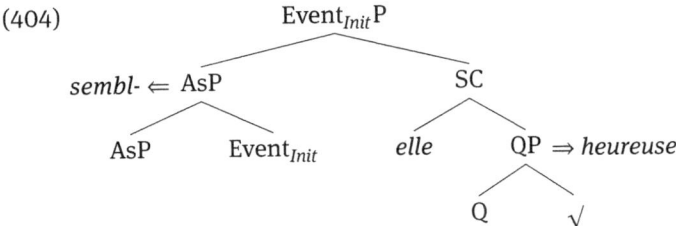

In accordance with what we said about complex specifiers in section 2 and section 6.4.2, this new derivation containing the verb, will continue as long as possible and merge tense features, person features and negation features if necessary.

The inflection on *sembl-* is thus achieved within the complex specifier. Without going into the details of the particular lexical items and lexical trees of French agreement and tense markers, which would go well beyond the confines of this book, we assume—in line with Estivalet & Meunier (2016)—that there is a systematic array of independent markers for Agreement and Tense on the verb. First, T_{PST} is merged within the complex specifier and spelled out as *-ai-* after snowball movement of the complement of T_{PAST}.[128]

(405)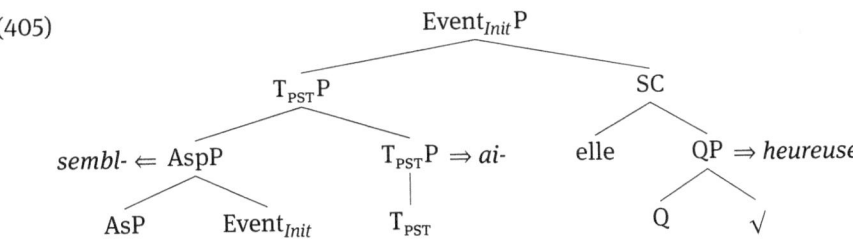

Second, third person singular will be merged, captured here by the feature [3], and will be spelled out as *-t*. The derivation is in (406).

(406)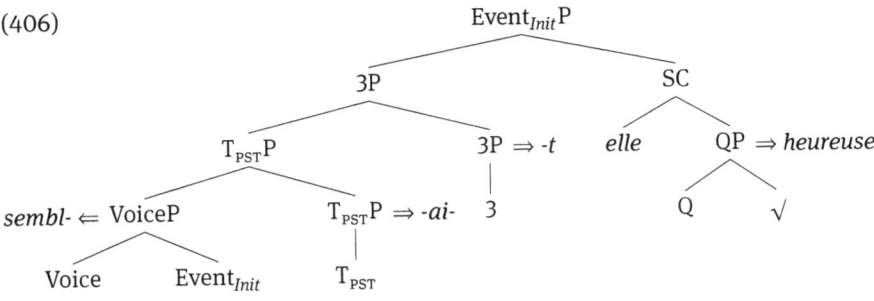

---

[128] In line with Estivalet & Meunier (2016) I assume that the thematic vowel *e* in *sembler* is derived from Latin *a*. In the past tense this *a* reappears, which is why I take the thematic vowel up in the spellout of Tense.

All features related to the verbal nano fseq have now been spelled out, so the complex specifier closes off and in a next step Neg is merged in the clausal spine. All regular movement options of the algorithm are available and will be tried, but without success. So the complex specifier for negation will be merged and the feature for negation, required by the fseq at that point will be merged and projected in the main spine. However, at the point when TP inside the complex specifier is merged, there will not be a way to spell out this feature. It is not possible to attract any constituent to this position inside the complex NegP, nor will movement lead to any spellout. As a consequence, inside this complex specifier, which is basically a new derivation in yet another new derivation, another complex specifier will be merged, which will allow us to spell out *ne*. The required default T-feature and the next polarity related feature in line (see discussion above) will be merged, i. e. Mood. This will allow for the spellout of *ne*. The derivation looks as in (407):

(407)

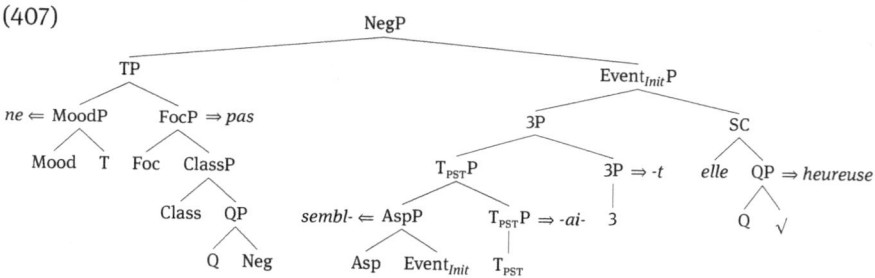

The complex specifier for negation will be closed after this, having merged all features required by the fseq for negation at that point and the main clausal spine will continue merging. AgrS is the first feature in line now. The derivation will first be probed for a constituent that can provide this feature (in conformity with the updated algorithm in chapter 6, section 6.4.2 (395)). The verbal constituent with the agreement features will be a candidate to satisfy the requirement of the fseq and will hence be moved. The agreement features, represented here by [3], will project AgrSP in the main spine. Next Mood will be required in the clausal spine, which we assume sits high up in the TP-domain (see Cinque 1999:76 for a more fine-grained distinction of Mood projections), the derivation will again first be probed in accordance with the updated algorithm in section 6.4.2 and the constituent spelling out *ne* will be attracted. Finally, the subject will move and project SubjP, attracted by the requirement of the fseq to merge Subj (one of the possible positions for subjects, as discussed in section 6.1).

(408)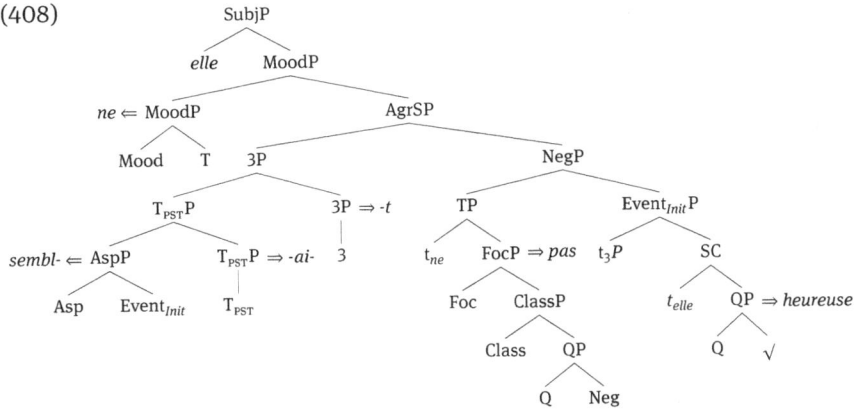

In sum, we discussed in this section how a simple copular clause can be derived in French within nanosyntax. We discussed how the updated algorithm, cf. chapter 6 section 6.4.2, allows complex constituents that are merged lower down to be attracted to satisfy the featural requirements of the fseq. Most importantly, we saw how *ne* was merged as a complex left branch within the complex left branch that spells out *pas*. In the next section we discuss how in CF a change in the structure of the lexicon pushes *ne* away, slowly turning it into an expletive negator.

7.3 Colloquial French

In present day spoken French, i. e. CF, *pas* has become the real sentence negator. The lexical tree for *pas* has grown in size. It has become a T^{NEG}-marker.

The evolution of *pas* is visible in the lexical items: *pas* spells out four layers now, (409c). As a consequence, *ne*, which is still part of the lexicon, becomes redundant, i. e. it is pushed away (push-chain approach), since merging *ne* in a complex specifier will not happen if the easier phrasal spellout option with *pas* is available.

(409)   a.   < /iN-/, [$_{QP}$ Q Neg] >
        b.   < /non/ [$_{ClassP}$ Class [$_{QP}$ Q Neg]]>
        c.   < /pas/ [$_{TP}$ T [$_{FocP}$ Foc [$_{ClassP}$ Class [$_{QP}$ Q Neg]]] >
        d.   < /ne/ [$_{MoodP}$ Mood T] >

At the point when it comes to merging the negative nanospine in the newly spawn derivation, there will be a spellout at the level of TP, i. e. *pas* (409c). There is no need for a movement internal to the new complex left branch and hence *ne* is no longer necessary to fulfill the requirements of sentential negation.

7.4 Two additional notes

7.4.1 A note on grammaticalisation and negative arguments

De Clercq (2017) briefly discusses the relation between grammaticalisation and the diachronic development for French worked out in this book. Often grammatical reanalysis is thought of as involving upward change along the functional hierarchy, i. e. a lexical item becomes functional over time due to structural or featural simplification (Roberts & Roussou (2003), Van Gelderen (2004)). We saw something similar for Jespersen's Cycle: new negative elements start out lower in the functional hierarchy, as predicate negators (Chatzopoulou 2013), and they climb up along the spine, until they reach the propositional level (Chatzopoulou 2013). The present account offers a novel way of looking at diachronic change, and more in particular at the Jespersen's Cycle. Within nanosyntax grammaticalisation does not only involve structural simplification (Roberts & Roussou 2003), but it involves both growing complexity and simplification of lexical items at the same time. For example, the introduction of *pas* as a negator in French in stage II of the Jespersen's Cycle leads to a competition with *ne*. The new negator wins the competition that is regulated by the Superset Principle. The old negator can either be reanalyzed (and lose features) or get out of use. Crucial in this approach is that change starts in the new item, i. e. in *pas*, which gains features rather than that the old negator loses features.

The process of grammaticalisation in general could be viewed as one involving the loss of grammatical features in certain lexical items, with a concomitant gain of these same features in different lexical items. This is because the features in themselves are not lost, i. e. there is an fseq, but there is a redistribution in the way these features are expressed. One might say that there is a law of Feature Conservation, which ensures that in the grammatical system as a whole, features are not lost. While feature loss may occur at the level of individual lexical items, it needs to be compensated for in other lexical items. I discuss this issue with respect to French negative concord in more detail in De Clercq (2019a).

7.4.2 A note on Afrikaans

Afrikaans has the well-know property that every negative marker or negative argument needs to be accompanied by a clause final marker *nie* (Waher 1978, den Besten 1986, Biberauer 2008, Biberauer & Zeijlstra 2012). In a copular clause the bipartite negation pattern that we see is illustrated in (410):

(410)   Hy is nie moeg nie
        he is NEG tired NEG
        'He is not tired.'

The clause final *nie* is an obligatory element in all possible sentences expressing sentential negation (Huddlestone 2010:42).[129] The contrast between the data in (411a) and (411b) confirms that clause final *nie* is crucial for the expression of sentential negation.

(411)   a. Hulle sal oor niks   baklei nie (en ons ook nie).
            they will over nothing fight   SN (and us also SN)
            "They won't fight over anything (and us neither)"
        b. Hulle sal oor niks   baklei (*en ons ook nie).
            they will over nothing fight   (and us also SN)
            "They will fight over nothing."(i. e. "They will fight over the smallest thing.")   (Huddlestone 2010:42)

We will not dwell on the concord and double negation patterns that arise in combination with negative arguments and adverbs (Biberauer & Zeijlstra 2012), but the bipartite pattern in (410) deserves our attention, since it presents us with a problem for the analysis proposed in the previous section. If bipartite negation is indeed the spellout of two pieces of the same negative spine, then it is unexpected that the same morpheme would be able to spell out these two different pieces. The default assumption under the current syntactic approach would be that the two lexical items *nie* must somehow be related since they are syncretic and they express negation. If they are related, then we expect there to be one lexical item in the lexicon for *nie* that can spell out both instances of *nie*. However, this is exactly where the problem lies. Since clause final *nie* can co-occur with n-words that can give rise to double negation, without contributing any extra negation itself, it seems that the clause final *nie* is more a scopal marker than a real negator. As such we need to get a non-negative element out of a spine that has [neg] at the bottom. Under the current version of the Superset Principle and the Elsewhere Principle this is not possible: the bottom feature of the spine, i. e. [neg], will always have to be part of the structure spelling out *nie*. One way out of this problem is that we assume – as for French BUF – that the clause final *nie* is spelling out the top layer in the negative spine and that the medial *nie* expresses the lower layers up until

---

[129] An exception is the environment in which two instances of *nie* would co-occur at the end of a sentence: the clause final one is deleted then. Biberauer (2008) explains the obligatory deletion of *nie* as a case of haplology.

the Foc^{NEG}-layer, including negation. However, this hypothesis implies that we assume that there are two different homophonous elements *nie* in the lexicon, each with a different structure. Another option is that we change how the fseq for negation is set up. Instead of having the negative feature at the bottom of the negative nanospine, we could argue that the negative feature comes at the top. If this is the case, the lexical item for *nie* could spell out both a negative sentential marker, including the upper layer, but also a positive element. However, this hypothesis has the disadvantage that the position for the negative feature in the nanospine is flexible and can be on top of any of the other non-negative features, depending on how many different negative markers there are in a language. Moreover, this structure for lexical items would imply that all negative markers can be used as positive elements as well, a claim which – though sometimes definitely true – seems an overgeneralisation. Both solutions work, but both solutions come with some disadvantages. I leave it for future work to decide what the best solution is.

7.5 Conclusion

The obligatory co-occurrence of both *ne* and *pas* in *le bon usage* French follows under my account from (i) the fact that both *ne* and *pas* are part of the same spine and (ii) the way the lexical items are stored in the lexicon, i.e the LI for *ne* is small and structurally deficient and cannot override *pas*. As a consequence, as long as *pas* is still a constituent negator, *ne* will be spelled out whenever sentential negation needs to be expressed. However, as soon as *pas* becomes a full-fledged sentential negator the structurally deficient *ne* is pushed away and can no longer serve as the spellout of the TP-layer in the negative nanospine.

Moreover, this case study of French negation showed that the nanosyntactic tenet that language variation boils down to differences in the size of lexical trees (Starke 2014b) is well-equipped to account for diachronic change. The change from bipartite negation in stage IIb of Jespersen's Cycle to the use of a postverbal negative marker in stage III is reflected by a change in size of the lexical items, as described above. Diachronic change is under the present account characterised by concomitant gain and loss in the feature structure of lexical items. Finally, we discussed two options to tackle bipartite negation in Afrikaans.

Part IV: **Remaining issues**

8 Other syntactic perspectives on negation

8.1 Introduction

The proposal presented in this book is a morpho-syntactic account of different types of predicate negators that turn out to be connected in more intriguing ways than we knew before. The absence of ABA patterns shows that negative markers across the functional-lexical divide are united in a meaningful way and can hence be decomposed in subatomic features. In addition, the syncretism patterns also provide an argument to treat all negative markers within one module of the grammar, i. e. syntax, and they indirectly suggest an fseq for lexical categories, i. e. V > N > A, which opens up interesting avenues for future research (Baker 2003).

At a surface level, the way of decomposing negation in this book finds its closest resemblance in the syntactic work by Poletto (2008, 2017) and is a natural extension of the cartographic work on negation in general (Zanuttini (1991), Haegeman (1995), Zanuttini (1997)). Moreover, as illustrated in De Clercq (2013, 2017) the account can be made compatible with the minimalist tradition, but since this defies the nanosyntactic principle 'one feature one head', it was deviated from in the present book.

In the present chapter I want to briefly discuss the proposal laid out in this book against the background of some of the syntactic literature on negation. Up until now I referred to the literature on negation where necessary, but never really embarked upon a comparison or discussion given the quite different nature of the proposal presented here. Nevertheless, this book is deeply embedded in the literature on negation and highly influenced by it. In what follows I will point out how the proposal in the present book compares to and deviates from proposals made by Zanuttini (1997), Poletto (2008, 2017) and Cormack & Smith (2002).[130]

8.2 Multiple NegPs

Since the postulation of a NegP by Pollock, researchers started thinking about how to capture the fact that negation seems to be able to surface in different positions in the clause.

---

[130] I refer the reader to Horn (2001b) for a detailed introduction into the philosophy, logic, semantics and pragmatics of negation and to Penka & Zeijlstra (2010), Haegeman & Lohndal (2013), De Swart (2016) for concise introductions to the vast topic of negation, each focusing on it from different angles.

Zanuttini (1997), whose work is deeply rooted in the cartographic tradition, studied the position of negative markers in combination with verbal predicates in 150 different dialects of Romance. Based on the position of these negative markers with respect to functional adverbs in the clausal spine (Cinque 1999), Zanuttini concludes that sentential negation can appear in at least four different positions which she labelled $NegP_1$, $NegP_2$, $NegP_3$ and $NegP_4$. The different positions are illustrated in the tree structure in (412), based on Zanuttini (1997:101).

(412)

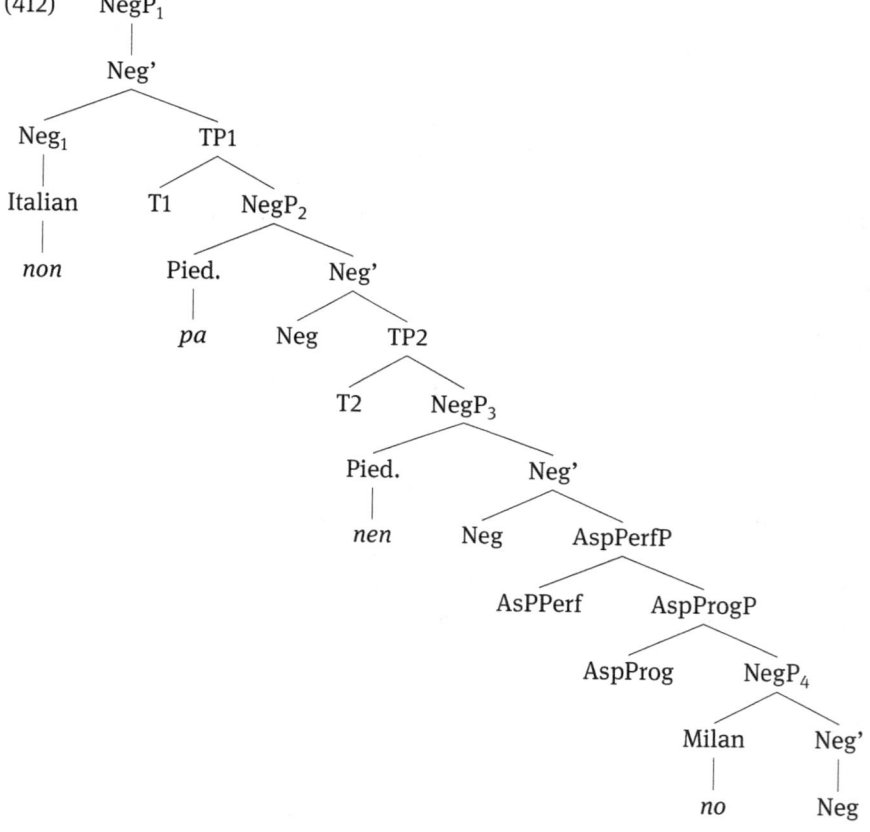

Neg1P is the position for negators which negate the clause on their own, as for instance Standard Italian *non*, (413), which is considered a head.[131]

---

[131] Zanuttini distinguishes between preverbal negators which negate the clause on their own and preverbal negators which do not negate the clause on their own. The former are in Neg1P, the latter are merged in Neg2P and head-move to be adjoined to a functional head in between Neg1P and TP.

(413)   Gianni non ha   telefonato a sua madre. (Standard Italian)
        Gianni NEG has called   to his mother
        'Gianni hasn't called his mother.'   (Zanuttini 1997:3)

NegP2 is the position for presuppositional negators like Piedmontese *pa*, (414), or Italian *mica*. These negators precede adverbs like *già* 'already' and *più* 'no more'.

(414)   A   l'è   pa gia   parti. (Piedmontese)
        S.CL S.CL.is NEG already left
        'He hasn't already left.'   (Zanuttini 1997:69)

NegP3 hosts negative markers like Piedmontese *nen* which precede an adverb like *sempre*, (415). Poletto (2017:83) argues this is the position for negative elements whose etymological origin is related to the meaning 'nothing'.

(415)   A   l'ha   nen dine   sempre tut.   (Piedmontese)
        S.CL S.CL.has NEG told.us always everything
        'He hasn't always told us everything.'   (Zanuttini 1997:73)

Negative markers like Milanese *no* which occur in a position lower than *sempre* 'always', (416), and higher than *tut cos* 'all' are hosted by NegP4.

(416)   L'a   semper pagà no i   tas. (Milanese)
        S.CL.has always paid NEG the taxes
        'It's always been the case that he hasn't paid taxes. (Zanuttini 1997:89)

Zanuttini hypothesizes that all markers which surface in NegP2, NegP3 and/or NegP4 need to move covertly to NegP1 at LF to give rise to sentential negation. Some further crucial properties of the negative markers in these positions are that only NegP1 can block subject clitic inversion, i.e. T to C movement. NegP1 and sometimes NegP2 can trigger a change in the morphology of the imperative, i.e. trigger allomorphy or suppletion, and interact with clitics, but NegP3 and NegP4 do not. NegP1 always requires negative concord, NegP2 and NegP3 only rarely and NegP4 never. Poletto (2017:86) provides a summary of these properties and this summary is repeated in table 8.1.

Zanuttini sees these properties as support for the claim that there must be four different positions for sentential negation. Poletto's work on negation starts from these four positions detected by Zanuttini, but she argues that instead of being merged in these positions, the negative markers move to these positions from a position within vP. The idea of negative markers that can move, can be traced to Cinque (1976), who identified that *mica* can also appear in preverbal position and hence must have moved there from the postverbal position where it usually

Table 8.1: Properties of negative markers, after Zanuttini (1997), Poletto (2017).

	Neg$_1$P	Neg$_2$P	Neg$_3$P	Neg$_4$P
Position	pre T	pre AnteriorT	pre genericAsp	pre vP
V to C interference	+	–	–	
Negative concord	+	+/–	–/(+)	–
Compatible with true imperatives	–	+/–	+	+
Reorders with clitics	+	+/–	–	–

surfaces. Also Manzini & Savoia (2011) argue that NegP$_3$ and NegP$_4$-markers occasionally appear in different positions than where they are supposed to occur on the basis of Zanuttini's proposal, even in very low positions, as illustrated by means of a Neg$_3$-marker in (417). The marker in (417) occurs below the adverb *yet*, while Zanuttini (1997) argues this type of negator sits above *yet*.

(417)   i dormu ŋku naint
          they sleep yet neg3
          'They don't yet sleep.'

In order to account for both the generalisations in Zanuttini's work and the exceptions to them in Manzini & Savoia (2011)'s work Poletto proposes that NegP is merged in a very low position in the structure, inside vP and that this NegP is internally complex, basically consisting of the four types of markers distinguished by Zanuttini. In addition to adding a movement hypothesis to Zanuttini's work, Poletto relates Zanutini's four positions to etymologically different types of negative markers.

> Each negative marker singled out by Zanuttini corresponds to an "etymological type" in the sense that all elements found in a given position have developed from homogeneous classes. (Poletto 2008:63)

Poletto labels the negative markers in NegP1 scalar negative markers. The negative markers in NegP2 she calls Minimizers, because of the historical origin of these negative markers as minimizers (Poletto 2017). The negators in NegP3 she refers to as quantifier phrases, because these negators are historically derived from a quantifier with the meaning 'nothing'. The negators in NegP4 are referred to as focus markers, because they are always stressed and because they take the same shape as the polarity particle 'no'. Poletto's main claim is that Pollock (1989)'s idea concerning French negative doubling, i.e. bipartite negation, should be pushed further to capture also instances of doubling and tripling in the North Italian dialects. While Pollock (1989) argued that the negativity of *ne ... pas* and the crucial interdependence of the two elements can be captured by splitting up the two parts of the negation over the head and the specifier of one functional projection, Poletto proposes to combine this idea with the need to capture Zanuttini's generalisations about multiple NegPs and the exceptions noted by Manzini & Savoia (2011). Therefore, NegP is decomposed into at least four features with the etymological labels discussed above. This entire complex NegP is basegenerated low.[132] Poletto (2008) argues for the Big NegP in (418), whereas Poletto (2017) argues for the similar but slightly more truncated structure in (419). I will discuss the implications for negative doubling with respect to her most recent proposal.

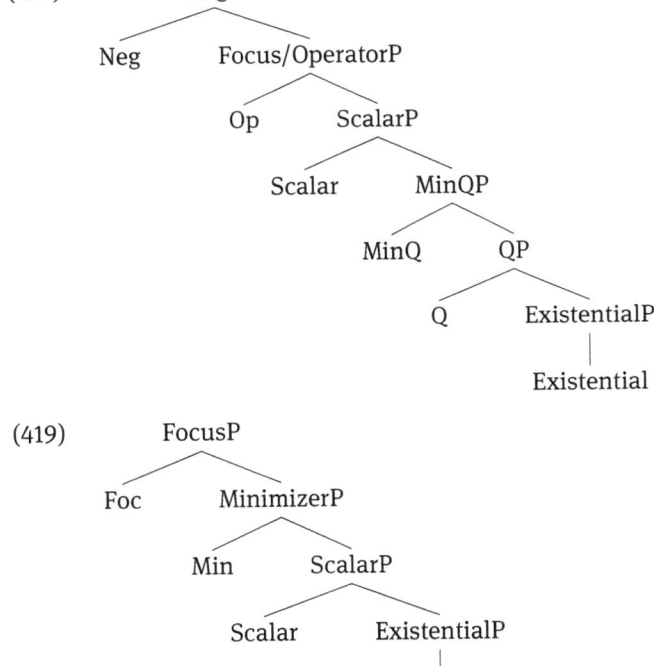

Poletto's Big NegP-analysis manages to capture cases of negative doubling, (420) and tripling, (421), in the Romance dialects.[133]

---

[132] The proposal that different components are one unit at some level of the derivation is not new and goes back to Kayne (1975)'s and Belletti (2005)'s proposal for DP doubling.
[133] Doubling or tripling involves the co-occurrence of two or three negative markers which together express one semantic negation. It should be distinguished from negative concord, which

(420) a. Nol   me piaze
        NEG.it me pleases
        'I do not like it.'
     b. Nol   me piaze   miga
        NEG.it me pleases not
        'I do not like it.'
     c. Nol   me piaze   gninte
        NEG.it me pleases nothing
        'I do not like it.'
     d. Nol   me piaze   NO
        NEG.it me pleases no
        'I do not like it.'

(421) a. No la go   miga magnada NO!
        NEG it have not eaten   not
        ' I did not eat it.'
     b. Nol   me piaze   gninte NO!
        NEG.it me pleases not   NOT
        'I do not like it at all.'

Poletto (2017:95–97) discusses that only certain patterns give rise to standard negation. Other patterns, like those with * in table 8.2 can only give rise to non-standard negation, "referring by the latter to those negative markers that can only occur under certain pragmatic conditions related to the speaker's or addressee's expectations." Poletto argues that more research needs to be done to understand why certain patterns do not occur to give rise to standard negation, whilst others do.

Table 8.2: (non)standard negation.

standard negation	Neg$_1$P	Neg$_2$P	Neg$_3$P	Neg$_4$P
Emilian area	yes	yes	–	–
Rhaetoromance area	yes	–	yes	–
Trentino area	yes		yes	
*	–	yes	yes	–
*	–	yes	–	yes
*	–	–	yes	yes

involves the co-occurrence of two (or more) negative indefinites or one or more negative indefinites and a negative marker.

Poletto (2008) base-generates the Big NegP on vP, because 'some negative markers show sensitivity to Aspect, which is located quite low in the IP' (Poletto 2008:58). In Garzonio & Poletto (2013) it is suggested that the base-position may even be within vP, a proposal that she also adopts in Poletto (2017). Poletto (2017:90) illustrates how the low predicate Big NegP interacts with the four positions distinguished by Zanuttini (1997):

(422)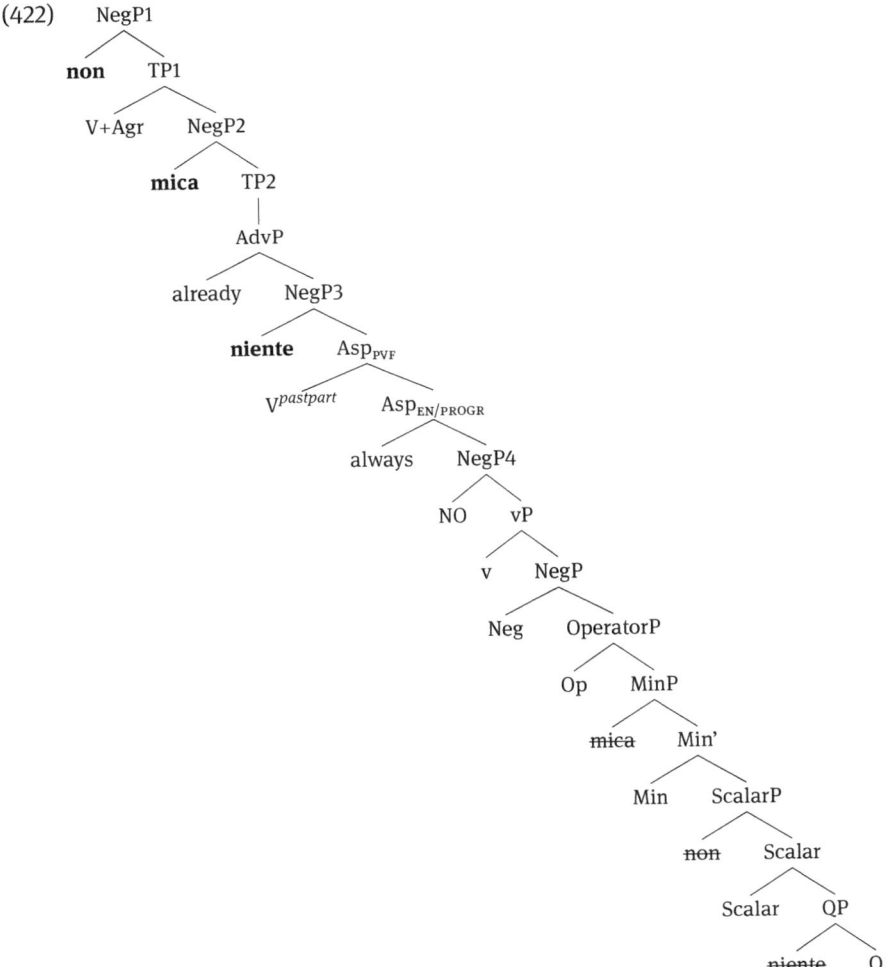

There are some crucial differences between the proposal in the present book and the proposals developed by Zanuttini and Poletto. I discuss them here. First, Poletto's and Zanuttini's proposal focuses on sentence negation. It reveals how within the dialects of one standard language, i. e. Italian, different strategies can be used to give rise to sentence negation, whereas I distinguish four positions that cut across the sentential-constituent-lexical divide, across the syntax-morphology divide and even across categorial divides (VP/AP). Their proposal does not involve negations that have traditionally been resorted under the labels constituent or lexical negation. In order to be able to evaluate Zanuttini's and Poletto's study with respect to mine, it is crucial to get a better overview per dialect of which negators can express sentential negation on their own, which negators could also give rise to constituent and lexical negation and which negators always need to co-occur with another negator. Only in this way can we get a systematic overview of how our approaches can be compared. What is for sure is that both Poletto's proposal and mine suggest that NegP can be merged very low in the structure, albeit that her proposal is different in merging the entire spine very low (as I also proposed in De Clercq (2013)), whilst the present book proposes to merge certain types of negators very low, whilst others are merged higher, depending on their featural properties. Second, the methodology used to arrive at the multiple positions is different in the current study and in Zanuttini's and Poletto's work. Whereas Zanuttini's work derives the four positions of negation in Italian dialects on the basis of the interactions with adverbs and syntactic properties like those listed in 8.1 and Poletto's work in addition investigates the etymological origin of the negators in these positions, the present account arrived at four different positions for negation on the basis of syncretism patterns between scopally different negative markers in a sample of 23 languages from different language families. Third, due to the fact that Zanuttini and Poletto zoom in on one particular type of negative marker in one group of languages, i. e. the Italian dialects, their results are necessarily different. While their work involves the interaction of sentential negation with temporal and aspectual adverbs, the current study aimed at understanding which negative markers can be ïNdexstacking stacked, i. e. which negations cancel each other out. It is therefore probable that a closer investigation of what I label T^{NEG}-marker and potentially also Foc^{NEG}-marker, leads to a more finegrained decomposition that captures possible TAM-alternations and that shows overlap with the four distinctions made in Zanuttini's and Poletto's work.[134] More concretely, what Zanuttini refers to as $NegP_1$ and $NegP_2$ most probably instantiates a decomposition of the sole position for negation that I distinguish above TP. However, the reason that I only have one is that the aim of my research was to discover which negative markers can give rise to stackable negation and I have

---

[134] My new project has this topic as its focus, i. e. studying negative allomorphy triggered by TAM-alternations.

not encountered a language in my sample where two so closely related negative markers can stack. The prediction is that the negative markers in NegP1 and NegP2 are not stackable in the sense that they will give rise to double negation together, which turns out to be true (cf. Poletto 2017). One of the two positions is possibly sensitive to alternations under the influence of TAM (cf. footnote 23 in chapter 3). Zanuttini's NegP3 and NegP4 could be compatible with the position for negation above clause internal FocP that I discussed. Once more it is my hypothesis that aspectual distinctions allow for these different positions between TP and vP, but that markers in those two positions will not give rise to a double negation reading together. More fine grained analyses of the sentential negative marker in interaction with the verbal domain are needed for all languages in my sample to see whether the distinctions Zanuttini/Poletto proposed are transferrable to other languages and language families. Fourth, the role of the lexicon is crucially different under both approaches. Even though Poletto dives into the internal structure of NegP by decomposing negation, the internal difference for instance between Italian *non* and French *ne* cannot be read off the position these markers get in the structure in (422). Both elements will be located in Poletto's ScalarP, even though *ne* cannot negate a sentence on its own in *le bon usage* French nor in Colloquial French (cf. chapter 7), whilst Italian *non* can do that. For Poletto (p. c.) the lexicon provides the crucial and necessary information to capture the distribution of these negative markers. Under the present proposal the internal structure of *non* and *ne* is crucially different, with *ne* being featurally defective as opposed to *non* (cf. 7). The distinction and distributional differences between negative markers is – under the present account – reflected in the size of the lexically stored trees. Fifth, the labels used for the decomposition of NegP are very different in Poletto's and my work, though some elements clearly return in both approaches. Poletto's work is deeply vested in tracing the etymological origin of the four positions distinguished by Zanuttini. Under the present account the scopal behaviour and distributional properties of a negative marker provided the label for the features inside the complex negative marker. Finally, the way bipartite negation is treated in both approaches is the aspect that can be best compared. Both approaches capture the intuition that the two parts involved in the expression of bipartite negation are spellouts of what is actually one unit. Furthermore, the approach in this book and Zanuttini/Poletto's approach is in many ways different since the study object is essentially very different: whilst the aim of the current study is to find syncretic markers across scopal divides, the aim of Z/P's work is to provide a fine-grained cartography of sentential negative markers.

Cormack & Smith (2002)'s approach to negation is also worth mentioning with respect to this book, since their work does not only discuss multiple positions for negation related to sentential negation, but they are also concerned about scopally different positions. They distinguish a position for echoic negation, one for polarity negation and a position for (what they refer to as) adverbial negation. In their system the LF interpretation of heads relates to the initial merge position of heads and is unaffected by subsequent movement, which is why they assume three different positions for negation to explain the contrasts in (423), and the ambiguities and interactions between negation and modality, as illustrated in (424)–(425).

(423)   a.   John often snores
       b.   *John not snores
       c.   John will not snore
       d.   *John snores not

(424)   a.   John may not come home late. MAY NOT / NOT MAY Edwin should not eat peanuts. SHOULD NOT / *NOT SHOULD

(425)   a.   Shouldn't you be at work? *Q SHOULD NOT /Q NOT SHOULD
       b.   Should you not eat meat? Q SHOULD NOT/ Q NOT SHOULD

Cormack & Smith (2002)'s echoic negation corresponds to a position in the left periphery, above C, devoted to negators like *n't* illustratedin (426).

(426)   Shouldn't you be at work?

Cormack and Smith's polar negation is illustrated in (427), and their adverbial or constituent negation is illustrated in (428).

(427)   a.   Leslie did not scream.
       b.   Leslie didn't scream.

(428)   The burglar might have not been in a hurry.

The LF sequence they propose is in (429) and apart from the three positions for negation it also consists of two positions for modals, of which the second one can also be filled by auxiliaries.

(429)   Echo C T (Adv1) Modal1 Pol (Adv2) Modal2/Aux ...(Adv) V

Even though this account recognizes the relevance of low scope negation for the syntax of negation and to capture the reading *can > not* in (430c), the account differs in many ways from the current proposal in not including lexical negation on the one hand and creating a dedicated position for echoic negation in the left periphery.

(430) a. John can not eat vegetables (deontic)
b. 'It is not the case that John is permitted to eat vegetables' NOT CAN
c. 'It is permitted that John not eat vegetables' CAN NOT

In the present study none of the languages under discussion had a wide scope dedicated negator in the left periphery that cannot at the same time also function as a T^{NEG}-marker. Therefore, I argue that what is a dedicated position for negation in Cormack & Smith (2002) is a derived position for negation in the present account, i. e. a position which interacts with other base-generated positions for negation and which can possibly be assimilated to the left peripheral FocP (as discussed in chapter 3). Furthermore, Cormack & Smith's (2002) Polarity negation is compatible with the position for T^{NEG}-markers in the present study and their adverbial negation overlaps with the position for negation related to low FocP in the present study, i.e. the Foc^{NEG}-marker. Even though the present study does not focus on the interaction with modality, it should be equipped to capture the same interactions, since the current system adopts similar positions as they do.

Other accounts for English that make use of two positions for negation are Moscati (2006), Temmerman (2012), Van Craenenbroeck & Temmerman (2017), Holmberg (2013). All these accounts distinguish a position above TP from a position above vP, which basically coincides with the two scopal positions that I discern above TP and vP and where I argue T^{NEG}- and Foc^{NEG}-marker-markers are generated.

8.3 Conclusion

In this section I discussed some syntactic approaches to negation which I consider very relevant for the present proposal. In particular I highlighted the similarities and differences between Zanuttini's and Poletto's approach to negation, two approaches which have at first sight most in common with the syntactic account developed in this book. However, I showed that the overlap is actually rather minimal, since their work focuses solely on sentential negative markers, whilst the present study is concerned with domains for negation that give rise to double negation. The main overlap consists in how negative doubling, i. e. bipartite negation, can be captured in both approaches. Finally, the chapter concludes with a short discussion of Cormack & Smith's (2002)'s work whose scope positions coincide with 2 positions also distinguished in the present account.

9 Semantics

9.1 Introduction

This book offers first and foremost a morpho-syntactic account of negative markers.[135] Nevertheless, in this chapter I would like to provide an onset for how the semantics of negation underlying this proposal could be looked at. More in particular, what I want to show is that the semantic effect of [Neg] can change depending on the syntactico-semantic features it interacts with. This chapter will present a case study to this effect, showing in detail how in the context of scales, [Neg] may give rise to contrary opposition. The general starting point is that the [Neg] feature that I have claimed to be present in all types of negative markers has a semantics which is that of logical (i.e. contradictory) negation. Concretely, I view negative markers as modifiers of predicates, in line with the proposal Collins & Postal (2014) make for negation in general:

(431) [Neg] takes X with semantic value $\lambda P_1 \ldots \lambda P_n [\ldots]$ and returns Y with semantic value $\lambda P_1 \ldots \lambda P_n \neg [\ldots]$

As Collins & Postal (2014:15) state, (431) 'is actually a schema for an infinite number of semantically different NEGs. : $\lambda P_1 \ldots \lambda P_n [\ldots]$. For propositional variables p, the negation is simply ¬p'.

Concretely, I will show how the scalar negators that are syntactically Q^{NEG}-markers contain a [Neg] feature with contradictory meaning, and how this underlying contradictory negator gives rise to contrary opposition. The idea is that the presence of the other features (Q, Class, Foc, T) inside negative markers determines the scope of the negative marker. In addition, the particular scopal environment may also affect the meaning of contradictory [Neg] and give rise to the different types of negation, functionally and semantically. However, this meaning is derived, since the basic meaning of [Neg] is contradiction.

Important to stress before we move on is the fact that even if a full semantic account were developed, this will not obviate the need for the syntax developed in this book. The reason for this is that two identical negations, i.e. negation with the same scope, cannot be stacked, as the empirical work in this book shows. In syntactic terms, negative markers, and the NegPs that host them, are always structurally separated from each other. This idea is one of the main results

---

135 Sections 9.2–9.6 of this chapter is based on joint work with Guido Vanden Wyngaerd (De Clercq & Vanden Wyngaerd 2018).

of this work and referred to as a *Neg-Neg constraint in De Clercq & Vanden Wyngaerd (2017b, 2019a) (cf. section 3.3.4). A simple semantic constraint against the stacking of negations will not do to capture this fact, since there is nothing semantically wrong with the stacking of multiple negative operators, as illustrated in (432).

(432)   ¬¬P(x)

9.2 Setting the scene

I shall illustrate the working of [Neg] in gradable adjectives with the following pair:

(433)   a.   Linus is tall.
        b.   Linus is short.

Neither of the adjectives in (433) features an overt negative marker, but as argued in De Clercq & Vanden Wyngaerd (2019a) (see also section 3.3.4 above), negative adjectives like *short* in (433b) do contain a [Neg] feature, i. e. they are the phrasal spellout of a structure like (434):

(434)

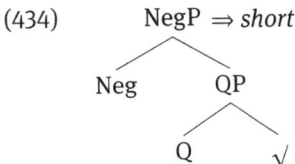

Scales involving physical dimensions like height have somewhat different properties from the scales involved in a pair like *happy-unhappy*, as I shall show in section 9.7 below. For now, I will use the pair in (433) even though it does not contain an overt negative marker, as the properties of the respective scales which are relevant in this context are not different.

It is a well-know property of antonymic pairs of gradable adjectives that they give rise to contrary opposition, i. e. the sentences of (433) cannot be true together, but they can be false together, namely in a situation where Linus is neither tall nor short, but of average height. As already pointed out in section 3.4 above, the same is true for the scalar negator *un-*, whereas a negative marker like *not* typically gives rise to contradictory opposition:

(435)   a.   Mark is happy.
        b.   Mark is unhappy.

(436) a. Linus is tall.
b. Linus is not tall.

Again, (436a) and (436b) cannot both be true, but now they cannot both be false either.[136] This is because Linus is either tall or not-tall, and cannot be anything in between. In contrast, there is a neutral area between *tall* and *short* which counts as neither tall nor short. This neutral area is represented by the dotted line in Figure 9.1. In contrast, there is no neutral area between the two red lines, which represent the domain of *tall* and *not tall*; nor is there one between the two blue lines of *short* and *not short*.

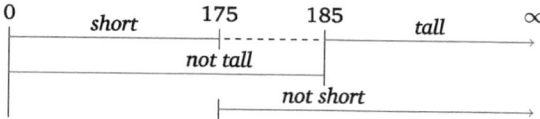

Figure 9.1: Contrary and contradictory opposition.

What we can conclude from that is that the sentential negator *not* gives rise to contradictory opposition, but that antonymic pairs like *tall-short* are related by contrary opposition (see also Horn 2001b).

A crucial question is why negation sometimes gives rise to contrary opposition, as in the case of antonymic adjectives or *un*-negated adjectives, and sometimes to contradictory opposition, as in the case of the sentence negator *not*. In what follows I argue that – in spite of the different internal structure of these negative markers – the same [Neg] feature is present in antonymic adjectives like *short*, a negative marker like *un-*, and the negator *not*. Differences in interpretation arise due to interaction of Neg with the surrounding features, also packaged with the internal structure of the negative marker itself. For Q^{NEG}-markers the feature that determines the shift of [Neg] to a contrary interpretation is a contextual standard related to the interpretation of gradable adjectives.

In section 9.3, we introduce the notion of an interval or extent, and show how positive and negative extents are related by a relation of contradictoriness. Sec-

---

136 I abstract away here from the fact that a sentence like (436b) may have a reading where *not tall* gets a stronger meaning, equivalent with *short*. Horn (2001b) takes this to be a pragmatic effect, which involves the pragmatic strengthening of a contradictory negation to a contrary one. Such pragmatic strengthening is not found with the negative pole of the scale (*not short*), nor with nonscalar predications (e. g. *John laughed-John didn't laugh*). Also see Krifka (2007), Ruytenbeek et al. (2017).

tion 9.4 discusses the context-dependence of gradable adjectives. In section 9.5 we show how the contrary opposition can arise from the presence of an underlying contradictory negation.

9.3 Extents

The analysis of gradable adjectives that we propose draws heavily on Seuren (1978), whose analysis is based on interval semantics, in which gradable adjectives are taken to denote intervals or extents (Seuren 1984, Von Stechow 1984, Löbner 1990, Kennedy 2001, Roelandt 2016).

An extent is a part of a scale. A scale $\langle S, <_{DIM} \rangle$ is a linearly ordered set of points along a dimension DIM. An extent E is a nonempty subset of S with the following property (Landman 1991:110):

(437) $\quad \forall p_1, p_2 \in E, \forall p_3 \in S, [(p_1 < p_3 < p_2) \rightarrow (p_3 \in E)]$

Assume further a degree function d_{DIM}, which maps any entity x which can be ordered along some dimension DIM onto a unique point on the scale $\langle S, <_{DIM} \rangle$. This unique point divides the scale into two intervals or extents, a positive and negative one, as defined in (438):

(438)   a. $POS_{DIM}(x) = \{p \in \langle S, <_{DIM} \rangle \mid p \leq d(x)\}$
        b. $NEG_{DIM}(x) = \{p \in \langle S, <_{DIM} \rangle \mid \neg[p \leq d(x)]\}$

Suppose, for example, that d_{HEIGHT}(Kurt) = 167; then the corresponding positive and negative extents can be represented as in (439) (the orientation of the square bracket indicates whether or not the point next to it is included in the extent).

(439)   a. POS_{HEIGHT}(Kurt) = [0, 167]
        b. NEG_{HEIGHT}(Kurt) =]167, ∞[

A graphical representation is given in Figure 9.2, with the red line the positive extent of x, and the blue line its negative extent.

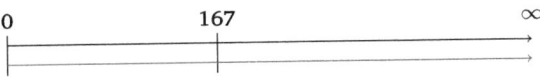

Figure 9.2: Positive and negative extent.

Intuitively, positive and negative extents entertain a relation of contradictoriness: together, they exhaust the universe (i. e. the entire scale), and there is no neutral area in between them. We formalise this idea by adopting the following definitions of contradiction and contrariety:

(440)   a.   Contradiction
$$A \cup B = \mathcal{U}$$
$$A \cap B = \varnothing$$
          b.   Contrariety
$$A \cup B \neq \mathcal{U}$$
$$A \cap B = \varnothing$$

Contradictory opposition involves a relation between two items where their set-theoretic union amounts to the Universe $\mathcal{U}$. In the case of contrariety, set-theoretic union yields less than the universe. In either case, the intersection of both sets is empty. Let us first show that this set-theoretic definition can be applied to propositions. This is done by taking the denotation of a proposition to be the set of situations in which it is true (Van Fraassen 1971). Two propositions are then contradictory if their union equals the Universe of all possible situations, and contrary if their union does not denote the Universe. In either case, their intersection will yield the empty set: the set of situations where both propositions are true is empty, i. e. they cannot be true together.

But the definitions in (440) also work to directly establish a relation of contradictoriness between extents, since extents are sets. By (440a), the relation between the positive and negative extent in (439) (and in the corresponding Figure 9.2) is a contradictory one: their union is the entire scale, and their intersection is empty. In the case of contrary opposition, the union of the two sets thus is less than the Universe: this can be seen in the top line of Figure 9.1, where the blue line of *short* and the red one of *tall* together do not amount to the entire scale. Here too, the intersection of the two sets is empty.

The contradictory nature of the opposition between positive and negative extents follows directly from the presence of logical negation (¬) in the definition of a negative extent in (438b) above. More concisely, we may therefore define a negative extent as follows (see also Von Stechow 1984, 2008):

(441) $NEG_{DIM}(x) = \neg POS_{DIM}(x)$

This will be important when we take the next step and look at the relationship between antonymic adjectives.

A crucial assumption is that positive gradable adjectives denote a positive extent, and negative gradable adjectives a negative extent, as shown in (442) for the pair *tall-short* (see also Kennedy 2001, Heim 2008):

(442) a. ⟦tall(x)⟧ = POS$_{HEIGHT}$(x)
       b. ⟦short(x)⟧ = NEG$_{HEIGHT}$(x)

That is, ⟦tall(x)⟧ is the set of degrees to which x is tall, whereas ⟦short(x)⟧ is the set of degrees to which x is not tall. The antonymic pair in (442) therefore stands in a relationship of contradictoriness, for the reasons just explained.

Given the equation in (441) above, we can now assume that negative scalar adjectives contain a logical negation in their internal structure (as proposed in De Clercq & Vanden Wyngaerd 2019a).

(443) ⟦short(x)⟧ = ⟦¬tall(x)⟧ = ¬POS$_{HEIGHT}$(x) = NEG$_{HEIGHT}$(x)

The arboreal representation of this is given in (444). Gradable adjectives involve a [Q] feature (cf. chapter 5), which semantically contributes an ordering. Negative gradable adjectives add a [Neg] feature.

(444)   NegP = ⟦short(x)⟧ =]r, ∞[$_{HEIGHT}$
          /   \
        Neg   QP = ⟦tall(x)⟧ = [0, r]$_{HEIGHT}$
              / \
             Q   √

Now this analysis obviously raises the question where the contrariness comes from in this (and similar) pairs of antonyms. In order to answer that question, we first need to consider the issue of the context-dependence of scalar adjectives.

9.4 Context-dependence

It has long been known that the interpretation of gradable adjectives is sensitive to a contextual standard (Wheeler 1972, Seuren 1978, Klein 1980, and much subsequent work). For example, a sentence like *Kurt is tall* does not mean that Kurt has a degree on the scale of height, but rather that Kurt's degree on the scale of height exceeds a contextually given standard. This standard may be made explicit, as in the following examples:

(445) a. Kurt is tall for a Bolivian.
       b. Kurt is not tall for a Swede.

Varying the standard may lead to the sentence changing its truth value; as a result, both sentences of (445) may be true together. If we take out the standard again, but interpret the implicit standard as in (445), this may lead to an apparent violation of the Law of Contradiction (LC: $\neg(p \land \neg p)$).

(446) a. Kurt is tall.
       b. Kurt is not tall.

These two sentences can be true together if we interpret (446a) as (445a) and (446b) as (445b). The LC can be upheld, however, by stipulating that in sentences with gradable adjectives, the (implicit) standard of comparison of a sentence and its negation needs to be held constant. The example then reveals the importance of the standard for the interpretation of scalar adjectives.

Following Seuren (1978), we take this contextual standard or average itself to be an extent, i.e. the context-sensitive interval A_C of average height, or the set of degrees that counts as neither tall nor short. For the above example, let the relevant extents be as in (447):[137]

(447) a. $A_S = [175, 185]$ (Swedish men)
       b. $A_B = [145, 155]$ (Bolivian men)

With this much in place, we are now ready to explain how the contradictory negation in the internal makeup of negative adjectives gives rise to contrary opposition.

9.5 Deriving contrariety from extent inclusion

Contrariety in pairs of antonymic adjectives is a direct consequence of the truth conditions on sentences with gradable adjectives. Following Seuren (1978), we formulate these truth conditions in terms of extent inclusion, as defined as in (448):

(448) For two extents X and Y,
       $X \subseteq Y \iff ((X \cap Y = X) \land (X \cup Y = Y))$.

A sentence like *Linus is tall* will be true if the positive extent of Linus's height includes the contextual average A_C. Similarly for negative adjectives, except that they involve a negative extent: *Kurt is short* is true in case the negative extent of Kurt's height includes A_C.

(449) a. $[\![\text{Linus is tall}]\!] = POS_{HEIGHT}(Linus) \supseteq A_C$
       b. $[\![\text{Kurt is short}]\!] = NEG_{HEIGHT}(Kurt) \supseteq A_C$

---

[137] https://en.wikipedia.org/wiki/List_of_average_human_height_worldwide

Figure 9.3 illustrates these inclusion relationships (where d(Linus) = 193 and d(Kurt) = 167). The bold red line is the positive extent of Linus' height, and it includes the interval of the average height of Swedish men, here called A_C. The bold blue line is the negative extent of Kurt's height, and it likewise includes the interval of the average height of Swedish men A_C. In this model, then, both sentences of (449) will come out as true.

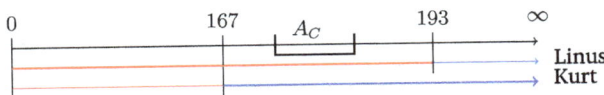

Figure 9.3: Extent inclusion in positive adjectives.

Now suppose Eva is of average height, e. g. d(Eva) = 182. Since this value is included in the contextual average A_C, neither the positive nor the negative extent of Eva's height will include A_C. This is shown in Figure 9.4. As a result, both the sentence *Eva is tall* and *Eva is short* will come out as false. This derives the contrary opposition of the latter two sentences, since they can both be false at the same time (though not both true at the same time, as the reader may verify).

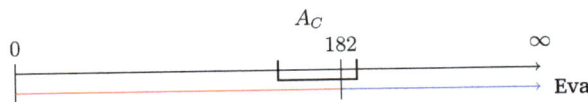

Figure 9.4: No inclusion with average height.

Now recall from above the contradictory pair in (436), repeated here:

(436) a. Linus is tall.
       b. Linus is not tall.

In line with our earlier analysis in terms of extent inclusion, (449b) will be true if the (positive) extent of Linus' height does not include the contextual average, as illustrated in (450b).

(450) a. ⟦Linus is tall⟧ = $POS_{HEIGHT}(Linus) \supseteq A_S$
       b. ⟦Linus is not tall⟧ = $POS_{HEIGHT}(Linus) \not\supseteq A_S$

This will be the case for any extent whose upper bound is lower than the upper bound of A_C. In our example of Swedish men (i. e. given that A_C = [175, 185]; see (447a) above), (450a) will come out as true for all values of d(x) equal to or higher than 185, since this will give rise to positive extents that do not include A_C, whose upper bound is 185. By the same reasoning, (450b) will be true for any d(x) that is lower than 185. It is easy to see that these two cases are exactly complementary: any value of x that makes (449a) true makes (449b) false, and vice versa. The net result is contradictory opposition. The reader may verify that the same works for the contradictory pair *short-not short*.

In sum, the analysis proposed takes antonymic pairs of adjectives to be related by a [Neg] feature, which gives rise to contradictory opposition. Contrariety follows from the way the scales work that are associated with gradable adjectives, in particular their dependence on a contextual standard. We have formulated the truth conditions of such adjectives in terms of an inclusion relation between two extents: one the one hand, a context-dependent average A_C; on the other, a positive extent for positive adjectives, and a negative extent for negative adjective ones.

9.6 Syntax

The syntax of gradable adjectives that we proposed above still leaves some issues to be addressed. Recall (from (444) above) that we assumed a [Neg] feature in the makeup of negative gradable adjectives, which contributes contradictory opposition:

(451) NegP = $]r, \infty[_{DIM}$
        ╱╲
    Neg   QP = $[0, r]_{DIM}$
            ╱╲
           Q   √

There are three issues with this structure that need to be addressed. The first is that it does not give us contrariety; the second that it lacks the aspect of context-dependence of gradable adjectives. Lastly, what (451) does not give us is a compositional way of getting from (451) to the truth condition for a sentence like *Linus is tall*, which involves an inclusion relationship between a positive or negative extent and the contextual average. It is from this inclusion relationship that contrariety is the consequence.

Before we go on to modify the syntactic structure in (451) to address these issues, we first discuss a number of cases where the contextual average is absent from the interpretation of the adjective.

(452)   a.   How tall is Kurt?

    b. Kurt is (more/less than) 1.5m tall.
    c. Kurt is that tall.
(453) a. Kurt is (half/twice) as tall as Lisa.
    b. Kurt is (not) as tall as Lisa.
    c. Kurt is taller than Lisa.
(454) a. Kurt is too tall for this suit.
    b. Kurt is tall enough to be a pilot.

What all these examples have in common is that the adjective *tall* itself does not make reference to a contextual standard. This is quite clearly seen in (452a), which is a question for a degree (any degree) on the scale of height. The other examples are all interpreted in terms of some standard or other, but one that is explicitly present in the sentences (e. g. *1.5m, that* (pointing), *Lisa's tallness, for this suit, to be a pilot*, suggesting that the adjective *tall* in these cases itself does not refer to such a standard. Following Seuren (1978), we call this the neutral use of *tall* (or *neutral tall* for short). The use of *tall* that involves reference to a contextual standard (e. g. (436a) above) we shall call *relative tall*.

It seems obvious that relative *tall* has a richer intension than neutral *tall*. The question is how the relation between both types of *tall* can be modelled. We suggest that it is a case of syncretism, i. e. one piece of phonology that is shared by different grammatical categories. In particular, we shall be assuming two things: (i) given their semantic relationship, relative *tall* is syntactically bigger than neutral *tall*, and (ii) the structure of relative *tall* contains that of neutral *tall*. We depict this analysis in the tree in (455).

(455)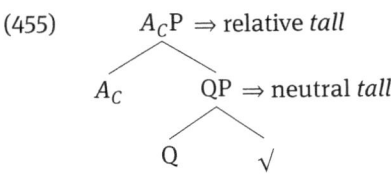

In comparison with our earlier tree, this tree adds the feature A_C for the contextual average at the top. The syncretism now arises in virtue of the fact that *tall* can spell out both QP (neutral *tall*) and A_CP (relative *tall*). The principle by which this happens is the Superset Principle (Starke 2009), repeated here for convenience:

(456) *Superset Principle*
    A lexical entry may spell out a syntactic node iff the lexical tree is identical to the syntactic tree, or if it contains the syntactic tree as a constituent.

Concretely, the lexical entry for *tall* would contain the entire tree in (455); this lexical entry could spell out the syntactic object QP, as well as A_CP.

Semantically, QP denotes a function from an individual to an extent: to get an extent we necessarily need a degree, and to get a degree, we need an individual who is the input to the degree function d(x) that maps the individual onto a degree. Using the λ-notation, the function for positive and negative gradable adjectives are given in (457):

(457) a. $\lambda x.POS_{DIM}(x)$
      b. $\lambda x.NEG_{DIM}(x)$

The head A_C then adds the contextual average, as well as the inclusion relation, as follows:

(458) a. $\lambda x.POS_{DIM}(x) \supset A_C$
      b. $\lambda x.NEG_{DIM}(x) \supset A_C$

Now the semantic relationship between neutral *tall* and relative *tall* can be represented as in (459):

(459) $A_CP = \lambda x.POS_{DIM}(x) \supset A_C$
        ╱╲
      A_C QP $= \lambda x.POS_{DIM}(x)$
              ╱╲
             Q   √

Negative adjectives differ from positive ones in the presence of a [Neg] feature, which transforms the positive extent into a negative one. The A_C head subsequently adds the contextual average and the inclusion relation.

(460) $A_CP = \lambda x.NEG_{DIM}(x) \supset A_C$
        ╱╲
      A_C NegP $= \lambda x.NEG_{DIM}(x)$
              ╱╲
            Neg   QP $= \lambda x.POS_{DIM}(x)$
                  ╱╲
                 Q   √

9.7 Un-marked antonyms

I now extend the analysis of the previous sections to negative gradable adjectives with overt negative morphology. As Seuren (1978) notes, the problem with some dimensions (which he calls parameters) is that they do not have a natural zero point. It happens to be the case that gradable adjectives that take negative morphemes like *un-* do not have such natural zero point. As is the case with the dimensional adjectives discussed above, a sentence like *Linus is happy* does not mean that Linus has a degree on the scale of happiness, but rather that Linus's degree on the scale of happiness exceeds a contextually given standard. Seuren proposes that the upper limit of the contextual average constitutes the zero for this type of scale without a naturally given zero. For a pair like *happy-unhappy* this means that the pair in (461) can be visualized as in Figure 9.5.

(461) a. Linus is happy.
       b. Kurt is unhappy.

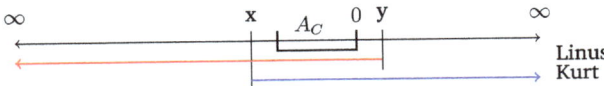

Figure 9.5: Negative and positive extents on the happiness scale.

The degree of happiness of Linus is indicated by the value y on the scale, and that of Kurt by x. Correspondingly, the red line is the positive extent of Linus' happiness, which is not bounded since the scale is open-ended on either side. The blue line is the negative extent of Kurt's happiness, which is also not bounded. Both include the contextual standard of what is understood to be happiness, indicated by A_C. Sentence (461a) is true if the contextual standard associated with happiness is included in the positive extent of Linus' happiness, and (461b) is true if the contextual standard is included in the negative extent of Kurt's happiness.

Since the opposition *happy-unhappy* is a contrary one, it can happen that someone is neither happy nor unhappy, i. e. both sentences of (462) can be false:

(462) a. Eva is happy.
       b. Eva is unhappy.

This is the case if Eva's degree of happiness falls in the A_C interval, like the value z in Figure 9.6.

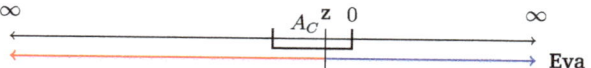

Figure 9.6: Contrariety as joint falsehood.

Neither Eva's negative extent, nor her positive extent include the contextual standard. So if Eva's degree of happiness is at any point which is contained in the extent A_C, then neither (462a) nor (462b) is true, because neither the positive nor the negative extent of her happiness includes the contextual standard. Since both are false then, the contrary opposition is derived. A slightly different syntax will be used for *happy* and *unhappy*, given that in the case of *unhappy* overt negative morphology is used, which will be inserted as a complex specifier in the main spine, projecting the negative semantics that was also present in *short*. Given that the features of the negative markers are at least partly a copy of the features present in the clausal spine, it is only the feature that has not yet been projected, i. e. Neg, which projects, since this is the one required by the fseq at that point, and the one that contributes new semantic information. This approach shows that the interface between syntax and semantics is one where syntax generates more features, some of which do not play a role at the level of semantic interpretation. It is possible that duplication of features is a phenomenon restricted to optional adverbial elements, like negative markers. However, more research is needed to confirm this.

(463)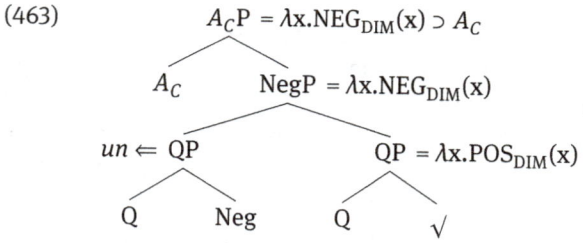

However, this does not mean that all features apart from the Neg-feature in for instance the complex negative specifier in (463) are meaningless for the computation. To the contrary, all these features steer insertion and selection. Due to the fact that negative markers are the spellout of a hierarchically ordered feature spine, negative markers can be different without the negation itself being different. The [Neg] feature has the same value, i. e. contributing contradictory negation in all negative markers that we introduced in this book. The difference between the negative markers arises due to the interaction with the surrounding featural make-up. In this particular case the feature [Q] matches the [Q] in the FSEQ, providing, together with the [A_C] feature, the featural context which influences the interpretation of the negation and the negative marker as a whole.

9.8 Conclusion

In this chapter we explored the interaction between the syntactic account developed in this book and the semantics of antonymic adjectival pairs with overt and covert negation. We developed an account for the well-known distinction between contrary and contradictory negation and argued that contrary negation can be derived from the interaction of interval semantics with the presence of a contextual standard, which can be present in the denotation of a gradable adjective.

10 Conclusion

This book started off with a discussion of Klima's well-known syntactic tests for sentence negation and constituent negation, arguing that there are languages, like Czech, that make use of the same negative marker for both sentence and constituent negation and languages like English that show more variation than the dichotomy suggests, especially when it comes to what is usually referred to as lexical negation. This triggered the questions what types of negative markers there are and how common the Czech and English pattern are in a more varied typological sample.

In order to provide an answer to these questions I argued for a four-way classification of scopally different negative markers, i. e. Q^{NEG}-markers, $Class^{NEG}$-markers, Foc^{NEG}-markers and T^{NEG}-markers, in predicative declarative main clauses with copular verbs and adjectival predicates in the simple present tense (chapter 3). This classification immediately shows that the dichotomy between sentence negation and constituent negation (cf. chapter 1) is too coarse to do justice to the realm of negative markers languages have at their disposal. The four-way classification was then used to systematically scrutinise 23 typologically varied languages for the negative markers they use (cf. chapter 4). It turned out that the negative markers in the languages investigated lay bare meaningful syncretism patterns, i. e. the negative markers can be ordered in such a way that there are no ABA patterns. In addition, it turned out that morphology also tracks the natural semantic scope of negation, i. e. the syncretisms can be ordered from wide to narrow scope (or vice versa), supporting the idea that morphology is not arbitrary (cf. section 4.3). We interpreted the absence of ABA patterns as an indication that scopally different negative markers are united at a deeper level of the grammar and captured this by decomposing negation into subatomic features, i. e. [T], [Foc], [Class], [Q] and [Neg], in line with the nanosyntactic programme introduced in chapter 2 and applied in chapter 5.

The present study further showed that negative markers across the lexical-functional divide share crucial properties and constitute a sequence of cumulative features, hence providing an argument to treat all negative markers in the same module of the grammar, i. e. syntax. This is done in chapters 5 and 6: it is demonstrated how both those markers that are typically considered part of the morphology and those that are typically treated in syntax can be inserted at the clausal level by means of the same spellout algorithm. Chapter 6 also provides full clausal derivations in nanosyntax in a first attempt to show how the nanolevel and the clausal level can be made to work together. Since there is little to no work providing derivations for full clauses in nanosyntax, this part of the book should be considered pioneering work to spark off discussion.

In addition this study also shows how the new nanosyntactic approach to negation is well-equipped to capture diachronic change and more in particular Jespersen's Cycle. Chapter 7 provides an analysis for the change from *le bon usage* French to Colloquial French in terms of changes in the size of lexical trees, as such providing support to Starke (2011b)'s claim that language variation boils down to the size of lexically stored trees.

The current book also offers a first proposal of a semantics for the syntactic framework offered in this book (cf. chapter 9). By means of extent semantics it is argued that contrariety arises as a consequence of the interaction of [Neg] with the contextual average that can project as a feature [A_C] on the scalarity-contributing Q. Chapter 9 also shows why semantics alone would never be sufficient to capture one of more striking generalisations that emerges from this book: negative markers with the same scope are never stacked immediately on top of each other without intervening layers of structure, i. e. there is a syntactic constraint against Neg-Neg, as also argued for in De Clercq & Vanden Wyngaerd (2019a), while there is no such constraint in semantics.

Just like the semantic proposal developed in chapter 9 could be further worked out to get a clearer idea of what the contribution is of the different types of negative markers, there are other topics related to this book that I keep for further research.

One of these topics is the study of negative markers that are in complementary distribution with the sentential negative markers taken up in this book, i. e. the so-called TAM-related negative allomorphs. They constitute a full research domain of their own. TAM-related negative allormorphs can never be stacked on the default sentential negative marker used in the indicative present tense and they seem a promising domain to shed light on the various positions for sentential negation that have been discerned by Zanuttini (1997), Cinque (1999), Poletto (2008) and Poletto (2017) (cf. discussion in chapter 8).

Another topic that is not addressed in this book is how to deal with concord and the nature of negative indefinites, such as English *no, nothing* or Czech n-words like *nikdo*, from the current perspective. I refer the reader to De Clercq (2019a) for a first proposal as to how to analyse n-words and the concord and double negation patterns they give rise to in French within a nanosyntactic framework.

Finally, the syncretism patterns amongst negative markers discussed in this book also uncover an intriguing functional sequence for lexical categories that has the following shape: V>N>A. The implications of this result have not been studied in this book, since they are far-reaching and they require further investigation (cf. the work by Baker (2003)). It is one of the many puzzles I would like to tackle in future work.

Bibliography

Aboh, Enoch. 2004. Snowballing movement and generalized pied-piping. In Anne Breitbarth & Henk van Riemsdijk (eds.), *Triggers*. 15–47. Berlin: Mouton de Gruyter.

Agmon, Galit. 2013. Negation of adjectives: Modern Hebrew. In Geoffrey Khan (ed.), *Encyclopedia of Hebrew language and linguistics*. Leiden/Boston: Brill.

Al-Sharifi, Budour & Louisa Sadler. 2009. The adjectival construct in Arabic. In: Miriam Butt & Tracy King (eds.), *Proceedings of LFG09*. 26–43. Stanford, California: CSLI Publications.

Alexiadou, Artemis & Elena Anagnostopoulou. 1998. Parametrizing Agr: word order, V-movement and EPP-checking. *Natural Language & Linguistic Theory* 16(3). 491–539.

Allen, Margaret Reece. 1978. *Morphological Investigations*. Storrs, CT: University of Connecticut dissertation.

Alsharif, Ahmad & Louisa Sadler. 2009. Negation in modern standard Arabic. In Miriam Butt & Tracy King (eds.), *Proceedings of LFG09*. 5–25. Stanford, California: CSLI Publications.

Amritavalli, Raghavachari, Karattuparambil Jayaseelan. 2005. Finiteness and negation in Dravidian. In Guglielmo Cinque & Richard S. Kayne (eds.), *The Oxford handbook of comparative syntax*. 178–220. Oxford University Press.

Aoun, Joseph, Elabbas Benmamoun & Lina Choueiri. 2010. *The syntax of Arabic*. Cambridge: Cambridge University Press.

Asher, R. E & T. C. Kumar. 1997. *Malayalam*. London: Routledge.

ATILF. 2003. Trésor de la langue française informatisée. http://atilf.atilf.fr.

Authier, Jean-Marc. 2013. Phase-edge features and the syntax of polarity particles. *Linguistic Inquiry* 44(3). 345–389.

Baerman, Matthew & Dunstan Brown. 2011. Case syncretism. In Matthew Dryer & Martin Haspelmath (eds.), *The world atlas of language structures online*. Munich: Max Planck Digital Library. http://wals.info/chapter/28.

Baerman, Matthew, Dunstan Brown & Greville Corbett. 2005. *The syntax-morphology interface: A study of syncretism*. Cambridge: Cambridge University Press.

Baker, Mark. 2003. *Lexical categories*. Cambridge: Cambridge University Press.

Baker, Mark & Jim McCloskey. 2007. On the relationship of typology to theoretical syntax. *Linguistic Typology* 11. 285–296.

Bar-Asher Siegal, Elitzur. 2015. Arguments in favor of an ambiguist approach. Paper presented at the Göttingen Workshop on Negation and Polarity.

Bar-Asher Siegal, Elitzur. 2015. The case for external sentential negation: Evidence from Jewish Babylonian Aramaic. *Linguistics* 53(3). 1031–1078.

Bar-Asher Siegal, Elitzur & Karen De Clercq. 2019. From negative cleft to external negator. In Miriam Bouzouita, Anne Breitbarth, Lieven Danckaert & Elisabeth Witzenhausen (eds.), *Cycles in language change*. 228–248. Oxford: Oxford University Press.

Baunaz, Lena, Karen De Clercq, Liliane Haegeman & Eric Lander (eds.). 2018. *Exploring nanosyntax*. Oxford: Oxford University Press.

Baunaz, Lena & Eric Lander. 2018a. Deconstructing categories syncretic with the nominal complementizer. *Glossa: a Journal of General Linguistics* 3(1). 31.1–27.

Baunaz, Lena & Eric Lander. 2018b. Nanosyntax: the basics. In Lena Baunaz, Karen De Clercq, Liliane Haegeman & Eric Lander (eds.), *Exploring nanosyntax*. 3–56. Oxford: Oxford University Press.

Belletti, Adriana. 1990. *Generalized verb movement: aspects of verb syntax*. Turin: Rosenberg & Sellier.
Belletti, Adriana. 2001. Inversion as focalization. In Aafke Hulk & Jean-Yves Pollock (eds.), *Subject inversion in Romance and the theory of universal grammar*. 60–90. New York: Oxford University Press.
Belletti, Adriana. 2004. Aspects of the low IP area. In Luigi Rizzi (ed.), *The Structure of IP and CP*, vol. 2 The Cartography of Syntactic Structures. 16–51. Oxford: Oxford University Press.
Belletti, Adriana. 2005. Extended doubling and the VP periphery. *Probus* 17(1). 1–35.
Benmamoun, Elabbas. 2000. *The feature structure of functional categories: a comparative study of Arabic dialects*. Oxford: Oxford University Press.
den Besten, Hans. 1986. Double negation and the genesis of Afrikaans. In Pieter Muysken & Norval Smith (eds.), *Substrate versus universals in creole genesis*. Amsterdam: John Benjamins.
Biberauer, Theresa. 2008. Doubling and omission: Insights from Afrikaans negation. In Sjef Barbiers, Margreet van der Ham, Olaf Koeneman & Marika Lekakou (eds.), *Microvariation in syntactic doubling*. 103–140. Bingley, UK: Emerald.
Biberauer, Theresa & Hedde Zeijlstra. 2012. Negative concord in Afrikaans: filling the typological gap. *Journal of Semantics* 29(3). 345–371.
Blake, Barry. 1994. *Case*. Cambridge: Cambridge University Press.
Bobaljik, Jonathan. 1995. *Morphosyntax: The syntax of verbal inflection*. Cambridge, MA: MIT dissertation.
Bobaljik, Jonathan. 2002. Realizing Germanic inflection: Why morphology does not drive syntax. *The Journal of Comparative Germanic Linguistics* 6. 129–167.
Bobaljik, Jonathan. 2012. *Universals in comparative morphology*. Cambridge, MA: MIT Press.
Booij, Geert & Jenny Audring. 2018. Category change in construction morphology. In Kristel Van Goethem, Muriel Norde, Evie Coussé & Gudrun Vanderbauwhede (eds.), *Category change from a constructional perspective*. 209–228. John Benjamins.
Borer, Hagit. 2005. *In name only*. Oxford: Oxford University Press.
Bošković, Željko. 2002. Expletives don't move. In Masako Hirotani (ed.), *Proceedings of NELS*, vol. 32. 21–40.
Bošković, Željko. 2005. On the locality of left branch extraction and the structure of NP. *Studia Linguistica* 59(1). 1–45.
Bowers, John. 1993. The syntax of predication. *Linguistic Inquiry* 24. 591–656.
Brandtler, Johan. 2006. On Aristotle and baldness – topic, reference, presupposition of existence and negation.
Brandtler, Johan. 2012. *The evaluability hypothesis. The syntax, semantics and pragmatics of polarity item licensing*. Amsterdam: John Benjamins.
Brasoveanu, Adrian, Karen De Clercq, Donka Farkas & Floris Roelofsen. 2014. Question tags and sentential negativity. *Lingua* 145. 173–193.
Breitbarth, Anne. 2009. A hybrid approach to Jespersen's cycle in West Germanic. *Journal of Comparative Germanic Linguistics* 12. 81–114.
Breitbarth, Anne, Karen De Clercq & Liliane Haegeman (eds.). 2013a. *Polarity emphasis: distribution and locus of licensing*. Lingua Special Issue, vol. 128.
Breitbarth, Anne, Karen De Clercq & Liliane Haegeman. 2013b. The syntax of polarity emphasis. *Lingua* 128. 1–8.
Breitbarth, Anne & Liliane Haegeman. 2010. Continuity is change: the long tail of Jespersen's cycle in Flemish. In Anne Breitbarth, Christopher Lucas, Sheila Watts & David Willis (eds.), *Continuity and change in grammar*. 61–76. Amsterdam: John Benjamins.

Breitbarth, Anne & Liliane Haegeman. 2014. The distribution of preverbal /en/ in (West) Flemish: syntactic and interpretive properties. *Lingua* 147. 69–86.

Breitbarth, Anne, Christopher Lucas & David Willis. 2013c. Incipient Jespersen's cycle: the (non-)grammaticalization of new negative markers. In Jürg Fleischer & Horst Simon (eds.), *Sprachwandelvergleich–comparing diachronies*. 141–162. Berlin: Mouton De Gruyter.

Bresnan, Joan. 2001. Explaining morphosyntactic competition. In Mark Baltin & Chris Collins (eds.), *Handbook of contemporary syntactic theory*. 1–44. MA: Blackwell.

Bresnan, Joan W. 1973. Syntax of Comparative Clause Construction in English. *Linguistic Inquiry* 4(3). 275–343.

Butler, Jonny. 2003. A minimalist treatment of modality. *Lingua* 113. 967–996.

Caha, Pavel. 2009. *The nanosyntax of case*. Tromsø: University of Tromsø dissertation.

Caha, Pavel. 2013. Explaining the structure of case paradigms by the mechanisms of nanosyntax. *Natural Language & Linguistic Theory* 31. 1015–1066.

Caha, Pavel. 2018. Notes on insertion in distributed morphology and nanosyntax. In Lena Baunaz, Karen De Clercq, Liliane Haegeman & Eric Lander (eds.), *Exploring nanosyntax*. 57–87. Oxford: Oxford University Press.

Caha, Pavel, Karen De Clercq & Guido Vanden Wyngaerd. 2019. The fine structure of the comparative. *Studia Linguistica* 73(3). 470–521. https://doi.org/10.1111/stul.12107.

Caha, Pavel & Marina Pantcheva. 2012. Contiguity beyond linearity. Talk at Decennium: The first 10 years of CASTL.

Cardinaletti, Anna. 1997. Agreement and control in expletive constructions. *Linguistic Inquiry* 28(3). 521–533.

Cardinaletti, Anna. 2004. Toward a cartography of subject position. In Luigi Rizzi (ed.), *The structure of CP and IP*. 115–165. New York: Oxford University Press.

Cardinaletti, Anna & Michal Starke. 1999. The typology of structural deficiency: a case study of the three classes of pronouns. In Henk van Riemsdijk (ed.), *Clitics in the languages of Europe*. 145–233. Berlin: Mouton de Gruyter.

Cattell, Ray. 1973. Negative transportation and tag questions. *Language* 49. 612–639.

Chang, Suk-Jin. 1996. *Korean*. John Benjamins.

Chatzopoulou, Katerina. 2011. Negation beyond fate. Renewal and inertia in the history of Greek negation. Paper presented at ICGL 10. Democritus University of Thrace, Komotini, Greece.

Chatzopoulou, Katerina. 2013. The particularity of Meillet's spiral. Presentation at Societas Linguistica Europea, University of Split, Croatia.

Chatzopoulou, Katerina & Anastasia Giannakidou. 2011. Negator selection in Attic Greek is a polarity phenomenon. Poster presented at the 13th International Diachronic Generative Syntax Conference, University of Pennsylvania.

Chomsky, Noam. 1957. *Syntactic structures*. The Hague: Mouton.

Chomsky, Noam. 1995. *The minimalist program*. Cambridge, Massachusetts: MIT Press.

Chomsky, Noam. 2001. Derivation by phase. In Michael Kenstowicz (ed.), *Ken Hale: A life in language*. 1–52. Cambridge, MA: MIT Press.

Christensen, Ken Ramshøj. 2005. *Interfaces. Negation-syntax-brain*. Aarhus: University of Aarhus/Aarhus University Hospital dissertation.

Chung, Inkie. 2007. Suppletive negation in Korean and distributed morphology. *Lingua* 117. 95–148.

Cinque, Guglielmo. 1976. Mica. In *Annali della Facoltà di Lettere e Filosofia dell' Università di Padova*, vol. 1. 101–112.

Cinque, Guglielmo. 1999. *Adverbs and functional heads: A cross-linguistic perspective*. Oxford: Oxford University Press.
Cinque, Guglielmo. 2010. *The syntax of adjectives: a comparative study*. Cambridge, MA: MIT Press.
Cinque, Guglielmo & Luigi Rizzi. 2008. The cartography of syntactic structures. *CISCL Working Papers* 2. 42–58.
Collins, Chris. 2002. Eliminating labels. In Samuel Epstein & Daniel Seely (eds.), *Derivation and explanation in the minimalist program*. 42–64. Cambridge, Mass.: MIT Press.
Collins, Chris. 2018. *NEG NEG. *Glossa* 3(1). 64.1–8.
Collins, Chris & Paul Postal. 2014. *Classical NEG raising*. Cambridge, MA: MIT Press.
Comrie, Bernard. 1989. *Language universals and linguistic typology*. Chicago: University of Chicago Press.
Coppen, P.A., W. Haeseryn & F. de Vriend. 2002. De elektronische ANS. http://ans.ruhosting.nl/e-ans/.
Cormack, Annabel & Neil Smith. 2002. Modals and negation in English. In Sjef Barbiers, Frits Beukema & William van der Wurf (eds.), *Modality and its interaction with the verbal system*. 133–163. Amsterdam: John Benjamins.
Corver, Norbert. 1997a. The internal syntax of the Dutch extended adjectival projection. *Natural Language & Linguistic Theory* 15. 289–368.
Corver, Norbert. 1997b. Much-support as a last resort. *Linguistic Inquiry* 28. 119–164.
Croft, William. 1991. The evolution of negation. *Journal of Linguistics* 27. 1–27.
Culicover, Peter. 1992. English tag questions in universal grammar. *Lingua* 88. 193–226.
Dahl, Östen. 1979. Typology of sentence negation. *Linguistics* 17. 79–106.
Dahl, Östen. 2010. Typology of negation. In Laurence Horn (ed.), *The expression of negation*. Berlin: Mouton de Gruyter.
Dan, Xu. 2006. *Typological change in Chinese syntax*. Oxford: Oxford University Press.
Danckaert, Lieven & Liliane Haegeman. 2017. Syntacticizing blends. The case of English wh-raising. In *Boundaries, phases and interfaces. Case studies in honor of violeta demonte*. Amsterdam and Philadelphia: John Benjamins.
Dayley, Jon. 1989a. *Tümpisa (Panamint) Shoshone dictionary*. Berkeley: University of California Press.
Dayley, Jon. 1989b. *Tümpisa (Panamint) Shoshone grammar*. Berkeley: University of California Press.
De Clercq, Karen. 2011. Squat, zero and no/nothing: syntactic negation vs. semantic negation. In Marion Elenbaas & Rick Nouwen (eds.), *Linguistics in the Netherlands 2011*. 14–24. Amsterdam: John Benjamins.
De Clercq, Karen. 2013. *A unified syntax of negation*. Ghent: Ghent University dissertation.
De Clercq, Karen. 2016. Decomposing Korean *mos* and *molu*. Talk at SinFonIJA 9, Brno, Czech Republic.
De Clercq, Karen. 2017. The nanosyntax of French negation. In Silvio Cruschina, Katharina Hartmann & Eva-Maria Remberger (eds.), *Studies on negation: Syntax, semantics, and variation*. 49–80. Vienna: Vienna University Press.
De Clercq, Karen. 2018. Syncretisms and the morphosyntax of negation. In Lena Baunaz, Karen De Clercq, Liliane Haegeman & Eric Lander (eds.), *Exploring nanosyntax*. 180–204. Oxford University Press.
De Clercq, Karen. 2019a. French negation, the superset principle and feature conservation. In Miriam Bouzouita, Anne Breitbarth, Lieven Danckaert & Elisabeth Witzenhausen (eds.),

Cycles in language change. 199–227. Oxford: Oxford University Press.
De Clercq, Karen. 2019b. Honorific and negative portmanteaus in Korean. Connecting roots and affixes. Workshop at Masaryk University, Brno, Czech Republic, 13–14 May 2019.
De Clercq, Karen. 2020. Types of negation, chapter 5. In Viviane Déprez & M. Teresa Espinal (eds.), *The Oxford Handbook of Negation*. 58–74. Oxford: Oxford University Press.
De Clercq, Karen & Guido Vanden Wyngaerd. 2017a. *ABA revisited: evidence from Czech and Latin degree morphology. *Glossa* 2(1). 69.1–32.
De Clercq, Karen & Guido Vanden Wyngaerd. 2017b. Why affixal negation is syntactic. In Aaron Kaplan, Abby Kaplan, Miranda McCarvel & Edward Rubin (eds.), *Proceedings of WCCFL 34*. 151–158. Sommerville, MA: Cascadilla Press.
De Clercq, Karen & Guido Vanden Wyngaerd. 2018. Adjectives and negation: deriving contrariety from contradiction. *Papers of the Linguistic Society of Belgium* 12. 1–19.
De Clercq, Karen & Guido Vanden Wyngaerd. 2019a. Negation and the functional sequence. *Natural Language & Linguistic Theory* 37(2). 425–460.
De Clercq, Karen & Guido Wyngaerd Vanden. 2019b. On the idiomatic nature of unproductive morphology. In Janine Berns & Elena Tribushinina (eds.), *Linguistics in the Netherlands 2019*. 99–114. Amsterdam: John Benjamins.
De Haan, Ferdinand. 1997. *The interaction of modality and negation. A typological study*. London & New York: Routledge.
De Swart, Henriette. 2010. *Expression and interpretation of negation: an OT typology*. Dordrecht: Springer.
De Swart, Henriette. 2016. Negation. In Maria Aloni & Paul Dekker (eds.), *The Cambridge handbook of formal semantics*. chap. 17, 467–489. Cambridge: Cambridge University Press.
Deal, Amy-Rose. 2009. The origin and content of expletives: evidence from 'selection'. *Syntax* 12. 285–323.
Derbyshire, Desmond. 1979. *Hixkaryana*. Amsterdam: North-Holland.
Detges, Ulrich & Richard Waltereit. 2002. Grammaticalization vs. reanalysis : A semantic-pragmatic account of functional change in grammar. *Zeitschrift für Sprachwissenschaft* 21. 151–195.
Dryer, Matthew. 2011. Position of tense-aspect affixes. In Matthew Dryer & Martin Haspelmath (eds.), *The world atlas of language structures online*. Munich: Max Planck Digital Library. http://wals.info/chapter/69.
Dryer, Matthew S. 1988. Universals of negative position. In Michael Hammond, Edith Moravcsik & Jessica Wirth (eds.), *Studies in syntactic typology*. Amsterdam and Philadelphia: John Benjamins.
Embick, David & Rolf Noyer. 2001. Movement operations after syntax. *Linguistic Inquiry* 32(4). 555–595.
Endo, Yoshio & Liliane Haegeman. 2014. Adverbial clauses and adverbial concord. In Shigeto Kawahara & Mika Igarashi (eds.), *Proceedings of FAJL 7: Formal approaches to Japanese linguistics* MIT Working Papers in Linguistics. 25–44. Cambridge, MA.
Epstein, Samuel & T. Daniel Seely. 2002. Rule applications as cycles in a level-free syntax. In Samuel David Epstein & T. Daniel Seely (eds.), *Derivation and explanation in the minimalist framework*. 65–89. Oxford: Blackwell.
Erlewine, Michael Yoshitaka & Hadas Kotek. 2018. Covert focus movement with pied-piping: Evidence from Tanglewood. *Linguistic Inquiry* 49(3). 441–463.

Ernst, Thomas. 1992. The phrase structure of English negation. *The Linguistic Review* 9. 109–144.
Estivalet, Gustavo & Fanny Meunier. 2016. Stem formation in French verbs: structure, rules, and allomorphy. *Languages* 1(2). 13:1–16.
Fabregas, Antonio. 2009. An argument for phrasal spell-out: indefinites and interrogatives in Spanish. *Nordlyd* 36. 129–168.
Farkas, Donka & Floris Roelofsen. 2012. Polar initiatives and polarity particle responses in an inquisitive discourse model. Manuscript.
Funk, W. P. 1971. Adjectives with negative prefixes in modern English and the problem of synonymy. *Zeitschrift für Anglistik und Amerikanistik* 19. 364–386.
Gajewski, Jon. 2011. Licensing strong NPIs. *Natural Language Semantics* 19(2). 109–148.
Garzonio, Jacopo & Cecilia Poletto. 2013. *Non* and its companions: on the big NegP hypothesis. Talk presented at ICL 19, University of Geneva.
Ghomeshi, Jila. 1996. *Projection and inflection: a study of Persian phrase structure*: University of Toronto dissertation.
Giannakidou, Anastasia. 1997. *The landscape of polarity items*. Groningen: University of Groningen dissertation.
Giannakidou, Anastasia. 1998. *Polarity sensitivity as (non)veridical dependency*. Amsterdam: John Benjamins.
Giannakidou, Anastasia. 2013. (Non)veridicality, evaluation, and event actualization: evidence from the subjunctive in relative clauses. In Maite Taboada & Rada Trnavac (eds.), *Nonveridicality and evaluation. Theoretical, computational and corpus approaches*. Leiden: Brill.
Giannakidou, Anastasia. 2016. Evaluative subjunctive and nonveridicality. In Joanna Blaszczak, Anastasia Giannakidou, Dorota Klimek-Jankowska & Krzysztof Migdalski (eds.), *Mood, aspect, modality revisited. New answers to old questions*. Chicago, IL: University of Chicago Press.
Gibert Sotelo, Elisabeth. 2017. *Source and negative prefixes: on the syntax-lexicon interface and the encoding of spatial relations*. Girona: Universitat de Girona dissertation.
Glinert, Lewis. 2013. Negation: Modern Hebrew. In Geoffrey Kahn (ed.), *Encyclopedia of Hebrew language and linguistics*. Leiden/Boston: Brill.
Göksel, Aslı & Celia Kerslake. 2005. *Turkish: A comprehensive grammar*. Routledge.
Greenberg, Joseph H. 1966. *Universals of language*. MA: MIT Press.
Grevisse, Maurice & Andre Goosse. [1936] 1993. *Le bon usage*. Paris: Duculot.
Grohmann, Kleanthes K. 2011. Anti-locality: too-close relations in grammar. In *The Oxford handbook of linguistic minimalism*. Oxford University Press.
Haegeman, Liliane. 1987a. Complement ellipsis in English: or how to cook without objects. In Anne-Marie Simon-Vandenbergen (ed.), *Studies in honour of René Derolez*. 248–261. Ghent, Belgium: Seminarie voor Engelse en Oud-Germaanse Taalkunde.
Haegeman, Liliane. 1987b. Register variation in English: some theoretical observations. *Journal of English Linguistics* 20. 230–248.
Haegeman, Liliane. 1995. *The syntax of negation*. Cambridge: Cambridge University Press.
Haegeman, Liliane. 2000. Negative inversion, the Neg-criterion and the structure of the CP. In Laurence Horn & Yasuhiko Kato (eds.), *Negation and polarity*. 29–69. Oxford: Oxford University Press.
Haegeman, Liliane. 2002. Adult null subjects in the non-pro-drop languages: two diary dialects. *Language Acquisition* 9. 329–346.

Haegeman, Liliane. 2006. Register variation: core grammar and periphery. In Keith Brown (ed.), *Encyclopedia of language and linguistics*. 468–474. Oxford: Elsevier.
Haegeman, Liliane & Tabea Ihsane. 1999. Subject ellipsis in embedded clauses in English. *Journal of English Language and Linguistics* 3. 117–145.
Haegeman, Liliane & Terje Lohndal. 2010. Negative concord and multiple agree: a case study of West-Flemish. *Linguistic Inquiry* 41(2). 181–211.
Haegeman, Liliane & Terje Lohndal. 2013. Negation. In Silvia Luraghi & Claudia Parodi (eds.), *The Bloomsbury companion to syntax*. Bloomsbury.
Hagstrom, Paul. 1997. Scope interactions and phrasal movement in Korean negation. *Harvard Studies in Korean Linguistics* 7. 254–268.
Hagstrom, Paul. 2000. Phrasal movement in Korean negation. *MIT Working Papers in Linguistics* 35.
Halle, Morris & Alec Marantz. 1993. Distributed morphology and the pieces of inflection. In Ken Hale & Jay Keyser (eds.), *The view from building 20*. 111–176. Cambridge, MA: MIT Press.
Hamawand, Zeki. 2009. *The semantics of English negative prefixes*. London: Equinox.
Han, Chung-Hye & Anthony Kroch. 2000. The rise of do-support in English: implications for clause structure. In Masako Hirotani, Andries Coetzee, Nancy Hall & Ji-yung Kim (eds.), *Proceedings of NELS 30*. GLSA Publications.
Han, Chung-Hye & Chungmin Lee. 2007. On negative imperatives in Korean. *Linguistic Inquiry* 38(2). 373–394.
Han, Chung-hye, Jeffrey Lidz & Julien Musolino. 2007. V-raising and grammar competition in Korean: Evidence from negation and quantifier scope. *Linguistic Inquiry* 38(1). 1–47.
Han, Chung-Hye & Maribel Romero. 2001. Negation, focus and alternative questions. *WCCFL* 20. 101–114.
Hansen, Maj-Britt Mosegaard. 2013. Negation in the history of French. In *The history of negation in the languages of Europe and the Mediterranean*. 51–76. Oxford University Press.
Harley, Heidi & Rolf Noyer. 1999. State-of-the-article: distributed morphology. *Glot International* 4. 3–9.
Harper, Douglas. 2013. Online etymology dictionary. http://www.etymonline.com.
Harwood, William. 2014. Rise of the auxiliaries: a case for auxiliary raising vs. affix lowering. *The Linguistic Review* 31. 295–362.
Haspelmath, Martin. 1997. *Indefinite pronouns*. Oxford: Oxford University Press.
Haspelmath, Martin. 2011. Negative indefinite pronouns and predicate negation. In Matthew S. Dryer & Martin Haspelmath (eds.), *The world atlas of language structures online*. Munich: Max Planck Digital Library. http://wals.info/chapter/115.
Heath, Jeffrey. 2002. *Jewish and muslim dialects of Moroccan Arabic*. New York: Routledge Curzon.
Heim, Irene. 2008. Decomposing antonyms? In Attle Grøn (ed.), *Proceedings of Sinn und Bedeutung*, vol. 16. 212–225. Oslo: ILOS.
Herburger, Elena. 2000. *What counts. Focus and quantification*. Cambridge, Mass.: MIT Press.
Hetzron, Robert (ed.). 1997. *The Semitic languages*. London: Routledge.
Hinds, John. 1986. *Japanese*. London: Croom Helm.
Hoffmann, J. J. 1876. *A Japanese grammar*. Brill.
Holes, Clive. [1995] 2004. *Modern Arabic: structures, functions and varieties*. Washington: Georgetown University Press.

Holmberg, Anders. 2003. Questions, answers, polarity and head movement in Germanic and Finnish. *Nordlyd* 31. 88–115.

Holmberg, Anders. 2013. The syntax of answers to polar questions in English and Swedish. *Lingua* 128. 32–50.

Holmberg, Anders. 2015. *The syntax of yes and no*. New York: Oxford University Press.

Holmes, Philip & Ian Hinchliffe. 2008 [1997]. *Swedish. an essential grammar*. Routledge 2nd edn.

Holton, David, Peter Mackridge & Irene Philippaki-Warburton. 2004. *Greek. An essential grammar of the modern language*. New York: Routledge.

Horn, Laurence. 1985. Metalinguistic negation and pragmatic ambiguity. *Language* 61. 121–174.

Horn, Laurence. 2001a. Flaubert triggers, squatitive negation, and other quirks of grammar. In Jack Hoeksema, Hotze Rullman, Victor Sanchez-Valencia & Ton van der Wouden (eds.), *Perspectives on Negation and Polarity items*. Amsterdam: John Benjamins.

Horn, Laurence. 2001b. *A natural history of negation*. Chicago, IL: The University of Chicago Press 2nd edn.

Horn, Laurence. 2005. An un-paper for the unsyntactician. In Salikoko Mufwene, Elaine Francis & Rebecca Wheeler (eds.), *Polymorphous linguistics. Jim McCawley's legacy*. 329–365. Cambridge, MA: MIT Press.

Huddlestone, Kathleen Maria. 2010. *Negative indefinites in Afrikaans*. Utrecht: Utrecht Univeristy dissertation.

Iatridou, Sabine, Elena Anagnostopoulou & Roumyana Izvorsk. 2001. Some observations about the form and meaning of the perfect. In Michael Kenstowicz (ed.), *Ken Hale: a life in language*. 189–238. Cambridge, MA: MIT Press.

Instituut voor de Nederlandse taal. 2013. Corpus Hedendaags Nederlands. http://corpushedendaagsnederlands.inl.nl.

Jackendoff, Ray. 1969. An interpretive theory of negation. *Foundations of Language* 5. 218–241.

Jackendoff, Ray. 1972. *Semantic interpretation in generative grammar*. Cambridge, Massachusetts: MIT Press.

Jackendoff, Ray. 1974. A Deep Structure Projection Rule. *Linguistic Inquiry* 5(4). 481–505.

Jakobson, Roman. 1962. Beitrag zur allgemeinen Kasuslehre: Gesamtbedeutungen der Russischen Kasus. In *Selected writings*, vol. 2. 23–71. The Hague: Mouton.

Janda, Laura & Charles Townsend. 2000. *Czech, vol. 125 Languages of the World/Materials*. Munich: Lincom Europa.

Jayaseelan, Karattuparambil. 2001. IP-internal topic and focus phrases. *Studia Linguistica* 55. 39–75.

Jayaseelan, Karattuparambil. 2008. Topic, focus and adverb positions in clause structure. *Nanzan Linguistics* 4. 43–68.

Jespersen, Otto. 1913. *A modern English grammar on historical principles*, vol. II. London: George Allen & Unwin.

Jespersen, Otto. 1917. *Negation in English and other languages*. København: A.F. Høst & Søn.

Jespersen, Otto. 1924. *The philosophy of grammar*. London: Allen and Unwin.

Johnston, Jason. 1996. *Systematic homonymy and the structure of morphological categories. Some lessons from paradigm geometry*: University of Sydney dissertation.

Kageyama, Taro & Hideki Kishimoto. 2016. *Handbook of Japanese lexicon and word formation*. Berlin: Walter de Gruyter.

Kandybowicz, Jason. 2013. Ways of emphatic scope-taking: from emphatic assertion in Nupe to the grammar of emphasis. *Lingua* 128. 51–71.

Karttunen, Lauri. 1973. Presuppositions of compound sentences. *Linguistic Inquiry* 4(2). 169–193.
Kayne, Richard. 1975. *French syntax*. Cambridge, Massachusetts: MIT Press.
Kayne, Richard. 1989. Null subjects and clitic climbing. In Osvaldo Jaeggli & Ken Safir (eds.), *The null subject parameter*. Dordrecht: Kluwer.
Kayne, Richard. 1993. Toward a modular theory of auxiliary selection. *Studia Linguistica* 47. 3–31.
Kayne, Richard. 2005. A note on the syntax of quantity in English. In Richard Kayne (ed.), *Movement and silence*. 176–214. New York: Oxford University Press.
Kelepir, Meltem. 2001. *Topics in Turkish syntax: Clausal structure and scope*. Cambridge, MA: MIT dissertation.
Kennedy, Christopher. 2001. On the monotonicity of polar adjectives. In Jack Hoeksema, Hotze Rullman, Victor Sanchez-Valencia & Ton van der Wouden (eds.), *Perspectives on negation and polarity items*. 201–221. Amsterdam: John Benjamins.
Kilian-Hatz, Christa. 2008. *A grammar of modern Khwe Quellen zur Khoisan Forschung*. Köln: Rüdiger Köppe Verlag.
Kim, Shin-Sook. 2010. The structures of modality in Korean. In Hiroki Maezawa & Azusa Yokogoshi (eds.), *Proceedings of the 6th workshop on Altaic formal linguistics (WAFL6)*. 171–180. Cambridge, MA: MIT Working Papers in Linguistics.
Kim-Renaud, Young-Key. 2009. *Korean: an essential grammar*. New York: Routledge.
Kiparsky, Paul. 1973. 'Elsewhere' in phonology. In Stephen Anderson & Paul Kiparsky (eds.), *A festschrift for Morris Halle*. 93–106. New York: Holt, Rinehart & Winston.
Kiparsky, Paul. 1982. Lexical morphology and phonology. In The Linguistic Society of Korea (ed.), *Linguistics in the morning calm*. 3–91. Seoul: Hanshin.
Kiparsky, Paul. 1983. Word formation and the lexicon. In Frances Ingemann (ed.), *Proceedings of the 1982 Mid-America linguistics conference*. 3–29. Lawrence: University of Kansas.
Kiparsky, Paul & Cleo Condoravdi. 2006. Tracking Jespersen's cycle. In Mark Janse, Brian Joseph & Angela Ralli (eds.), *Proceedings of the 2nd internation conference of Modern Greek dialects and linguistic theory*. 172–197. Patras: University of Patras.
Kiss, Katalin. 1996. Two subject positions in English. *The Linguistic Review* 13. 119–142.
Kiss, Katalin. 2004. *The syntax of Hungarian*. Cambridge: Cambridge University Press.
Kjellmer, Göran. 2005. Negated adjectives in modern English. *Studia Neophilologica* 77(2). 156–170.
Klaus, Abels. 2003. *Successive cyclicity, anti-locality and adposition stranding*. Storrs, CT: University of Connecticut dissertation.
Klein, Ewan. 1980. A semantics for positive and comparative adjectives. *Linguistics and Philosophy* 4. 1–45.
Klima, Edward. 1964. Negation in English. In Jerry Fodor & Jerrold Katz (eds.), *The structure of language*. 246–323. Englewood Cliffs, NJ: Prentice-Hall.
Kovarikova, Dominika, Lucie Chlumska & Vaclav Cvrcek. 2012. What belongs in a dictionary? The example of negation in Czech. In Ruth Vatvedt Fjeld & Julie Matilde Torjusen (eds.), *Proceedings of the 15th Euralex international congress*. 822–827. University of Oslo.
Kratzer, Angelika. 1989. Stage-level and individual-level predicates. In Emmon Bach, Angelika Kratzer & Barbara Partee (eds.), *Papers on quantification*. Amherst, MA: University of Massachusetts.
Krifka, Manfred. 2007. Negated antonyms: Creating and flling the gap. In Uli Sauerland & Penka Stateva (eds.), *Presupposition and implicature in compositional semantics*. 163–177.

Houndmills: Palgrave Macmillan.
Krishnamurti, Bhadriraju. 2003. *The Dravidian languages*. New York: Cambridge University Press.
Kroch, Anthony. 1989. Function and grammar in the history of English periphrastic *do*. In Ralph Fasold & Deborah Schiffrin (eds.), *Language variation and change*. Amsterdam: Benjamins.
Kunjan Pillai, Surnad (ed.) 1965. *Malayalam lexicon*. Thiruvananthapuram: International school of Dravidian linguistics.
Kwak, Saera. 2010. Negation in Persian. *Iranian Studies* 43(4). 621–636.
Ladusaw, William. 1979. *Polarity sensitivity as inherent scope relations*. Austin, TX: University of Texas dissertation.
Lafkioui, Mena B. 2013. Reinventing negation patterns in Moroccan Arabic. 978-3-11-029232-9. hal-01411665.
Laka, Itziar. 1990. *Negation in syntax: On the nature of functional categories and projections*: MIT dissertation.
Laka, Itziar. 1991. Negation in syntax: On the nature of functional categories and projections. *ASJU* XXV(1). 65–136.
Laka, Itziar. 1994. *On the syntax of negation*. New York: Garland Publishing.
Lambton, Ann. 2003. *Persian grammar*. Cambridge: Cambridge University Press.
Lander, Eric. 2015. Intraparadigmatic cyclic and roll-up derivations in the Old Norse reinforced demonstrative. *The Linguistic Review* 32(4). 777–817.
Lander, Eric. 2016. *The nanosyntax of the Northwest Germanic reinforced demonstrative*. Ghent: Ghent University dissertation.
Landman, Fred. 1991. *Structures for semantics*. Dordrecht: Kluwer.
Larson, Richard & Hiroko Yamakido. 2008. Exafe and the deep position of nominal modifiers. In Louise McNally & Christopher Kennedy (eds.), *Adjectives and adverbs*. 43–70. Oxford: Oxford University Press.
Lasnik, Howard. 1981. Restricting the theory of transformations. In Norbert Hornstein & David Lightfoot (eds.), *Explanation in linguistics*. London: Longman.
Lehrer, Adrienne. 2002. Paradigmatic relations of exclusion and opposition I: gradable antonymy and complementarity. In Alan Cruse (ed.), *Lexicologie: ein internationales Handbuch zur Natur und Struktur von Wörtern und Wortschätzen*, vol. 21. 498–506. Mouton de Gruyter.
Li, Charles N. & Sandra A. Thompson. 1981. *Mandarin Chinese: a functional reference grammar*. Berkeley, CA: University of California Press.
Lieber, Rochelle. 1981. *On the organisation of the lexicon*. Cambridge, MA: MIT dissertation.
Lindblom, Camille. 2014. Negation in Dravidian languages. a descriptive typological study on verbal and non-verbal negation in simple declarative sentences. Master thesis, Stockholm University.
Löbner, Sebastian. 1990. *Wahr neben Falsch. Duale Operatoren als die Quantoren natürlicher Sprache*. Tübingen: Max Niemeyer.
Lucas, Christopher. 2009. *The development of negation in Arabic and Afro-Asiatic*: Cambridge University dissertation.
Mackridge, Peter. 1985. *The modern Greek language. A descriptive analysis of standard modern Greek*. Oxford: Oxford University Press.
Malamud, Sophia & Tamina Stephenson. 2011. Three ways to avoid commitments: Declarative force modifiers in the conversational scoreboard. In Artstein Ron, Mark Core, David

DeVault, Kallirroi Georgila, Elsi Kaiser & Amanda Stent (eds.), *SemDial 2011: Proceedings of the 15th Workshop on the Semantics and Pragmatics of Dialogue.* 74–83. Los Angeles, CA.
Manzini, M. Rita & Leonardo M. Savoia. 2011. *Grammatical categories: Variation in Romance languages*. Cambridge: Cambridge University Press.
Martin, Samuel E. 1975. *A reference grammar of Japanese*. London: Yale University Press.
Massam, Diane & Yves Roberge. 1989. Recipe context null objects in English. *Linguistic Inquiry* 20(1). 134–139.
Mathew, Rosmin. 2013. Recursion of FocP in Malayalam. In Katharina Hartmann & Tonjes Veenstra (eds.), *Cleft structures*. 251–268. Amsterdam: John Benjamins.
McCawley, James. 1968. Lexical insertion in a transformational grammar without deep structure. *CLS* 4. 71–80.
McCawley, James. 1991. Contrastive negation and metalinguistic negation. *CLS (The Parasession on Negation)* 27. 189–206.
McCawley, James. 1998. *The syntactic phenomena of English*. Chicago: University of Chicago Press.
McCloskey, Jim. 1997. Subjecthood and subject positions. In Liliane Haegeman (ed.), *Elements of grammar. Handbook in generative syntax.* 197–235. Dordrecht: Kluwer.
McCloskey, Jim. 2011. Polarity and case licensing: The cartography of the inflectional layer in Irish. Talk presented at GIST 3: Cartographic Structures and Beyond. Ghent University.
Meillet, Antoine. 1921. L'évolution des formes grammaticales. *Scientia* 12. 384–400.
Miestamo, Matti. 2005. *Standard negation. The negation of declarative verbal main clauses in a typological perspective*. Berlin: Mouton de Gruyter.
Miestamo, Matti. 2007. Negation. An overview of typological research. *Language and Linguistics Compass* 1(5). 552–570.
Mohanan, K. P. 1982. Infinitival subjects, government, and abstract case. *Linguistic Inquiry* 13. 323–327.
Mohanan, Tara & Karuvannur P. Mohanan. 1999. Two forms of 'be' in malayalam. Paper presented at LFG 99.
Moinzadeh, Ahmad. 2005. A new approach to the ezafe phrase in Persian. *CLO* 33. 43–64.
Moscati, Vincenzo. 2006. *The scope of negation*. Siena: University of Siena dissertation.
Moscati, Vincenzo. 2010. *Negation raising: logical form and linguistic variation*. Cambridge: Cambridge Scholars Publishing.
Moscati, Vincenzo. 2012. The cartography of negative markers: why negation breaks the assumption of LF/PF isomorphism. In Valentina Bianchi & Christiano Chesi (eds.), *Enjoy linguistics! Papers offered to Luigi Rizzi on the occasion of his 60th birthday*. 1–7. Siena, Italy: CISCL Press.
Muller, Claude. 1991. *La négation en français : syntaxe, sémantique et éléments de comparaison avec les autres langues romanes*. Genève: Librairie Droz.
Müller, Gereon. 2004. Phase impenetrability and wh-intervention. In Arthur Stepanov, Gisbert Fanselow & Ralf Vogel (eds.), *Minimality effects in syntax*. 289–325. Berlin: Mouton de Gruyter.
Nair, Ravi Sankar S. 2012. *A grammar of Malayalam*. Language in India.
Naughton, James. 2005. *Czech. An essential grammar*. New York: Routledge.
Neeleman, Ad & Kriszta Szendröi. 2007. Radical pro-drop and the morphology of pronouns. *Linguistic Inquiry* 38. 671–714.
Neeleman, Ad & Reiko Vermeulen. 2012. Types of focus and their interactions with negation. In

Ad Neeleman & Reiko Vermeulen (eds.), *The syntax of topic, focus and contrast*. 227–264. Berlin/Boston: Walter de Gruyter.

Newell, Heather. 2008. *Aspects of the morphology and phonology of phases*. Montreal: McGill University dissertation.

Nyberg, Joacim. 2012. Negation in Japanese. Exam paper, Stockholm University.

Ouhalla, Jamal. 1990. Sentential negation, relativized minimality and the aspectual status of auxiliaries. *The Linguistic Review* 7. 183–231.

Ouhalla, Jamal. 1991. *Functional categories and parametric variation*. New York: Routledge.

Ouhalla, Jamal. 1993. Negation, focus and tense: the Arabic *maa* and *laa*. *Rivista di Linguistica* 5. 275–300.

Pantcheva, Marina. 2009. Directional expressions cross-linguistically. Nanosyntax and lexicalization. *Nordlyd* 36(1). 7–39.

Pantcheva, Marina. 2011. *Decomposing path: The nanosyntax of directional expressions*. Tromsø: University of Tromsø dissertation.

Penka, Doris. 2011. *Negative indefinites*. Oxford: Oxford University Press.

Penka, Doris & Hedde Zeijlstra. 2010. Negation and polarity: an introduction. *Natural Language & Linguistic Theory* 28. 771–786.

Pesetsky, David. 1985. Morphology and logical form. *Linguistic Inquiry* 16. 193–246.

Po-Ching, Yip & Don Rimmington. 2006 [1997]. *Chinese. An essential grammar*. New York: Routledge.

Poletto, Cecilia. 2008. On negative doubling. Ms. University of Venice.

Poletto, Cecilia. 2017. Negative doubling: in favor of a big NegP analysis. In Silvio Cruschina, Katharina Hartmann & Eva-Maria Remberger (eds.), *Studies on negation: syntax, semantics and variation*. Göttingen: Vienna University Press.

Poletto, Cecilia & Raffaella Zanuttini. 2013. Emphasis as reduplication: evidence from *sì che/no che* sentences. *Lingua* 128. 124–141.

Pollock, Jean-Yves. 1989. Verb movement, universal grammar and the structure of IP. *Linguistic Inquiry* 20. 365–424.

Posner, Rebecca. 1985. Post-verbal negation in non-standard French: a historical and comparative view. *Romance Philology* 39. 170–197.

Progovac, Ljiljana. 2006. The syntax of nonsententials: small clauses and phrases at the root. In Ljiljana Progovac, Kate Paesani, Eugenia Casielles & Ellen Barton (eds.), *The syntax of nonsententials. Multidisciplinary perspectives*. 33–72. Amsterdam: John Benjamins.

Quirk, Randolph, Sidney Greenbaum, Geoffrey Leech & Jan Svartvik. 1985. *A comprehensive grammar of the English language*. London: Longman.

Rajaonarimanana, Narivelo. 2001. *Grammaire moderne de la langue Malgache*. Paris: Langues mondes. L'Asiathèque.

Ramchand, Gillian. 2008. *Verb meaning and the lexicon*. Cambridge, Massachusetts: MIT Press.

Rasoloson, Janie. 2001. *Malagasy-English. English-Malagasy. Dictionary and phrasebook*. New York: Hippocrene books.

Reuben, Levy. 1951. *Persian language*. New York: Philosophical Library.

Richards, Marc. 2007. On feature inheritance: an argument from the phase impenetrability condition. *Linguistic Inquiry* 38. 563–572.

Ritter, Elizabeth & Martina Wiltschko. 2014. The composition of INFL. An exploration of tense, tenseless languages and tenseless constructions. *Natural Language & Linguistic Theory* 32. 1331–1386.

Rizzi, Luigi. 1981. Nominative marking in Italian infinitives and the nominative island constraint. In Frank Heny (ed.), *Binding and filtering*. London: Croom Helm.
Rizzi, Luigi. 1990. *Relativized minimality*. Cambridge, Massachusetts: MIT Press.
Rizzi, Luigi. 1997. The fine structure of the left periphery. In Liliane Haegeman (ed.), *Elements of grammar. Handbook in generative syntax*. 281–337. Dordrecht: Kluwer.
Rizzi, Luigi. 2004. Locality and left periphery. In Adriana Belletti (ed.), *Structures and beyond*. 223–251. Oxford University Press.
Rizzi, Luigi & Ian Roberts. 1996. Complex inversion in French. In Adriana Belletti & Luigi Rizzi (eds.), *Parameters and functional heads*. 91–116. Oxford University Press.
Roberts, Ian. 1985. Agreement parameters and the development of English modal auxiliaries. *Natural Language & Linguistic Theory* 3(1). 21–58.
Roberts, Ian. 1993. *Verbs and diachronic syntax*. Dordrecht: Kluwer.
Roberts, Ian. 2007. *Diachronic syntax*. Oxford University Press.
Roberts, Ian & Anna Roussou. 2003. *Syntactic change. A minimalist approach to grammaticalization*. Cambridge: Cambridge University Press.
Rocquet, Amélie. 2013. *Splitting objects. A nanosyntactic account of direct object marking*. Ghent: Ghent University dissertation.
Roelandt, Koen. 2016. *Most or the art of compositionality: Dutch* de/het meeste *at the syntax-semantics interface*. Brussels: KU Leuven dissertation.
Roeper, Thomas. 1999. Universal bilingualism. *Bilingualism: Language and cognition* 2(3). 169–186.
Rooryck, Johan. 2017. A compositional analysis of French negation. Ms. Leiden University.
Rounds, Carol. 2001. *Hungarian. An essential grammar*. New York: Routledge.
Rowlett, Paul. 1998a. A non-overt negative operator in French. *Probus* 10. 185–206.
Rowlett, Paul. 1998b. *Sentential negation in French*. Oxford: Oxford University Press.
Ruytenbeek, Nicolas, Steven Verheyen & Benjamin Spector. 2017. Asymmetric inference towards the antonym: Experiments into the polarity and morphology of negated adjectives. *Glossa* 2. 92.1–27.
Ryding, Karin. 2005. *A reference grammar of modern standard Arabic*. Cambridge: Cambridge University Press.
Samiian, Vida. 1983. *Structure of phrasal categories in Persian: an X-bar analysis*. Los Angeles, CA: UCLA dissertation.
Sansom, George Bailey. 1928. *An historical grammar of Japanese*. Oxford: Clarendon Press.
Selkirk, Elisabeth. 1982. *The syntax of words*. Cambridge, MA: MIT Press.
Selkirk, Elisabeth O. 1984. *Phonology and syntax : the relation between sound and structure*. Cambridge, Mass.: MIT Press.
Sells, Peter. 2000. Raising and the order of clausal constituents in the Philippine languages. In Ileana Paul, Vivianne Phillips & Lisa Travis (eds.), *Formal issues in Austronesian linguistics*. 117–144. Dordrecht: Kluwer.
Seuren, Pieter. 1976. Echo: Een studie in negatie. In Geert Koefoed & Arnold Evers (eds.), *Lijnen van taaltheoretisch onderzoek*. 160–184. Groningen: Tjeenk Willink.
Seuren, Pieter. 1978. The structure and selection of positive and negative gradable adjectives. In Donka Farkas, Wesley Jacobsen & Karol Todrys (eds.), *Papers from the parasession on the lexicon*. 336–346. Chicago: Chicago Linguistic Society.
Seuren, Pieter. 1984. The comparative revisited. *Journal of Semantics* 3. 109–141.
Shibatani, Masayoshi. 1990. *The languages of Japan*. Cambridge: Cambridge University Press.

Shlonsky, Ur. 2010. The cartographic enterprise in syntax. *Language and Linguistics Compass* 4(6). 417–429.
Siegel, Dorothy. 1974. *Topics in English morphology*. Cambridge, MA: MIT dissertation.
Siegel, Dorothy. 1978. *Topics in English morphology*. New York: Garland Publishing.
Van der Sijs, Nicoline. 2010. Etymologiebank. http://www.etymologiebank.nl.
Simpson, Andrew & Zoe Wu. 2002. Agreement, shells, and focus. *Language* 78(2). 287–313.
Sohn, Ho-Min. 1999. *The Korean language*. Cambridge: Cambridge University Press.
Stalnaker, Robert. 1978. Assertion. In Peter Cole (ed.), *Syntax and semantics. pragmatics*. 315–332. New York: Academic Press.
Starke, Michal. 2004. On the inexistence of specifiers and the nature of heads. In Adriana Belletti (ed.), *Structures and beyond, vol. 3 The Cartography of Syntactic Structures*. 252–268. Oxford: Oxford University Press.
Starke, Michal. 2009. Nanosyntax: A short primer to a new approach to language. *Nordlyd* 36. 1–6.
Starke, Michal. 2011a. Nanosyntax, part I. Lecture series at GIST, Ghent.
Starke, Michal. 2011b. Towards an elegant solution to language variation: Variation reduces to the size of lexically stored trees. Ms., Tromsø University.
Starke, Michal. 2014a. Cleaning up the lexicon. *Linguistic Analysis* 39. 245–256.
Starke, Michal. 2014b. Towards elegant parameters: Language variation reduces to the size of lexically-stored trees. In M. Carme Picallo (ed.), *Linguistic variation in the minimalist framework*. 140–152. Oxford: Oxford University Press.
Starke, Michal. 2017. Resolving (DAT = ACC) ≠ GEN. *Glossa* 2(1). 104.1–8.
Starke, Michal. 2018. Complex left branches, spellout, and prefixes. In Lena Baunaz, Karen De Clercq, Liliane Haegeman & Eric Lander (eds.), *Exploring nanosyntax*. 239–249. Oxford: Oxford University Press.
Storoshenko, Dennis Ryan. 2004. *Negation scope and phrase structure in Japanese*. Burnaby, BC: Simon Fraser University MA thesis.
Stowell, Tim. 1981. *Origins of phrase structure*. Cambridge, MA: MIT dissertation.
Stowell, Tim. 1983. Subjects across categories. *The Linguistic Review* 2. 285–312.
Swan, Michael. 2005. *Practical English usage*. Oxford: Oxford University Press.
Tabaian, Hessam. 1974. *Conjunction, relativization and complementation in Persian*. Boulder, CO: University of Colorado dissertation.
Taleghani, Azita. 2006. *Modality, aspect and negation*. Tucson, AZ: University of Arizona dissertation.
Taleghani, Azita. 2008. *Modality, aspect and negation*. Amsterdam: John Benjamins.
Taraldsen, Tarald. 2012. *ABA and the representation of features in syntax. Talk presented at BCGL 7, Brussels.
Taraldsen Medová, Lucie & Bartosz Wiland. 2019. Semelfactives are bigger than degree achievements. *Natural Language & Linguistic Theory* 37. 1463–1513.
Taylor, Insup & Martin M. Taylor. 2014. *Writing and literacy in Chinese, Korean and Japanese*. Amsterdam: John Benjamins.
Temmerman, Tanja. 2012. *Multidominance, ellipsis and quantifier scope*. Leiden: Leiden University dissertation.
Thoms, Gary. 2017. Linguistic variation and English dialect syntax: the amn't gap. EGG Summer school, Olomouc.
Van Craenenbroeck, Jeroen. 2010. *The syntax of ellipsis: evidence from Dutch dialects*. Oxford: Oxford University Press.

Van Craenenbroeck, Jeroen & Tanja Temmerman. 2017. How (not) to elide negation. *Syntax* 20. 41–76.
Van der Auwera, Johan. 2009. The Jespersen cycles. In Elly van Gelderen (ed.), *Cyclical change*. 35–71. Amsterdam: Benjamins.
Van der Auwera, Johan & Annemie Neuckermans. 2004. Jespersen's cycle and the interaction of predicate and quantifier negation in Flemish. In Bernd Kortmann (ed.), *Typology meets dialectology. Dialect grammar from a cross-linguistic perspective*. 454–478. Berlin: Mouton de Gruyter.
Van Fraassen, Bas. 1971. *Formal semantics and logic. New York-London*: Macmillan.
Van Gelderen, Elly. 2004. Economy, innovation, and prescriptivism: From Spec to Head and Head to Head. *The Journal of Comparative Germanic Linguistics* 7(1). 59–98.
Vanden Wyngaerd, Guido. 1999. Positively polar. *Studia Linguistica* 23. 209–226.
Vanden Wyngaerd, Guido. 2018. The feature structure of pronouns: a probe into multidimensional paradigms. In Lena Baunaz, Karen De Clercq, Liliane Haegeman & Eric Lander (eds.), *Exploring nanosyntax*. 277–304. Oxford: Oxford University Press.
Vanden Wyngaerd, Guido, Michal Starke, Karen De Clercq & Pavel Caha. 2020. How to be positive. *Glossa* 5(1) 23. 1–34.
Veselinova, Ljuba. 2013. Negative existentials: a cross-linguistic study. *Rivista di Linguistica* 25(1). 107–145.
Veselinova, Ljuba. 2014. The negative existential cycle revisited. *Linguistics* 52(6). 1327–1369.
Vikner, Sten. 1995. *Verb movement and expletive subjects in the Germanic languages*. Oxford: Oxford University Press.
Von Stechow, Arnim. 1984. My reaction to Cresswell's, Hellan's and Seuren's comments. *Journal of Semantics* 3. 183–199.
Von Stechow, Arnim. 2008. The temporal degree adjectives *früh(er)/spät(er)* 'early(er)/late(r)' and the semantics of the positive. In Anastasia Giannakidou & Monika Rathert (eds.), *Quantification, definiteness, and nominalization*. 214–233. Oxford University Press.
Wade, Terence. 2011 [1992, 2000]. *A comprehensive Russian grammar*. Chichester, UK: Wiley-Blackwell.
Waher, Hester. 1978. *Die probleem van die bereik van die ontkenning met spesiale verwijsing na Afrikaans*. Cape Town: University of Cape Town dissertation.
Warren, Beatrice. 1984. *Classifying adjectives*. Gothenburg: Acta Universitatis Gothoburgensis.
Watters, John R. 1979. Focus in Aghem. In Larry M. Hyman (ed.), *Aghem grammatical structure* Southern California Occasional Papers in Linguistics 7. Los Angeles, CA: USC.
Weerman, Fred & Jacqueline Evers-Vermeul. 2002. Pronouns and case. *Lingua* 112. 301–338.
Weir, Andrew. 2009. Article drop in english headlinese. Master thesis, University College London.
Weir, Andrew. 2012. Left edge deletion in English and subject omission in diaries. *English Language and Linguistics* 16(1). 105–129.
Weir, Andrew. 2017. Object drop and article drop in reduced written register. In *Linguistic variation*, vol. 17 2. 157–185. John Benjamins.
Whaley, Lindsay. 1997. *An introduction to language typology: The unity and diversity of language*. Newbury Park, CA: SAGE Publications.
Wheeler, Samuel. 1972. Attributives and their modifiers. *Noûs* 6. 310–334.
Wiland, Bartosz. 2019. *The spell-out algorithm and lexicalization patterns. slavic verbs and complementizers*. Berlin: Language Science Press. https://langsci-press.org/catalog/book/242.

Wilder, Chris. 2013. English 'emphatic *do*'. *Lingua* 128. 142–171.
Williams, Alexander. 2009. Themes, cumulativity, and resultatives: comments on Kratzer 2003. *Linguistic Inquiry* 40(4). 686–700.
Williams, Edwin. 1980. Predication. *Linguistic Inquiry* 11. 203–238.
Williams, Edwin. 1981. Argument structure and morphology. *The Linguistic Review* 1. 81–114.
Williams, Edwin. 2003. *Representation theory*. Cambridge, MA: MIT Press.
Willis, David. 2011. A minimalist approach to Jespersen's Cycle in Welsh. In Dianne Jonas, John Whitman & Andrew Garrrett (eds.), *Grammatical change: origins, natures, outcomes*. 93–119. Oxford University Press.
Willis, David, Christopher Lucas & Anne Breitbarth (eds.). 2013. *The development of negation in the languages of Europe and the Mediterranean*, vol. 1 Case Studies. Oxford: Oxford University Press.
Willmott, Jo. 2008. Not in the mood: Modality and negation in the history of Greek. Talk presented at the 29th Annual Meeting of the Department of Linguistics, Thessaloniki.
Yang, Charles. 2017. How to wake up irregular (and speechless). In Claire Bowern, Laurence Horn & Rafaella Zanuttini (eds.), *On looking into words (and beyond)*. 211–233. Berlin: Language Science Press.
Zanuttini, Raffaella. 1991. *Syntactic properties of sentential negation: A comparative study of Romance languages*: University of Pennsylvania dissertation.
Zanuttini, Raffaella. 1997. *Negation and clausal structure*. Oxford: Oxford University Press.
Zeijlstra, Hedde. 2004a. *Sentential negation and negative concord*. Utrecht: Utrecht University dissertation.
Zeijlstra, Hedde. 2004b. Syntactic vs. semantic negation. In Cécile Meier & Matthias Weisgerber (eds.), *Proceedings of the conference sub8–sinn und bedeutung*, vol. 177 Arbeitspapier. Konstanz: Universität Konstanz.
Zeijlstra, Hedde. 2009. On French negation. In Iksoo Kwon, Hanna Pritchett & Justin Spence (eds.), *Proceedings of the 35th annual meeting of the Berkely Linguistics Society*. 447–458. Berkeley, California: BLS. http://ling.auf.net/lingbuzz/000885.
Zimmer, Karl. 1964. *Affixal negation in English and other languages* Supplement to *Word*, Monograph 5.
Zwart, Jan-Wouter. 1997. *Morphosyntax of verb movement*. Dordrecht: Kluwer.
Zwarts, Frans. 1995. Nonveridical contexts. *Linguistic Analysis* 25(1). 286–312.
Zwarts, Frans. 1998. Three types of polarity. In Fritz Hamm & Erhard Hinrichs (eds.), *Plurality and quantification*. 177–238. Kluwer.
Zwarts, Joost. 1992. *X-bar-syntax–X-bar-semantics: on the interpretation of functional and lexical heads*. Utrecht: Utrecht University dissertation.
Zwicky, Arnold & Geoffrey Pullum. 1983. Cliticisation vs. inflection: English *n't*. *Language* 59(3). 502–513.

Index

*ABA 6, 11, 26, 31, 205, 230
*Neg-Neg constraint 53, 160, 217, 231

A_CP 225
adjectival construct 103
adverbial modifier 44, 68, 74, 89, 96, 107, 121, 124, 128, 131
adverbial negation 214, 215
affixal negation 38
Afrikaans 42, 192, 200
algorithm 161
Altaic 77, 86
Ancient Greek 71, 120, 127, 130
antonymic adjective 220
antonymic pair 217, 221, 224
antonyms 133
Aristotle 32, 39
asymmetric 193
Austronesian 86, 136
Azerbaijani 95, 96

backtracking 22, 190
Big NegP 209, 211
bilingual 78
bipartite negation 37, 42, 46, 63, 74–76, 116, 117, 140, 191–202, 208, 213, 215
Blackfoot 33

Carib 129, 132
cartography 9, 149, 205, 206, 213
case 10–27, 31, 32, 144, 146
case compounding 14, 20
case hierarchy 22
case sequence 11
case stacking 14
Central Khoisan 113
characterising 94, 95, 168
characterising function 57, 66, 71, 89, 102, 105, 116, 118, 128, 167
Chinese 31, 77, 87, 144, 183
Class^{NEG}-marker 6, 36, 48, 49, 57–60, 66, 72, 78–81, 83, 85, 88, 89, 93–99, 102, 103, 105–107, 111, 112, 114, 116–118, 120–123, 126–131, 139, 140, 144–155, 170, 230
Classical Arabic 94, 102

classification 31, 59
classifying function 57, 72, 95, 98, 102, 105, 114, 116, 130, 167, 168
ClassP 48, 49, 168–170
cleft 91, 93, 111
clitic 181–183
Colloquial French 42, 90, 151, 192–202, 213, 231
competition 159, 173, 175, 180
complex left branch 161
complex specifier 159–191, 196, 197, 228
constituent negation 3–5, 31, 38, 46, 51, 68, 92, 96, 107, 111, 133, 134, 192, 194, 202, 212, 230
construct phrase 103
containment 150
context-dependence 221, 224
contextual average 224–229, 231
contextual presupposition 109
contextual standard 218, 221–224, 227
contiguous syncretisms 136
contradictory negation 6, 33, 54–56, 68, 69, 72, 74, 81, 98, 99, 102, 104, 105, 107, 125, 130, 216–229
contradictory opposition 216–229
contrariety 66
contrary negation 6, 33, 54–56, 71, 89, 94, 95, 99, 100, 102, 105, 112, 116, 118, 120, 124–126, 130, 133, 216–229, 231
contrary opposition 216–229
contrastive negation 44, 57, 68, 74, 96, 107, 117, 121, 128, 131, 133, 154
copula 31, 91, 92, 99, 103, 108, 111, 114, 120, 127, 128, 131, 132, 154, 161, 164, 183, 185, 192, 196, 199, 200, 230
copular clause 36, 48, 61
Croft's Cycle 101, 103, 110, 183
cumulative classification 12, 14, 147
cyclic movement 22
Cyclic Override 18, 24, 26
cyclic phrasal movement 20
cyclic spellout 9
Czech 129–132, 135, 173, 230, 231

decomposition 7, 12–15, 31, 32, 143, 145–150, 192, 205, 212, 213
degree function 219
deictic 49
denial 69, 104, 117
denying function 57
diachronic change 192–202
dimension 217, 219, 227
discontinuous negation 116
double negation 69, 75, 127, 140, 192, 201, 213, 215
Dravidian 86, 111
– Proto-Dravidian 111
Dutch 53, 127
– Flemish 127

East-Slavic 135
echo negation 172, 214
Elsewhere Condition 17, 26
Elsewhere Principle 148, 153, 180, 201
embracing negation 75, 116
English 152, 159–191, 230
existential 109, 115
existential verb 122, 183
extent 218–224
extent semantics 231
external negation 32, 38, 39, 41
external syntax 159–191
Ezāfe 107

Faithfulness Condition 166, 188
featural deficiency 194, 213
Finno-Ugric 118
Foc^{NEG}-marker 6, 36, 42–48, 57–61, 68, 73, 74, 83–85, 88, 89, 92, 96, 99–101, 104, 105, 107, 108, 110, 111, 115–118, 121, 123, 124, 127–129, 131, 133, 134, 139, 140, 144–155, 161, 184, 212, 215, 230
FocP 46–48, 213
focus 43–48, 208
focus field 121
focus value 45
Free Choice 166, 184
French 37, 42, 46, 51, 53, 87, 151, 173, 231
fseq 24, 25, 36, 37, 53, 159–162, 170–172, 188, 189, 196, 198, 200, 202, 228, 231
function 33, 57–59

functional-lexical divide 143, 205

genres 79
German 87
gradability 124, 167, 168, 180, 184
gradable 168
gradable adjective 217–229
gradablity 50
grammaticalisation 151, 200
Gungbe 64

Halkomelem 33
Hebrew 123–127, 173
Hixkaryana 31, 132–135
hole 172
homonymy 27
Hungarian 99, 118–123, 127, 173, 183

iDaafa 103
idioms 173
implicational universal 63, 64
Indo-European 86, 129
– Proto-Indo-European 150
inflectional affix 181, 183
interval semantics 219
Italian 47, 143, 151, 212, 213

Japanese 77, 86–90
Jespersen's Cycle 76, 77, 118, 191–202, 231

Kalahari Khoe 113
Khwe 31, 113–116
Kimeru 64
Korean 65, 77–86, 99, 141

Late Insertion 9, 15
Latin 51, 71, 120, 130, 150
Law of Contradiction 222
Law of Feature Conservation 200
le bon usage French 42, 65, 70, 90, 118, 139, 150, 151, 192–202, 213, 231
Level I 52
Level II 52
lexical insertion 15
lexical negation 38, 212, 214, 230
lexical-functional divide 139, 230
lexicalisation 15

Macedonian 135

Malagasy 136
Malayalam 108, 183
Mandarin Chinese 98, 102, 103, 141
merge-f 23, 24
merge-XP 23
metalinguistic negation 57, 68, 172
Middle Way 63
Minimize Junk 17, 148
minimizers 151, 208
modal 81
Modern Greek 10, 11, 43, 51, 62, 65–70
Modern Standard Arabic 102–105, 144, 183
modifying function 57
Moroccan Arabic 116–118, 144, 148
morphological gap 182
morphological negation 38
multiple NegPs 205–215

nanosyntax 6–27, 31, 141, 143–155, 159–191, 194, 199, 200, 202, 230, 231
negation sequence 143–146
negative adjective 217–229
negative classifier marker 33
negative cleft 38
negative concord 42, 75, 127, 140, 201, 207, 209, 231
negative doubling 42, 75, 208, 209, 215
negative existential 110
negative existential cycle 101
negative existential verb 92, 122, 183
negative extent 220–224, 226
negative focus marker 33
negative indefinite 32, 38, 75, 210, 231
negative nanospine 155, 159, 161, 163, 170, 172, 191
negative scalar quantity marker 33
negative tense marker 33
negative tripling 209
NegFirst 153
NegP 36–38, 140, 154, 160–163, 171, 172, 176, 205–216
nexal negation 3, 39–43
non-scalar 36
North Italian 208

Old English 151
ordinary value 45

Persian 105–108, 144
phrasal spellout 9, 15, 19, 176, 183, 189, 199
plug 172
pointers 173–175, 177, 178, 188, 191
polar focus 172
polarity emphasis 38, 172
polarity marker 38, 68, 73
polarity negation 214
PolP 37
positive adjective 229
positive extent 220–224, 226
POST 22, 153, 159, 165, 173, 178, 181, 191
post-syntactic lexicon 152
pragmatic strengthening 99, 102, 124
PRE 22, 153, 159, 164, 165, 178, 181, 191
predicate denial 3, 32, 35, 39–43
predicate negation 3, 32, 35, 44–48
predicate term negation 3, 33, 35, 44, 49, 51
privation 113, 125
propositional negation 32, 38, 39, 41
pull-chain approach 193
push-chain approach 193, 194

Q-word 53
Q^{NEG}-marker 6, 35, 36, 50–53, 57–60, 65, 70, 79–81, 83, 85, 88–90, 93–95, 97–99, 102, 103, 105–107, 111–114, 116–120, 123–125, 127–131, 133, 144–155, 159, 173–175, 177, 178, 216, 218, 230
QP 50–53, 170, 184, 225, 226
quantifier 208
question tag-test 3, 41
question tags 3, 41, 43

reduplicative tags 3
Romance 206, 209
Russian 135

ΣP 37
scalar 208
scalarity 177
scale 216, 217, 224
scopal properties 32–34, 59
scope position 35–53
scope properties 144
semantic properties 33, 54–56, 59
Semitic 102, 123

sentence negation 3–5, 31, 32, 37, 39–43, 47, 75, 76, 81, 84, 90, 96, 99, 116, 120, 121, 123, 131, 143, 151, 153, 154, 192–195, 199, 201, 202, 207, 211–213, 215, 230
Sino-Korean 77–79, 82
Sino-Tibetan 86
Slovene 15–20
small clause 44, 69, 184, 196
snowball movement 20–22, 25
South-Slavic 135
speaker presupposition 172
special negation 3, 51
spellout 9–26, 152–155, 198
spellout algorithm 15, 22–26, 163, 164, 166, 169, 170, 174, 186, 189, 191, 196, 230
spellout-driven movement 16, 23
Split K 13
Split NegP 143, 151
stacking 8, 33–35, 59, 61, 65, 69, 72–74, 84, 94–97, 100, 106, 108, 112, 120, 128, 131, 139, 144, 212, 216
stacking test 39
standard negation 66, 110, 132, 210
standard negator 61, 93, 108
structural containment 14
structural contiguity 11
structural deficiency 195, 202
structural relatedness 143
sub-classification 12, 13, 146, 148
subjunctive 43
Superset Principle 17, 26, 153, 167, 168, 179, 180, 200, 201, 225

suppletion 82, 88, 92, 101, 103, 115, 122, 131, 173, 174, 183, 207
Swahili 64
Swedish 95, 96
syncretism 3, 6, 7, 10–12, 15, 17, 26, 27, 31, 32, 60, 64, 70, 105, 113, 116, 132, 139, 143–146, 148, 159, 173, 213, 225
syncretism pattern 62, 63, 65, 67, 74, 77–79, 85, 86, 90, 91, 98, 100, 102, 106, 123, 136, 140, 141, 143, 144, 148, 168, 191, 205, 212, 230, 231
syntax-morphology divide 143

T^{NEG}-marker 6, 36, 39–43, 57–62, 69, 74–77, 83–85, 89, 91, 92, 96, 99–101, 103, 104, 107, 108, 110, 111, 114, 115, 117, 118, 121–124, 127–129, 131, 132, 134, 144–155, 164, 199, 212, 215, 230
TAM 43, 62, 101, 212, 231
Turkish 91, 97, 183
typology 6
Tümpisa Shoshone 136

Universal Case Containment Hypothesis 14
Universal Case Contiguity Hypothesis 14, 144, 145
Universal Negation Contiguity Hypothesis 144, 148
Uto-Aztecan 136

vowel harmony 118

West-Slavic 129
West-Tocharian 14, 20

www.ingramcontent.com/pod-product-compliance
Lightning Source LLC
Chambersburg PA
CBHW070758230426
43665CB00017B/2410